Henry Guernsey Hubbard

Insects Affecting the Orange

Henry Guernsey Hubbard

Insects Affecting the Orange

ISBN/EAN: 9783743320772

Manufactured in Europe, USA, Canada, Australia, Japa

Cover: Foto ©ninafisch / pixelio.de

Manufactured and distributed by brebook publishing software (www.brebook.com)

Henry Guernsey Hubbard

Insects Affecting the Orange

INSECTS

AFFECTING THE

ORANGE.

REPORT ON THE INSECTS AFFECTING THE CULTURE OF THE ORANGE AND OTHER PLANTS OF THE CITRUS FAMILY, WITH PRACTICAL SUGGESTIONS FOR THEIR CONTROL OR EXTERMINATION, MADE, UNDER DIRECTION OF THE ENTOMOLOGIST,

BY

H. G. HUBBARD.

WITH PLATES AND WOOD-CUTS.

WASHINGTON:
GOVERNMENT PRINTING OFFICE.
1885.

JOINT RESOLUTION AUTHORIZING THE PRINTING OF FIVE THOUSAND COPIES OF A SPECIAL REPORT ON INSECTS AFFECTING THE ORANGE TREE.

Resolved by the House of Representatives (the Senate concurring), That there be printed 5,000 copies of a special report from the Department of Agriculture on insects affecting the orange tree, with the necessary illustrations, 2,500 copies of which shall be for the use of the House of Representatives, 1,500 for the use of the Senate, and 1,000 for the use of the Department of Agriculture.

JULY 6, 1882.

TABLE OF CONTENTS.

	Page.
LETTER OF TRANSMITTAL	vii
LETTER OF SUBMITTAL	ix

INTRODUCTION.

INJURIES BY INSECTS DISTINGUISHED FROM ORGANIC DISEASE 1
Diseases affecting the condition of the plant;—die-back, 1—bark-fungus, 2—foot-rot;—smut, 3—splitting of fruit, 4—dropping of fruit, 5.

THE INSECT FAUNA OF THE ORANGE 5
Attraction which the orange tree has for insects, 5—injurious insects;—beneficial insects, 6—innocuous insects;—importance of distinguishing friends from foes, 7—presence of certain injurious insects indicated by ants, 8.

SYSTEMS OF CULTIVATION 8
Influence of shade upon the increase of insect pests, 8—clean culture or mulching preferable to cropping young groves;—seasons of greatest insect activity, 9—the proper months for applying remedies, 10.

PART I.—COCCIDÆ [SCALE-INSECTS OR BARK-LICE].

CHAPTER I.

CHARACTERS OF THE COCCIDÆ AND COMMENCEMENT OF THE CONSIDERATION OF THE SUBFAMILY DIASPINÆ 13
General characters of Bark-lice and their relations to other insects;—products of Bark-lice, 13—division into subfamilies, 14—life-history of the Diaspinæ;—the larva, 15—growth of the scale, 16—the females;—the males, 17—periods of development;—nature of the scale-covering, 18—Long Scale, 19—life-history, 21—broods, 22—parasites, 23—origin and spread, 24.

CHAPTER II.

DIASPINÆ—*Continued* 26
Purple Scale, 26—Red Scale of Florida, 28—Red Scale of California, 32—White Scale, 35—Chaff Scale, 37—the Orange Chionaspis, 40.

CHAPTER III.

DIASPINÆ—*Continued*—RAVAGES OF THE ARMORED SCALES 42
Bark-lice everywhere present in orange groves, 42—relative importance of the several species as pests;—agencies which assist their distribution, 43—influence of the wind, 44—enfeebled condition of the plant favorable to their increase;—usual course of the pest, 45—the popular belief that the scales are thrown off at the ends of the branches;—influence of climate, 46—effect of frost;—natural checks, 47.

CHAPTER IV.

LECANINÆ—THE NAKED OR WAXY SCALES.................................... 48
General characters and life-history of the subfamily;—the Turtle-back Scale;—Broad Scale, 48—growth;—habits, 49—broods;—honey-dew and ants;—parasites, 50—the Black Scale of California, 53—the Hemispherical Scale, 55—the Wax Scale, 56—the Barnacle Scale, 59—extent of injuries and relative importance of the species, 61—smut, 62.

CHAPTER V.

COCCINÆ—THE MEALY-BUGS 63
Characteristics of the subfamily;—food plants, 63—the Destructive Mealy-bug, 64—the Cottony Cushion Scale, 66.

CHAPTER VI.

INSECTS PREYING UPON BARK-LICE... 69
Enumeration of external enemies;—work of Mites, 69—internal parasites;—ants as friends and enemies, 70—Lady-birds, 71—parasites of the Lady-birds, 74—the Scale-eating Epitragus, 75—the Scale-eating Dakruma, 76—the Pale Dakruma;—the Scale-eating Tineid, 77—the Spider-legged Soldier-bug, 78—hemipterous enemies of the Mealy-bug, 79—Lace-wings, 80—predatory Mites, 81—Glover's Mite, 82—the Hairy Mite;—the Spearhead Mite;—the Spotted Mite, 83—Mites preying on Mealy-bug, 84—Long-bodied Mite;—the Orbicular Mite, 85.

CHAPTER VII.

MEANS OF DEFENSE AGAINST SCALE-INSECTS—REMEDIES...................... 86
Introduction of Scale-insects upon imported plants, 86—infection from nursery stock, 87—protection afforded by hedges and trees, 88—plants available for hedges;—benefits of inside pruning and cleanliness, 89—scrubbing the trunks;—palmetto brushes, 90—ineffectual popular remedies;—fumes of sulphur fatal to the plant;—impossibility of introducing insecticides into the sap through the roots, 91—or by inoculation;—fighting Scale with fertilizers;—effective remedies;—kerosene;—milk and kerosene emulsion, 92—soap and kerosene emulsion;—unrefined kerosene injurious;—effect of kerosene upon the Orange, 94—applications best made in spring;—whale-oil soap, 95—potash and soda lyes, 96—carbolic acid, 97—sulphurated lime, 98—bisulphide of carbon;—sulphuric acid;—sulphate of iron;—ammonia;—silicate of soda, 99—various common remedies of little value;—the application of remedies;—fineness and force of spray;—cyclone nozzle, 100—complete outfit mounted on a cart;—necessity of repeated applications, 101—proper seasons for applying remedies, 102.

PART II.—MISCELLANEOUS INSECTS AFFECTING THE ORANGE.

CHAPTER VIII.

RUST OF THE ORANGE... 105
Nature of rust;—discoloration of the fruit;—not produced by a fungus, 105—origin of rust;—reasons for considering it the work of a Mite;—the Mite on the leaves;—first appearance on the fruit, 106—attacks of the Mite always followed by rust;—development of rust subsequent to the departure of the Mites;—description of the Rust-mite, 107—growth from the egg to the adult, 108—food, habits, and numerical abundance, 109—

TABLE OF CONTENTS.

RUST OF THE ORANGE—Continued.
effect of sunshine and shade upon the Mites;—rust-rings on the fruit, 110—influence of the weather;—means of dissemination, 111—ravages of the Rust-mite confined to Citrus plants;—effect of attacks upon the foliage;—rusted fruit, 112—origin and spread of the Mite;—periods of increase;—geographical distribution;—remedies;—influence of soil, 113—fruit less liable to rust on low land;—preventive measures;—effect of reducing radiation;—protection afforded by wind-breaks, 114—application of insecticides;—whale-oil soap, 115—sulphur, 116—natural sulphur water;—kerosene;—carbolic acid, 118—potash;—pyrethrum, 119—lime;—ashes;—caution;—danger of making applications during winter, 120.

CHAPTER IX.

INSECTS AFFECTING THE ROOT, CROWN, TRUNK, AND BRANCHES.

ROOT AND CROWN.. 121
Tap-root borers;—white ants, 121—description and habits of the common species;—injuries to Orange, 121—the work of Termites distinguished from that of other insects;—buried wood and stumps a source of danger, 123—needful precautions;—remedies;—exposure to light;—applications of hot water;—pyrethrum;—kerosene;—bisulphide of carbon, 124—ashes;—lime and sulphur;—means of saving girdled trees;—a larger species of Termite, 125.
TRUNK AND BRANCHES.. 125
The Common Orange Sawyer, 125—injuries the result of careless pruning;—the tree protected by its gum;—precautions to be observed in pruning;—means of destroying the borers, 127—the Twig-girdler, 128—wood-eating habits of an ant (*Solenopsis*), 129—means of destroying their colonies, 130—methods of preventing ants from ascending the trees, 131.

CHAPTER X.

INSECTS AFFECTING THE TWIGS AND LEAVES.

HYMENOPTERA,—A leaf-eating ant, 132.
COLEOPTERA,—Brachys ovata, 132—Odontota rubra;—the Orange Leaf-notcher and other weevils slightly injurious to the leaves, 133.
ORTHOPTERA,—The Angular-winged Katydid, 134—the Lubber Grasshopper, 135—other locusts, 136.
LEPIDOPTERA,—The Orange Dog, 137—defensive measures, 138—parasites, 139—slug caterpillars and stinging caterpillars;—Lagoa opercularis, 140—the Saddle-back Caterpillar, 141—the Hag-moth Caterpillar, 142—the Skiff Caterpillar, 143—Bag-worms;—the Common Bag-worm, 145—provision made by the female for the safety of her eggs, 145—construction of its basket by the young;—parasites, 146—the Northern Bag-worm, 147—the Cylindrical Bag-worm;—the Orange Basket-worm, 148—small (undescribed) Bag-worm, 149—cocoons of Artace on Orange;—the Grassworm, 150—Leaf-rollers, 151—the Cork-colored Leaf-roller, 152—parasites, 153—the Sulphur-colored Leaf-roller;—a larger Leaf-roller; Webmakers;—the Orange-leaf Nothris, 154—the Orange Web-worm, 155—insects associated with the Orange Web-worm, 156.
HEMIPTERA,—The Orange Aphis, 157—birth of the young;—destructive powers;—enemies and parasites, 158—the Green Soldier-bug, 159—account of its ravages at West Apopka, Fla., 160—the Thick-thighed Metapodius, 162—other sucking bugs, 163.

CHAPTER XI.

INSECTS AFFECTING THE BLOSSOM AND FRUIT—SCAVENGER INSECTS.

	Page.
AFFECTING THE BLOSSOMS..	164

The Orange Thrips, 164.

AFFECTING THE FRUIT.........:.. 165

The Cotton Stainer, 165—the Leaf-footed Bug, 168—the Mexican Fruit Worm, 169.

SCAVENGERS.. 170

Insects feeding upon dead wood and bark;—tree-inhabiting ants, 170—the Orange Sawyer considered as a useful insect;—the Flat-headed Borer,' 171—the Cylindrical Bark-borer, 173—other insects boring in orange wood, 174—insects found in bleeding wounds and sores;—insects feeding upon decaying fruit;—Sap-beetles, 175—the Wine-fly of the Orange, 176—other insects found in injured fruit, 177—insects in dry fruit;—white ants in fruit, 178.

CHAPTER XII.

PREDATORY INSECTS.

INSECTS PREYING UPON PLANT-LICE ....:..... 180

Lady-birds;—Scymnus caudalis, 180—Syrphus flies;—life-history, 181—the Four-spotted Aphis-fly, 183—the Dusky-winged Aphis-fly;—the Ruddy Aphis-fly, 184—the Pruinose Aphis-fly, 185.

OTHER PREDATORY INSECTS FREQUENTING THE ORANGE 186

Wasps;—Polistes americanus, 186—the Vase-maker Wasp, 187—the Camel-crickets or Soothsayers, 188—the Carolina Mantis, 189—the Slender Mantis (Missouriensis ?), 190—Soldier-bugs;—the Spider-legged Soldier-bug;—the Rapacious Soldier-bug, 191—the Wheel-bug, 192.

INNOXIOUS INSECTS... 193

Case-bearers on Orange;—the Orange Case-bearing Tineid, 193;—Bark-cleaners, 193—Psocus venosus Burm., 193—the Orange Psocus, 194.

APPENDICES.

APPENDIX·I.

THE MEALY-BUG AT ORANGE LAKE, FLORIDA.....................:........ 197

APPENDIX II.

EXPERIMENTS WITH INSECTICIDES 199

Table I—Kerosene emulsions, 199; Table II—Whale-oil soap, 202; Table III—Lye solutions, 204; Table IV—Crude carbolic acid (oil of creosote), 206; Table V—Bisulphide of carbon, 209; Table VI—Silicate of soda, 211.

APPENDIX III.

THE COITION OF BAG-WORMS 213

NOTES.

Note 1, Additional parasites of Ceroplastes, 215—Note 2, Scale-eating Tineid, 215—Note 3, Telenomus from Leptocorisa eggs, 215—Note 4, Heteroptera feeding on Dactylopius, 215—Note 5, Perilitus from cocoon of Chrysopa, 215—Notes 6, 7, 8, 9, 10, Descriptions of Orange Mites, 216—Note 11, Composition of sulphurated lime, 217—Note 12, Miotropis parasitic on Platynota, 217—Note 13, Goniozus parasitic on Platynota, 217—Note 14, Larger Leaf-roller of the Orange, 217—Note 15, Orange-eating Tineid, 218—Note 16, Pteromalus from Pruinose Aphis-fly, 218—Note 17, Chrysis from Eumenes fraterna, 218.

LETTER OF TRANSMITTAL.

DEPARTMENT OF AGRICULTURE,
DIVISION OF ENTOMOLOGY,
Washington, D. C., May 20, 1885.

SIR: I have the honor to transmit herewith a special report which was ordered by Congress upon the "Insects affecting the Orange Tree." This report has been prepared by Mr. H. G. Hubbard, who has been employed as a special agent at Crescent City, Fla., and who has devoted his time for nearly four years in studying the insects that affect the Orange, and especially in practical experiments to counteract their injuries. It is but uttering a deserved compliment to say that the practical results of his labors have been most satisfactory, and mark an important era in the history of orange-growing in the United States.

The trees of the Citrus family are particularly subject to the disastrous ravages of various species of Scale-insects, which not infrequently thwart all effort to raise a grove. It is to these that the present report is chiefly devoted, and to their control that the greatest efforts were made.

Mr. Hubbard's work was confined to Florida, but the remedies are applicable to other orange-growing sections of the country. Prof. J. H. Comstock had already published much upon the Scale-insects affecting the Orange in California in the report of this Department for 1880, and his work has been very freely used in the present report.

The delay in the printing of the report has been partly due to the ill health from which Mr. Hubbard has suffered during the past year, and which has necessitated considerable office work, in which I have had the assistance, which I take pleasure in acknowledging, of Messrs. Howard, Schwarz, and Pergande.

Respectfully,

C. V. RILEY,
Entomologist.

Hon. NORMAN J. COLMAN,
Commissioner of Agriculture.

LETTER OF SUBMITTAL.

CRESCENT CITY, FLA., *March* 25, 1885.

SIR: I have the honor to submit the following report upon insects that affect the culture of the Orange. The investigations conducted under your direction, and which form the basis of this report, were begun upon my arrival in the field in Florida, in August, 1881, and continued until March, 1882. The work was resumed in June, 1882, and I returned to Florida in September, remaining in the field twenty-three months, or until August, 1884.

At your request, a preliminary report upon Scale-insects of the Orange, with special reference to remedies and their application, was prepared in advance of the final report, and was included in the Report of the Entomologist for 1882.

A treatise upon Rust of the Orange, including the essential part of Chapter VIII of this report, was prepared in the spring of 1883, and short extracts from this and other portions of the final report have appeared in the Bulletins of the Entomological Division. The full treatise upon Rust, with illustrations, is included in the Annual Report of the Entomologist for 1884.

In the preparation of the present work a single object has been kept in view, namely, to afford practical aid to the orange-grower in the warfare which must be waged with insect foes. Technical terms, which might render the treatise unintelligible to non-entomological readers, have been as far as possible excluded from the text, and in the descriptions of insects which fall within the scope of these investigations an attempt has been made to render the various forms recognizable to an intelligent observer, by the use of popular language, aided in many cases by figures, and without a resort to intricacies of description, such as would be imperatively demanded for specific identification.

Nevertheless, that the work may not prove of less advantage to the student of entomology, and to the investigator who may seek to correct, advance, or complete the many imperfect observations here recorded, references to more complete descriptions elsewhere published are given when deemed necessary, and descriptions of new insects, with other purely technical matters, are relegated to notes and appendices at the end of the volume.

Although my own observations have not extended beyond the State of Florida, and the accessible notes of observers elsewhere are few and meager, the first part of the work, that relating to Bark-lice, will be found applicable to any region where the Orange is grown, since these universal enemies of the Orange are as cosmopolitan as the plant itself. This part of the work, moreover, includes, in addition to those species which have been the subjects of original investigation in Florida, such notes as have been published upon the Californian species, and which have not as yet made their appearance upon the Orange in the East.

Of the miscellaneous insects considered in the second part of this report, by far the greater number are known only in Florida or Louisiana, and are not likely to make their appearance in the Pacific States.

In a record of observations extending over several years of daily and almost constant work in orange groves, it will not seem strange if many of the facts observed by previous investigators are found repeated in the following pages, and if credit is not always given for priority of discovery in matters relating to the habits of insects, such as may be verified in every orange grove, more intricate researches, or such as have not been reobserved, are always accompanied by the proper references. In this way contributions of interest to orange-growers have been extracted from the writings of well-known entomologists, and particularly from notes and published treatises on orange insects by Glover, Ashmead, and Comstock.

Finally, to your direction and guidance is attributable much of whatever valuable may result from my work; and the influence of your own scientific researches, not less than your personal co-operation, has lightened the labor and made the preparation of this report a pleasant task.

Respectfully submitted,

H. G. HUBBARD,
Special Agent.

Prof. C. V. RILEY,
Entomologist.

INTRODUCTION.

INJURIES BY INSECTS DISTINGUISHED FROM ORGANIC DISEASE

DISEASES AFFECTING THE CONDITION OF THE PLANT.

In plants, as in animals, the outward symptoms of disease do not always indicate plainly the cause of the physical disturbance. There is often need of skilful diagnosis before it is possible to intelligently apply a remedy.

Naturally, in exogenous plants, whose vital growing parts are near the surface, we look for the most part to external enemies for the cause of disease, and especially upon insects, the natural foes of the vegetable world, suspicion falls most readily and with greatest reason. Do the leaves of an orange tree turn yellow and fall to the ground, some worm, we suspect, is gnawing at the root, or Scale-insects are sapping the vital fluids from the bark. Are the blossoms blasted, the fruit dropping or splitting, we are inclined to lay the blame upon some sucking bug or upon some, it may be, harmless insect that we chance to see upon the plant.

But these phenomena are not always attributable to insect agencies, although they are often correctly so assigned. They are frequently the result of pathological disturbances, as obscure in their origin as are many diseases of animals.

As the object of the present treatise is solely to make known to orange growers the insect enemies and friends with which they have to deal, we cannot here enter upon a discussion of the principles of vegetable hygiene as applied to orange trees.

There are, however, several organic diseases which in their effect upon the tree closely copy the work of insects, and it is desirable that they should be clearly distinguished. We may, therefore, at the outset briefly examine the forms of fungus and other affections most commonly met with on plants of the citrus family, and give their distinguishing characters, with so much as is certainly known or can be plainly conjectured concerning their nature or origin.

DIE-BACK.—(Plate II, Fig. 1.) This is a disease of the bark and young wood, affecting chiefly the tender shoots. These grow to a length of 1 foot or 18 inches, and then become stunted, and finally die. Trees affected with this disease continually push out new growth which soon dies back, and finally the older portions of the tree become affected and gradually succumb.

A morbid growth undoubtedly of fungus origin invariably accompanies the disease in its advanced stages. This appears first as discolored patches or slight swellings, which gradually become confluent, and finally burst, forming an eruption of brownish color. The older branches become covered with ridges of exfoliated bark and exudations of gum, presenting an unsightly appearance, not unlike that of "Black-knot" on the plum.

The peculiar microscopic fungus which causes "die-back" is undoubtedly well known to mycologists. The disease yields readily to treatment with dilute carbolic or creosote washes, and is curable by these simple means, provided the exciting cause is removed. This fact may be regarded as confirmatory of its fungus character. The term "die-back" has been applied to several other diseases of the orange, and even to injuries from frost, but the affection above described is the one which is generally known under this name.

The exciting cause of "die-back" has been variously ascribed to over-fertilization, deep planting, imperfect drainage, the presence of humic acid in the soil, and finally to insects. While there is good reason to suppose that conditions of the soil, or of cultivation unfavorable to the growth of the plant, render it liable to the attacks of fungus diseases, there is no evidence that in this case its presence is due to the depredations of insects. It is true that the dead and dying branches of trees affected with die-back attract boring insects of various sorts, but these are found to belong to wood-eating kinds, which act as scavengers merely, and have no connection with the disease itself.

BARK-FUNGUS.—(Plate II, Fig. 2.) Many forms of lichens attach themselves to the trunk of the Orange, in common with other trees, and flourish abundantly in dark and damp situations. There are, however, several mold-like fungi found more exclusively upon the Orange and its allies. These bear a deceptive resemblance to incrustations of Scale-insect.

Of these fungi the one most readily mistaken for Scale-insects commonly appears upon the trunk and branches as little hard excrescences of gray color, which, in wet weather, burst, disclosing a white cottony interior, from which they are often confounded with the "Mealy Bug," (*Dactylopius*). The resemblance to the Coccid is increased when the white spicules, a bundle of which fills each little fungus cup, are beaten out by rains, and felted upon the bark in a mold-like coating. The fungus is confined to the surface of the bark, and appears to germinate exclusively among the *débris* of Scale-insects. It is always found upon trunks that have long been coated with Chaff Scale (*Parlatoria pergandii*). It may also be found upon the leaves when they have become infested with this scale, and is easily removed by gentle friction between the fingers, coming off with the scales, and showing no close attachment to the surface of the leaf.

The fungus feeds upon the substance of the dead or vacated scales, and is not directly parasitic upon the plant. It is extremely injurious, however, by reason of the closely-felted coating which is formed, causing the bark to harden and the tree to become "hide-bound."

FOOT-ROT.—This disease appears only upon sweet seedling orange trees, most frequently between the ages of nine and twelve years, and often bears a deceptive resemblance to the work of insects. It takes the form of cancerous sores, which destroy the cambium layer of the bark. The sores are confined, except in rare instances, to the foot or collar of the tree, and begin as little cavities filled with fermenting sap and having an offensive, sour odor. These cavities extend their boundaries, the outer bark dries and cracks, allowing the sap to exude and run down upon the outside. Sometimes winding channels are formed in the inner bark by the burrowing of the pus, and when these are laid bare by the knife the resemblance to the track of a "Sawyer," or coleopterous borer, is very striking. When the sores become extensive the dead outer bark above them sloughs away, exposing the dry wood beneath. At this stage the disease is liable to be mistaken for the work of "Woodlice" or White-ants (Termites), which will, moreover, very likely have made their appearance. The characteristic mark by which the galleries of termites may most readily be distinguished from sores of foot-rot consists of a lining of comminuted wood with which these insects always smooth the walls of their tunnels and chambers. If this is wanting in any of the wounds, even though termites be seen in the immediate vicinity, they cannot be the authors of the mischief.

Foot-rot usually ends by girdling and killing the tree. Like cancer in animals, it is sometimes successfully treated by a free use of the knife, although this frequently serves only to aggravate the difficulty and increase the area of the disease.

Antiseptic treatment with lotions and poultices containing carbolic acid might prove beneficial, but seems never to have been tried. A remedy that has been found practicable, if taken in time, is to plant at the foot of the diseased tree young stocks of the Sour Orange, which is never affected by the disease, and as soon as they have established themselves, to graft them into the trunk two feet or more above the ground. These supplementary stocks will in time replace the original roots and form a new crown, while supporting and preserving the life of the tree.

Many insects, attracted by the fermenting sap, resort to these sores. They are all scavengers, feeding only upon the lifeless bark and sap, or else innocuous and predatory species, such as lurk in dark, cool places everywhere.

SMUT.—A deposit resembling soot is found upon the leaves and bark of trees which have been infested with certain kinds of bark-lice. It is not confined to the Orange, but is found upon the Oleander, the Olive, and many other plants, and always follows the attacks of Lecanium, Ceroplastes, and other Coccids which produce honey-dew.

The Gall-berry, *Ilex glabra*, a wild plant which grows in great abundance in the sterile "flat woods" of Florida, and which is much infested by Ceroplastes scale, is often blackened by it over many acres in extent.

Prof. W. G. Farlow, in a paper entitled "On a Disease of Olive and Orange Trees occurring in California in the Spring and Summer of 1875," describes and figures this smut, and shows it to be a fungus. He determines it to be *Capnodium citri* Berkeley & Desmazières, a species occurring on Orange, &c., in Europe, and says that it seems nearly or quite identical with the *Fumago salicina* of older writers. (See Tulasne, "Carpologia Fungorum," Pl. XXXIV, Figs. 14 and 20.) In the same paper it is shown, from botanical considerations, that it does not feed on the plant, but on the honey-dew ejected by insects.

Smut upon orange trees has long been known, and its nature and origin have formed the subject of many curious speculations.

In a rare work, published at Nice, in 1806, and entitled "Histoire Naturelle de la Morfée, ou de l'Infection de la Famille des Orangers; par l'Abbé Loquez," this fungus is described, and also the Bark-louse connected with it, and the two are treated as jointly constituting a disease of the Orange, which at that time ravaged the gardens of Italy and southern France.*

Both the fungus and the insect being nourished, according to the author's view, upon the superabundant juices of the plant, he proposes to remedy the disorders produced by their combined attack by depriving the tree of moisture, and by the dessication of its juices.

Smut probably does no more injury than would be occasioned by a similar coating of soot or other fine powder coating the leaves and growing parts of the plant. But as it is never seen except in conjunction with the destructive insects above mentioned, it is not very easy to determine what proportion of the damage is attributable to the fungus alone.

SPLITTING OF FRUIT.—Moore, in his treatise on Orange Culture, says: "The cracking of fruit is occasioned by any suspension of the growth of the fruit, and a consequent hardening of the rind, followed by a sudden flow of sap from any stimulating cause, as highly fertilizing a bearing grove, especially during summer, or a wet spell following a dry." Certain sap-loving beetles of the family *Nitidulidæ*, and also vinegar or pomace flies, attack the split fruit both on the tree and after it has fallen to the ground. The larvæ, which they produce in vast numbers, penetrate the pulp, and cause it to rot with great rapidity.

Many persons, finding the split fruit infested with these grubs and

---

* The Bark-louse is called by the author *Coccus hesperidum* Linn.; but his minute and excellent account of the insect and its habits clearly indicate that it was a species of Mealy-bug (*Dactylopius*).

maggots, are disposed to consider them the originators of the mischief. A sound orange is, however, most perfectly protected by its oily rind against the attacks of these and most other insects, and it has been found that they die of starvation rather than penetrate it to reach the pulp within.

DROPPING OF FRUIT.—Sucking-bugs (Hemiptera) of several kinds attack the orange, and their punctures invariably cause the fruit to drop and rot.

All fruit trees drop their fruit from causes more or less obscure, but in some way connected with the condition of the plant. The Orange is no exception to this rule, but whenever the loss of fruit is attributable to the bites or punctures of insects, the depredators themselves may be readily discovered, as all are of large size and easily seen.

WINTER-KILLED BRANCHES.—Borers and mining insects are commonly found in dead twigs and branches killed by frost in severe winters. They need occasion no alarm, as they are chiefly scavengers, subsisting upon the dead wood and bark, and seldom do injury to the living parts of the plant.

THE INSECT FAUNA OF THE ORANGE.

ATTRACTION WHICH THE ORANGE TREE HAS FOR INSECTS.—The dark green and glossy foliage of the orange tree, its dense shade, vigorous growth, and above all the succulence of the young shoots and leaves, render it unusually attractive to insects, not only of leaf-eating kinds, which are general feeders, but also to many predatory and innocuous insects which lurk in cool and shady places or seek protection among sheltering leaves.

Thus many kinds of insects are seen about the trees, some of them injurious, some beneficial, and some occasional visitants, whose presence is without significance for good or ill. In general, it may be said that those which are most visible to the casual observer, and which appear to seek no concealment, are not injurious. They are, as a rule, predatory insects, such as the wasps and sucking-bugs, which prowl about the trees in search of prey, or harmless flies and bees, visiting the flowers for nectar, or sporting among the foliage.

The injurious species generally lie concealed. They hide in folded leaves, excrete a scale, or form a covering of sticks and bark. Many of them are of small size, or, if large, they have some device for their better concealment, and by some peculiarity of form or of coloration they are made to resemble portions of the plant on which they rest, and thus escape observation. The large green "Katydid" readily passes for a leaf, and in spite of its size is very difficult to detect among the foliage. The "Orange Dog," a caterpillar more than $2\frac{1}{2}$ inches long, is so marked with brown and white as to be inconspicuous when resting upon the bark, from its resemblance to a lichen-covered twig. Its chrysalis presents a still more striking example of the same protective resemblance.

INJURIOUS INSECTS.—First in importance are the Bark-lice (Coccidæ). These sap the life of the tree at its source. The vital juices are sucked up, and probably also poisoned, as the blood of animals sometimes is by the sucking parasites which infest them.

Of insects injuring the root, little is known. As has been shown, "Wood-lice" (Termites) are very often injurious just beneath the surface of the ground, and there are some as yet unknown larvæ which are said to bore into the tap-root at a considerable depth. The trunk has few enemies, except Bark-lice, some species of which prefer to attack that part.

The leaves and twigs, being those portions which offer the greatest extent of exposed surface and the greatest variety of food, support also the largest number of depredating enemies. A large proportion of the leaf eaters feed indiscriminately upon many plants. Such are nearly all the locusts, grasshoppers, and crickets, many caterpillars, and some true bugs which injure by suction. The latter, however, for the most part confine their attentions to the tender shoots, blossom buds and fruit.

With many of these insects the injury is limited to the gnawing of a few leaves, and their importance to the orange-grower is not great. Others, on account of their large size and voracity, defoliate the trees and do appreciable damage.

The tender budding stalks furnish particular species of insects with their especial food; certain other species feed upon the budding leaves in the earlier part of their lives, and, when adult, select them as places of deposit for their eggs. These do especial harm in checking the advancing growth, nipping it in the bud, and inflicting far greater damage than those which confine their attacks to mature parts of the plant.

Injury to the blossom buds and young fruit is caused by certain sucking-bugs (Hemiptera), and the fruit as it approaches maturity is attacked by insects of the same family, whose punctures cause it to drop from the trees and rot.

A minute mite, which appears to be one of the few forms of insect life peculiar to plants of the citrus family, infests the leaves and green fruit, causing upon the rind of the latter a discoloration known as " rust."

BENEFICIAL INSECTS.—Under this head are included a great variety of predaceous insects and parasites, without whose aid in checking the horde of depredators, the cultivation, not only of the Orange, but of most other plants, would be an impossibility.

Every order of insects furnishes its predatory species; which are to a greater or less extent beneficial in destroying the plant-eating kinds upon orange trees. The paper wasps, which hang their nests to the branches, are employed in seeking out spiders and leaf-rolling caterpillars, with which to feed their helpless young. The Lady-birds (Coccinellidæ) and their soft-bodied young, with other beetles seen upon the trunk and branches, are busily engaged in the good work of tearing off the scales of Bark-lice and feeding upon the Coccids and their eggs. Wherever is found a tender shoot infested with a colony of Aphides, there, in the midst of the swarming Plant-lice, will be found the slug-like larvæ of predaceous flies (*Syrphus*, etc.), gradually but surely reducing their numbers, in spite of the marvelous powers of reproduction and fecundity of the Plant-lice. Upon the leaves the active young of the Lace-wing (*Chrysopa*) may be seen trundling their little heaps of refuse, beneath which the insect lurks in ambush for its prey. Among the smaller forms, whose operations are invisible to the unassisted eye, are numerous predatory mites, which swarm among the Bark-lice, and greatly aid in holding them in check.

First in importance among beneficial insects, although least in size, and most difficult of observation, are the true parasites, which live within the bodies, and even inhabit the eggs of other insects, and, after having eaten and destroyed their host, issue as minute and active winged insects. Few, if any, of the insect depredators upon the Orange are without internal parasites, belonging with few exceptions to the *Hymenoptera*, an order of four-winged insects of which the bees and wasps are types.

Owing to their small size, and the concealment in which they pass the greater portion of their lives, parasites are themselves seldom seen, but the extent of their operations is sometimes rendered apparent by the great mortality which follows their attacks upon an invading army of plant enemies. Sometimes the presence of a parasite within its body is indicated by a change of form or color which the parasitized insect undergoes before its death, and in any case, after death, the work of the parasite is plainly shown by the round hole which, in issuing, it leaves behind in the body or the protective covering of its host.

INNOCUOUS INSECTS.—Of these little need be said except that their number is legion. Their importance to the agriculturist consists in the liability of their being mistaken for noxious insects, and thus diverting attention from the real depredators.

Many harmless insects, which are so frequently seen upon the orange tree that they may be considered its regular attendants, are to a certain extent beneficial, and either feed upon the various mosses and fungi which accumulate upon the trunk and branches, or upon the lifeless wood and bark of dead portions of the tree.

IMPORTANCE OF DISTINGUISHING FRIENDS FROM FOES.—Although little can be done to increase the efficiency of beneficial insects, much good can at times be accomplished by refraining from interference with their operations. The orange-grower often does injury to his own interests through lack of knowledge in distinguishing friends from foes, and by the indiscriminate killing of all insects which he finds upon his trees.

Horticulturists cannot be expected to acquire a technical knowledge of insects attainable only by specialists, but the entomologist can offer in many cases practical suggestions to aid in protecting the beneficial while accomplishing the destruction of the injurious species. In these pages, wherever our present knowledge permits, the ways and means of securing this advantage will be indicated, and it is hoped, by the aid of plain descriptions and figures, to render recognizable to the orange-grower some of the more important beneficial insects with which he is concerned, as well as the destructive kinds with which he must contend.

PRESENCE OF CERTAIN INJURIOUS INSECTS INDICATED BY ANTS.—Many of the Bark-lice (Coccidæ), as well as the common Plant-louse (Aphis) of the Orange produce sweetish secretions, which are greatly relished by ants; indeed, with some species, the honey-dew ejected by these insects appears to furnish the greater part of their food. At all events, whenever any of these nectar-giving insects exist upon an orange tree, ants will be found in attendance upon them, and a stream of ants ascending and descending the trunk of the tree is an infallible indication of their presence.

The ascending line of ants readily guides the eye to the spot among the twigs and leaves where these enemies lie concealed, and they are especially useful in indicating the whereabouts of incipient colonies, which may thus be destroyed before they have greatly increased, and by their numbers and the extent of their injuries have forced themselves upon our notice.

Young orange trees are particularly liable to suffer injury from Aphis and the soft-bodied, nectar-producing Coccidæ. In the nursery, where the greatest attention should be given to prevent stunting and loss of growth, we may pass rapidly along the rows, and by the presence of ants upon the stocks detect at a glance those plants upon which the pests have obtained a foothold.

SYSTEMS OF CULTIVATION.

INFLUENCE OF SHADE UPON THE INCREASE OF INSECT PESTS.—Most insects love shade. Some, and among the number Scale-insects, the worst pests of the Orange, prefer the darkness and dampness produced by dense masses of foliage. Plants, on the other hand, require light and air, for want of which the inner branches pine and lose vitality, a condition which also greatly favors the reproduction of Scale-insects.

The good advice of the horticulturist, "Prune back excessive branch growth, give and keep an open head to the tree," may be supplemented and sustained by that of the entomologist, "Let in light and air." Let this not, however, be construed as indorsing the practice of trimming high the trunks, and depriving them of their spreading lower branches, their best and most natural protection against extremes of heat and cold.

CLEAN CULTURE OR MULCHING PREFERABLE TO CROPPING YOUNG GROVES.—The practice of planting crops between the rows of young orange trees is not without certain evil consequences in attracting depredators. Many of these do indirect damage only. Cotton, for instance, is attacked by the Cotton Worm (*Aletia xylina*) which, after stripping the cotton plants of their leaves, gather upon the orange trees and make their cocoons between the leaves. The orange trees are fouled with their webs and tangles, which foster Scale-insects.

A very appreciable amount of damage is always inflicted by locusts or grasshoppers (Acrididæ) when succulent plants, like Cotton or Cow Pea, are planted in young groves; and when the system of allowing weeds to grow about the trees is pursued, the loss of growth from these insects is sometimes very serious. Older trees do not greatly suffer, and are, moreover, able to spare a portion of their foliage; but very young trees when surrounded by weeds are more or less defoliated and checked in growth. The tops of young trees being small and low their leaders and tender shoots are gnawed and destroyed as fast as they appear, and most of the summer growth may thus be lost.

Objection is sometimes made to mulching orange trees with leaves or vegetable refuse, on the ground that the mulch attracts and harbors insects. Most of the insects which lurk in such places, however, are predaceous species, and may be considered either harmless or beneficial. Very few of them are injurious to the orange tree.

White ants (Termites) must be considered an exception to this rule. They are attracted by decaying vegetable matter, especially by dead wood, and sometimes attack the living tree at or beneath the surface of the ground. To avoid attracting such dangerous neighbors care should be had in mulching to leave the crown of the tree uncovered and exposed to the light and air. It is also best to exclude from the mulch all solid masses of wood material, such as chips and branches.

It is to be noted in regard to the common practice of scattering in the grove and about the trees bits of wood, bark, branches or logs, and allowing them to decay upon the ground, that the danger from this system of fertilizing is not always immediate, but consists rather in attracting termites and inducing them to establish colonies in the vicinity of the trees, which may indeed escape injury while an abundant supply of dead wood remains, but are liable to be attacked if this should become dry or partially exhausted.

SEASONS OF GREATEST INSECT ACTIVITY.—Although in Florida some insects breed continuously throughout the year, there is a very general winter rest from November or December to January or February, according to the severity of the season. The awakening in spring is gradual and not sudden as at the North.

In February most of the species of insects injurious to the Orange make their appearance, and in May and June attain their greatest activity.

During July and August there is a marked lull in the insect world. Many forms disappear, to return again in September.

The most effective time to wage a war of extermination against insect pests can only be determined satisfactorily by a special study of each case, but, if a general rule be required, June and September may be indicated as the months in which especial efforts should be made to rid the groves of insect enemies. For fighting Scale-insects, however, the month of March or April, if the season be a late one, will be found the best in all the year.

PART I.

COCCIDÆ.

[SCALE-INSECTS OR BARK-LICE.]

CHAPTER I.

CHARACTERS OF THE COCCIDÆ AND COMMENCEMENT OF THE CONSIDERATION OF THE SUBFAMILY DIASPINÆ.

GENERAL CHARACTERS OF THE COCCIDÆ AND THEIR RELATIONS TO OTHER INSECTS.

The Scale-insects or Bark-lice, as they are more comprehensively called, constitute a striking group of insects, remarkable for the peculiarities of their development. In this family the females never progress to the winged state; on the contrary, in many of the species, after a short larval period, they undergo a change of form, and retrograde, becoming, when adult, mere living egg-sacks, with organs only of the simplest sorts, such as are needed for reproducing their kind, and to support a degraded, almost plant-like existence.

The males, on the other hand, advance further and pass through the usual metamorphoses of insects, finally appearing as winged insects. They differ, however, from other insects of the order Homoptera in possessing but one pair of wings; the hind pair (*halteres*) being aborted, and reduced to stumps, which are provided with a hook that grapples the fore-wing, and apparently aids in steadying or directing flight. The existence of the male after reaching the adult state is fleeting; he seeks out and impregnates one or more females of his kind, and then dies, living at most a day or two, and taking in the mean time no food. Indeed, in this final stage the insect is entirely unprovided with mouth organs or digestive apparatus of any sort.

Bark-lice commonly excrete a covering, which may be of a horny, resinous, waxy, or powdery nature. Some of these coverings afford products of use in the arts; the white wax of commerce and lac, from which shell-lac is formed, are substances of this sort. The dried-up bodies of certain other species yield purple or red dyes, of which the best known in modern times is cochineal. Many of the species, and especially the naked kinds, eject honey-dew, a sweetish liquid, which is greedily lapped up by ants, bees, wasps, and many other insects. A sort of solidified honey-dew, called "manna," is produced by a Bark-louse (*Gossyparia mannipara* Ehrenberg); it collects in considerable quantities upon the tamarix trees in Arabia, and is thought by some to have been the heaven-sent manna that nourished the Hebrews in their wanderings. Even in our day it is given as food to invalids, and has a limited use in pharmacy.

DIVISION INTO SUBFAMILIES.

The species of Coccidæ, according to their varied forms and the diverse nature of their coverings, are divided into several groups or subfamilies.

Three groups are represented in the southern United States, and embrace all the species doing injury to orange trees. The characters given below will suffice for the proper arrangement of the species falling within the scope of this treatise.

I. DIASPINÆ.—This subfamily embraces those species which form a thin, horny scale, supplemented by the molted skins of the insect. Example, the Long Scale of the Orange, *Mytilaspis gloverii*.

II. LECANINÆ.—The species of this division form no true scale; they are either naked or covered with a thick coating of waxy material. The naked species have, however, toughened skins, which, after the death of the insect, remain adhering to the bark, and then somewhat resemble the scales of the Diaspinæ. Example, the Turtle-back Scale, *Lecanium hesperidum*.

III. COCCINÆ.—This division includes soft-bodied Bark-lice, called "Mealy-bugs" because of their loose coverings of white, fibrous wax, in the form of a powder, or of long and delicate plates and filaments, easily destroyed by a touch. Example, the common Mealy-bug, *Dactylopius destructor*.

In the first of these groups (Diaspinæ) the change from an active, roving larva, possessed of legs, to a fixed and memberless, sack-like animal, takes place very soon after birth. The scale also is a complete and separate structure, permanently fastened to the bark, and large enough to include not only the body of the mother insect, but also her eggs.

In the second group (Lecaninæ) the form of the larva is retained much longer than in the first group, and the insects, though very sluggish in habit, do not become absolutely fixed upon the bark until they are distended with eggs or young. The legs also are not lost, but gradually become useless as the insect increases in size, and are finally lost to sight under the swollen body.

In the third group (Coccinæ) the form of the larva is retained by the females through life, and is obscured, but not altered, by the formation of an egg-sack, or by light coatings of wax.* The organs of locomotion are retained, and the females in most of the species move about freely, even after they have begun to produce young.

Thus in structure and habits the Diaspinæ differ most widely from other insects, the Coccinæ least, while the Lecaninæ hold in this respect an intermediate position.

---

*Except in *Kermes*, a genus with which orange-growers are not likely to become concerned.

DIASPINÆ.

(THE ARMORED SCALES.)

[Plate III, and Figures 1 and 2.]*

LIFE-HISTORY OF THE ARMORED SCALES.

The larva.—When the young Bark-louse first makes its appearance from beneath the protecting scale of its mother, it is a minute, oval, flattened creature, provided with all the organs usually possessed by the young of insects; namely, six legs, a pair of antennæ in front and

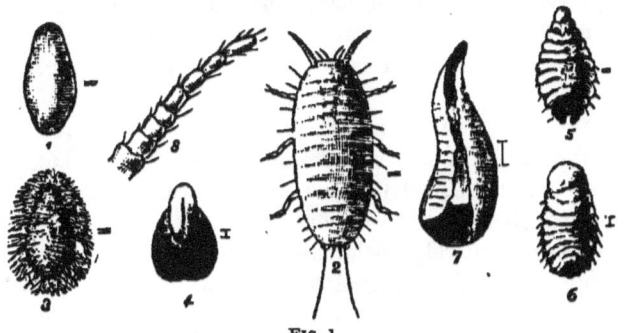

FIG. 1.—1, egg—natural size, scarcely ¹⁄₁₀₀ inch; 2, larva as it appears when running over the twigs—natural length, ¹⁄₁₀₀ inch; 3, its appearance soon after becoming fixed; 4, appearance of scale after the second plate is formed; 5, form of louse (ventral view) soon after losing its members; 6, form of louse when full grown; 7, fully formed scales, containing louse, as it appears from the under side, when raised; 8, highly magnified antenna of the larva—by an error eight joints, instead of seven, the correct number, are shown in the drawing. (After Riley.)

a pair of bristles behind, simple eyes on the sides of the head, and a short sucking beak.

At first the young larva moves restlessly about, with a lumbering gait, by no means sluggish, yet markedly less rapid than that of the minute and active mites which are often found in company with it. The object of its wanderings is simply to find a suitable spot upon the bark in which to insert its sucking tube or beak. Usually within a few hours after leaving the parent scale the young Bark-louse has become a fixture upon the surface of the plant; the sucking mouth-parts, which consist of a bundle of four slender hairs, grow rapidly until they greatly exceed the body of the insect in length, and, penetrating deeply into the tissues of the plant, can never after-

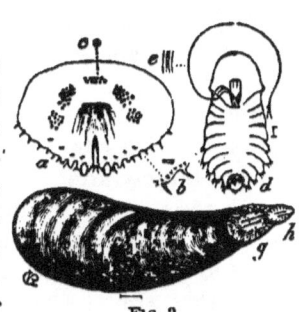

FIG. 2.—*a*, terminal joint of the female; *b*, spines upon the border; *c*, excretory pores; *d*, pregnant female; *e*, structure of proboscis, showing four components; *f*, excretory scale, showing successive layers; *g*, second, or medial, scale; *h*, larval, or first scale. (After Riley.)

---

*Figures 1 and 2 illustrate the mode of growth in *Mytilaspis pomorum* Bouché, the Oyster-shell Bark-louse of the Apple. They are reproduced from the First and Fifth Missouri Entomological Reports (1868 and 1872), in which the facts essential to a complete knowledge of the life-history of Diaspinous Scale-insects are fully set forth by Prof. C. V. Riley.

wards be removed by the Coccid, but firmly anchor it in place. When pulled by force from the bark these long bristles separate and curl up, and the insect is powerless to reinsert them or to again attach itself to the plant, and must inevitably die of starvation.

As soon as the young Bark-louse begins to feed upon the juices of the plant excretions of wax commence to exude from its body. There first appear along the sides and at the end of the body long curled threads of white wax. These form a tangled mass, enveloping the insect; but this first covering is very delicate, and after a time it partially or entirely disappears, owing to the action of the weather. It is succeeded by a covering formed in a similar manner, but of denser texture. This second covering is more persistent; it is in fact the beginning of the permanent scale.

For two or three weeks after the formation of the infantile scale is completed the external appearance of the insect does not change, but within a new body gradually forms and separates from the larva skin until the latter becomes a loosened envelope, from which finally the new-formed insect entirely withdraws its body, passing through a split in the under side. The molted skin is not abandoned, however, but remains, partly covering the Coccid above, and ultimately forms the summit or the extremity of the permanent scale.

With the old larva skin are cast off the now useless members of the larva, and the insect takes the form of a fleshy sack of very simple construction. The joints of the body are indicated by fleshy folds, and the hair-like mouth-tube projects from the under side near one end of the body. The thin outer edge of the last or anal joint of the body is furnished with minute, horny lobes and spines, and its upper and lower surfaces present numerous pores, through which flows a viscid liquid, the material which on hardening forms the protecting scale. On the under side of the last joint can also be plainly seen the vaginal opening, through which pass the eggs or young.

Immediately after molting the body of the Coccid expands, so that it can no longer be entirely covered by the cast skin of the larva, and a portion of the broad terminal joint projects beyond its edge; but the exposed parts are soon flooded with a glutinous fluid, issuing from the pores that stud its surface, and this in a few minutes hardens, and forms an extension of the covering.

During the growth of the insect which follows the molting of the larva skin, the scale covering receives repeated additions of these thin laminæ, each of which underlies and projects slightly beyond the preceding layer, and the scale constantly increases in size and in solidity; while at all times the outer edge remains the thinnest, and therefore the most vulnerable point. Thus the process of growth at this stage is seen to be analogous to that of snails or oysters, which form their shells in an exactly similar manner.

A considerable interval having elapsed after the first molt, the females again cast their skins; but their form at this time remains unchanged. The second skin like the first remains in place and forms a part of the scale; it is, however, less distinctly visible than the first larval skin, being covered with more or less of the thick excreted material.

Soon after the second molt the females are impregnated by the males. From this time until the scales reach their full size their growth is very rapid. In the linear scales (*Mytilaspis*) the females not only increase in size as their bodies become distended with eggs, but they also shift somewhat their position under the scale, so that finally, at the smaller end, that portion which lies immediately under the molted skins is left vacant. To permit this movement sufficient slack is given the flexible sucking tube between its junction with the body and the point at which it enters the bark.

The eggs are now laid under the scale, beginning at the outer edge. As they are deposited, the body of the female shrinks, and gradually retreats to its former position, leaving the outer portion of the scale filled with eggs. When all her eggs are laid the depleted female shrivels and dries up, and life in her exhausted body gradually becomes extinct.

The Males.—As crawling larvæ, and during the time that their scales are forming, the males are indistinguishable from the females; but after the first molt differences begin to appear, and the scales of the males become recognizable by their form or color, although the insects themselves are not markedly different until after the second molt.

Shortly before the second molt of the females the males also cast their skins a second time, and in so doing change to the pupa state. In the pupa, the legs, wings, and other parts of the perfect insect are gradually formed under a mask-like skin, in which the new form is obscurely outlined.

At the second molt the male ejects the skin from its scale, while in the female it remains and forms a part of the scale itself. In the male growth ceases with this molt; but the scale of the female is at this stage less than half its full size; the male scale is therefore much smaller and thinner than that of the other sex, and the first larva skin, but not the second, forms part of its structure.

After remaining a week or sometimes less in the pupa state the pupal envelope is rent and torn from its limbs by the perfect insect. This operation takes place under the scale, and the winged fly leaves its shelter only after a rest of several hours, which, indeed, may be prolonged into days if the weather does not happen to be propitious. The exit of the fly is made by pushing up a portion of the outer edge of the scale. In the elongate scales of Mytilaspis, the escape of the male is facilitated by a thin joint in the scale, which permits the broad end to be lifted as a flap. The body of the male terminates in a spine-shaped organ, by means of which it is enabled to reach and fertilize the females under their scales.

Prof. J. H. Comstock, whose minute and exhaustive study of the life-histories of certain of our common Scale-insects has left little to be added by subsequent observers, has pointed out that the lives of these insects are divided by their metamorphoses into nearly equal intervals. In the words of this author, "the three intervals between the birth of the female and the first molt, between the latter and the second molt, and between this and the beginning of oviposition are about equal."* The first molt in the male, and also its second molt, or entrance into pupa, take place at nearly the same time with the molts of the female. The existence of the male, however, terminates before the completion of the third interval by the female.

The interval in which the eggs are laid and hatched, and the young larvæ desert the parent scale, is about equal to the preceding intervals. This fourth period completes the cycle of development, and its close witnesses the death of the female, following the departure of her progeny.

During the spring and early summer, in the laboratory at Washington, twenty days appears to have been the mean duration of each interval; in the open air in Florida there is considerable acceleration, due to the warmer climate. This is apparent especially in the later stages of development, which are greatly shortened in summer. The first molt usually takes place within twenty days after hatching, but this first period, although more constant than the following, varies with the season or in different species, from sixteen to twenty-four days. The whole cycle, or brood period in winter, may cover three months, but in summer, it is reduced to five or six weeks.

Nature of the scale covering.—As was first clearly pointed out by Prof. C. V. Riley (see Fifth Missouri Entomological Report, p. 80) the scale of the Diaspinæ is a shield-like structure, covering the insect above, and wholly or partially protecting it beneath. It is constructed, as we have seen, in part of the molted skins of the insect, but mainly of a horny excretion, covering or surrounding the latter, and deposited by the Coccid in numerous fine, overlapping layers. The under layer is thinner, and, although perhaps a separate piece, is firmly united to the upper scale at the edges, so that the latter appear to be turned under at the sides. In the long scales the ventral plate consists of a flange along each side, leaving in the middle an open crevice; but in the oval or circular scales it forms an unbroken shield, which entirely separates the body of the insect from contact with the bark.

The scale is permanently fastened upon the tree, and so closely molded to its surface that the pores of the bark or the stomata of the leaf are seen plainly stamped upon it when removed.

The materials of which the scale is constructed are very indestructi-

---

* Report of Commissioner of Agriculture for 1880, p. 280.

ble, and well serve to protect the helpless organism which they surround, both from the action of the weather and the attacks of external enemies. The molted skins consist of *chitine*, a substance which forms the hard external parts of nearly all insects, and the excreted portion of the scale is composed of a sort of hardened wax, having the toughness of horn.

The upper scale is therefore impervious to most liquids, and is not soluble in acid or alkaline solutions strong enough to injure the plant. It resists the action of oils and of bisulphide of carbon, an almost universal solvent. Many insecticides are therefore inoperative, and all insoluble substances, such as sulphur, etc., are clearly useless, as they do not reach the eggs or mature insects. The thinner, ventral scale is not impervious to the more volatile oils or to alcoholic solutions, some of which reach and kill the insect by penetration through the bark.

As the scale, like the shell of the snail, is formed by successive additions, and keeps pace in its growth with that of the body of the insect within, its vulnerable point is the growing end, and there are times during its formation when the posterior extremity of the insect projects slightly beyond it and becomes exposed to the action of penetrating liquids. This is particularly the case at the critical periods when the Coccid sheds its skin. But when the scale is fully completed and tightly sealed at all points, no insect is more difficult to reach and to destroy.

LONG SCALE.

(*Mytilaspis gloverii*, Packard.)

[Plate III, fig. 2; IV; and Fig. 3.]

Growth of the Scale.—In the Long Scale the increase in size takes place chiefly in one direction, producing a linear body, which may be either straight or curved in the form of a cornucopia. The first molt or cast skin of the wandering larva forms its extreme tip, but the delicate film of wax which at first covered this skin disappears, or leaves traces only in the form of two minute projections, and its surface exhibits more or less plainly marked indications of the body-joints of the young louse. Beyond, and partly underlying the shield-shaped first larva skin, is that of the second molt, but this skin is overlaid and imbedded in the substance of the scale, so that its oval outline is faintly visible beneath the coating of horn. The scale increases in width during the first half of its growth, after which the width remains the same and the sides are parallel.

The plate which forms the underside is firmly united to the upper portion of the scale, and projects beyond it on the sides, forming thin flanges, that greatly increase the tenacity of its hold upon the bark. The ventral plate does not entirely cover the under surface, but is divided in the middle, leaving a long, narrow slit, through which the body of the insect comes in contact with the bark.

The Scale of the Female is brownish, about 3^{mm} ($\frac{1}{100}$ inch) in length, and less than one-fourth as wide; there is, however, great variation in size, and dwarfed or malformed scales are numerous. When crowded the scales are apt to be warped and curved, although normally they are straight.

The Scale of the Male is much smaller than that of the female, quite uniformly 1^{mm} ($\frac{1}{100}$ inch) in length, and very seldom curved.

The colors, varying shades of brown, are lighter, and incline to yellow in the males and young, but become dark mahogany-brown in the older females. The brighter color of the forming scales gives warning of the increase of the pest, and to a practiced eye discloses the age and progress of the brood, even when scattered or mingled with the *débris* of former broods.

In the aggregate, the scales, when densely clustered, have a reddish hue, which has caused this species to be known in some localities as the "Red Scale."

Female Coccid.—The body is an elongate, flattened sack, rounded at the extremities and divided into segments or joints. The posterior segment is bordered with spines and plates of microscopic fineness. During the growth of the insect this segment is the widest portion of the body, and upon its surface, as upon a trowel, are laid the successive additions to the scale. After impregnation it loses its prominence, through the swelling of the intermediate joints of the body.

The young and growing females are translucent, waxy white, with the thin outer edge of the last joint yellowish (*chitinous*). As they grow older, they are tinged with amethyst, and toward the end of their lives become dark purple in color.

The adult female is 1.3^{mm} ($\frac{5}{100}$ inch) in length. Its sucking beak considerably exceeds the body in length. The structural details are given in the Report of the Commissioner of Agriculture for 1880, page 323.

Male Coccid.—The male is a minute fly, $\frac{1}{100}$ inch in length. Its body is

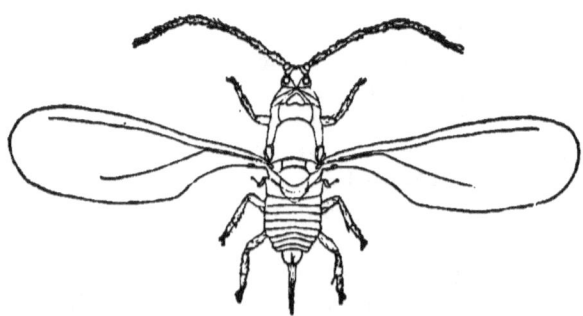

FIG. 3.—*Mytilaspis gloverii* (Pack.), male. (After Comstock.)

pale pink in color, and three or four times as long as wide. The different joints of which it is composed are very closely united, but are indicated upon the naked surface by a variety of lines, some of which inclose shield-shaped plates. Toward the head these plates are small and more or less triangular; upon the middle portion, to which the wings are attached, they are large and with rounded sides. The abdominal extremity is divided into short, transverse joints.

The head is small, and bears upon its apex a pair of rather heavy, many-jointed antennæ, equal to the body in length, and clothed with short hairs. The mouth-organs are wanting, but in their place are seen black dots, which are said to be supplementary eyes. The true eyes are also black in color, and are visible on the sides of the head.

The front pair of legs is placed well forward, and a wide interval separates it from the second and third pairs, which underlie the abdomen. The wings are long, membranous paddles, strengthened by a vein with a single branch, and supported by the aborted hind wings, or balancers, as they are called. The latter are minute, and terminate in a hook which grapples a pocket in the front wing. Although quite large, the wings and also the legs are weak and rather imperfect organs of locomotion, and the insect's powers of flight are not good. The sexual organs, on the other hand, are well developed, and consist externally of a long, stout spine or style at the end of the body.

Eggs.—The eggs are elongate-oval. The first laid are white; those laid later are tinged with purple. All become purple before hatching.

Young Coccid.—The newly-hatched larva is sometimes white, but usually more or less tinged and mottled with purple. It is oval and flattened, and does not exceed $\frac{1}{100}$ of an inch in length. The body is divided into a number of unequal joints; the first of these constitutes the head, and bears a pair of short antennæ, provided with bristles; minute eyes, widely separated, on each margin, and mouth-organs beneath united to form a sucking beak. The body terminates in two bristles of extreme fineness, which bend downwards, and are dragged after the insect as it walks.

Life-history.—The development and formation of the scale in the Diaspinæ has already been described. The history of the Long Scale presents few peculiarities. The newly-hatched larva wanders about for a very short time. As soon as it has settled upon the bark it begins to emit along its sides threads of wax, which in a few days form a white film, and gradually cover the body, beginning from behind and ending in front in two short, horn-like projections. Some of the threads stand out from the rest; being long and curly, they are fragile and easily broken by the wind, but in calm weather they sometimes accumulate, and form cottony tufts or tangles.

This first covering is evanescent, but traces of it remain in the horn-like projections on the sides of the head.

The casting off of the larva skin, or first molt, takes place eighteen or twenty days after birth, and immediately after this the formation of the true scale is begun. The first layers of horn are united to the hinder end of the larva skin, and partly underlie it. They are thin and transparent, but as each successive layer adds to their thickness, they develop a yellow color, which darkens at length to brown.

In the new form assumed by the insect after the molt the hinder end is broadly dilated, and as this portion of the body forms and determines the width of the scale, the latter for awhile increases in width as it grows in length. After the second molt in the female the extremity of the body ceases to grow in width, and the portion of the scale formed after this molt is linear, *i. e.*, has the sides parallel.

The second molt of the female occurs at the age of six or seven weeks. The male molts and changes to pupa a week or ten days earlier, and as the time required for this transition period is quite short, during the time that the females are casting their skins many of the males complete their transformations and issue from their scales as winged flies.

After the second molt the scale of the female continues to grow, and more than doubles its length, but increases little in width.

In nine or ten weeks from her birth the female begins to deposit eggs. At this time her body, although greatly elongated and distended with ova, does not entirely fill the scale; a space equal to about one-quarter of its entire length is left vacant at the upper or narrow end. The female is able, by means of the serrated edges of her body, to make a slight forward and backward movement within this vacant space.

The eggs are laid in two rows, and are placed obliquely, the eggs of one row alternating and interlocking at the ends with those of the other. The number of eggs laid by a single female varies greatly, but rarely exceeds thirty. The deposition of her eggs occupies the female from one to three weeks, according to the season. The eggs hatch within one week, unless retarded by cold weather. The first laid, those at the outer end, are the first to hatch, but the young lice usually remain several days under the parent scale. The egg-shells are left in place in the scale, but their arrangement is somewhat disturbed by the movements of the latest hatched young in making their escape.

The female after depositing all her eggs is much shrunken, and becomes very dark purple in color. The end of her existence is passed in that portion of the scale which she occupied at the time of the last molt.

Brood Periods.—There are at least three and sometimes four generations of Long Scale during the year, but the division into separate broods is not as distinct and clearly defined as with many other insects. The open winters in countries where the Orange is grown permit continuous breeding throughout the year, and at all seasons scales in every stage of development may be found upon the trees.

Not only does the time required by the insect for its development vary greatly in different seasons, and under varying conditions, but also individual insects in each brood undergo their transformations at unequal intervals, some far outstripping the rest and others lagging behind. This scattering in early broods confuses the succeeding ones and renders it impossible to assign to each an exact season or invariable duration. But although the limits of each brood cannot be exactly defined, the general progress in development may be known at any time by the condition of the majority of the scales.

Thus there are times when the number of migrating young reaches a maximum, and the application of remedies then proves particularly effective.

Three such periods occur: The first in spring, usually in March, but sometimes extending into April; the second in June or July; the third in September or October. During the winter months, if the season is a mild one, there is a fourth, very irregular brood beginning in January and continuing through this and the following month. The spring brood that follows is greatly confused. In cold and rainy winters the hatching process is retarded, and the appearance of the larvæ on the return of warm weather is more nearly simultaneous than in ordinary seasons.

Parasites.—Upon closely examining a branch or leaf infested with scales of *Mytilaspis gloverii*, there will always be found a certain number which have through their upper surface a small, round hole. The scales thus perforated are invariably females which have not quite completed their growth. They are empty or occupied by mites or other intruders, and the only trace of the original inhabitant which they contain is its dry, distended skin; this is also pierced with a round hole, placed directly beneath the one in the outer shell.

These are the exit holes of Hymenopterous parasites, the most effective enemies of the Scale-insect, and which, after destroying the maker of the scale, and after completing their own transformations in its room, have eaten their way through its skin and its shell, appearing finally as minute four-winged flies, both male and female.

The female parasite, when seeking to deposit her eggs, probes about the edges of the scale in order to find, if possible, an open crevice through which to insert her slender ovipositor. Failing in this she bores directly through the scale, using her ovipositor as a drill, and in this way inserts within the body of the Coccid a single egg.

The footless grub that hatches from this egg lives within the body of the Scale-insect and gradually consumes it. When nothing is left but the empty skin of its host the little parasite, now swollen to an almost globular form, transforms first to a pupa, and then to the perfect fly, which at last makes its appearance through a hole eaten in the walls that surround it.

Several distinct species of these minute parasites attack the Long Scale. They are about $\frac{3}{100}$ inch in length, with an expanse of wing equal to nearly twice their length. The head is large, with large compound eyes, and three minute simple eyes (*ocelli*) like jewels set upon its vertex. The body is rather short and thick. The wings are transparent and beautifully iridescent; they are strengthened for a portion of their length by a stout vein, placed very near the margin, and having a short spur or branch at or near the end of the vein. The front wings are broader outwards and rounded at the tips. The hind wings are narrow and more pointed at the ends. The antennæ are elbowed, and clubbed at the ends; they arise from the anterior face of the head, in front of the eyes.

In *Aphelinus fuscipennis* Howard, the general color is yellow, with a black band across the head behind the eyes, and several dusky bands upon the body. The wings are clouded with patches of smoky brown. Length, 0.6^{mm} ($\frac{2}{100}$ inch).

Aphycus flavus Howard, is uniformly yellow in color, with clear wings. Length, 1.2^{mm}, ($\frac{5}{100}$ inch).

Under the name *Aphelinus aspidioticola*, Mr. Ashmead (Orange Insects, page 7) describes another parasite of the Long Scale, which has a reddish brown or dusky body, yellowish legs, and clear wings. It is $\frac{2}{100}$ inch in length. According to Mr. Howard, this insect is not an *Aphelinus*, but belongs to an unknown genus of another family.

These parasites attack the female Long Scale insect about the time of her impregnation, and their egg is deposited, not simply beneath the scale, or, as some writers have affirmed, among the eggs of the Coccid, but within the body of the Coccid itself. The presence of the parasite within her body destroys the fecundity of the Scale-insect and she finally dies without reproducing her kind.

So effective are the attacks of these internal enemies, that not less than 25 per cent. of the scales are destroyed by them, and at times their numbers increase to such an extent that colonies of Long Scale are reduced almost to extermination.

Observations made at various seasons of the year indicate a greater abundance of the parasites in fall and winter, but they are unfailing attendants upon every brood of the Scale-insect. The result of twenty-five detailed examinations in early spring gives an average of 76 per cent. of the scales destroyed by Hymenopterous parasites. Ten examinations during the summer months give an average of 35 per cent., or one-half that of spring. Fifteen observations in autumn and the beginning of winter give an average of 40 per cent. of scales parasitized.

The activity of these insects is not perceptibly diminished by cool weather, which on the other hand greatly retards the development of the Scale insect. It is not therefore surprising that three-quarters of the winter brood perish from the attacks of these enemies.

Geographical Distribution. First appearance in the United States.—The Long Scale is supposed to have originated in China, and to have spread thence to the orange groves of southern Europe and the United States. According to one authority[*] it made its appearance in Florida in 1838 [†]

---

[*] Brown's "Trees of America," cited by Glover, Rept. Commissioner Patents for 1855, Agriculture, p. 117. See also Report for 1858, p. 266.
[†] Ashmead (Orange Insects, p. 1) gives the date 1835.

at Mandarin, on the Saint John's River, and was first seen in the grove of Mr. H. B. Robinson, upon trees purchased in New York from a ship from China.

In 1840 it was carried to Saint Augustine on trees obtained at Mandarin, and spread rapidly through the groves of that vicinity. Fifteen years later the same author records the spread of the pest throughout all the groves then existing in the State, and says: "Most of the cultivated orange trees in Florida have also been injured by them, their tops and branches having been generally destroyed. Their roots and stems, it is true, remain alive and annually send forth young shoots, only to share the fate of their predecessors."

The disastrous results of this invasion, which, twenty-five years ago, brought ruin to the orange industry, and seemed likely to end in the extermination of the Orange in this country, were due no doubt to the almost complete absence of parasites at the first advent of the Scale-insect, and for some years after it had obtained a foothold. Glover, writing in 1857 an account of the ravages of this Scale-insect in Florida, notes the complete absence of parasites, although flies belonging to the family of the *Chalcididæ* were found to do efficient service in destroying Bark-lice of other and indigenous species.*

At the present day, although this Scale-insect is everywhere disseminated in the groves of Florida and Louisiana, and likewise infests the wild orange trees, however remote from cultivated plantations, the destructive hordes are held in check by the effective attacks of parasites everywhere accompanying the Bark-lice, and increasing with their increase, so that no general onslaught of the Long Scale at least is likely ever again to occur in this country, and only local irruptions of the pest need be feared.

---

* Report of Commissioner of Patents for 1858, Agriculture.

CHAPTER II.

DIASPINÆ—Continued.

PURPLE SCALE.

(*Mytilaspis citricola*, Packard.)

[Plate III, Fig. 1, 1a, 1b, 1c.]

Scale of Female.—The scale of this species is larger than that of the Long Scale. Large females exceed 3^{mm} ($\frac{12}{100}$ inch) in length. The form is broadly trumpet-shaped, increasing in width behind, sometimes curved, like a cornucopia, but never with the sides parallel. The surface is smooth and even glossy, and the color varies with age from light to dark red-brown and purple. The molted larva skins are very plainly indicated; they are browned by the sun so as to appear scorched.

Scale of Male.—The scale of the male is less than half as long as that of the female ($1.4^{mm} = \frac{6}{100}$ inch); it is also more linear in shape, and uniformly dark purple in color. The thin hinge is always indicated by a line of lighter color across the upper surface of the scale, near the outer end.

The purple color of the male scales gives the mass of scales in the aggregate a characteristic hue, which readily distinguishes this species from all others found upon the Orange.

Female.—The insect within, as well as its outer covering, has a broader and less linear form than the Long Scale. The two species also differ in the number and structure of the microscopic plates and spines, with which the margins of the last two joints of the body are armed. The number of excreting pores and spinnerets is greater in *M. citricola* than in *M. gloverii*.

Mature females of the Purple Scale are 1.3^{mm} ($\frac{5}{100}$ inch) in length, and occupy less than half the space within their completed scales. The color is white, tinged with yellow at the extremities.

Male.—The male and also its pupa are pale amethyst in color. The perfect insect is about 1^{mm} ($\frac{4}{100}$ inch) in length, and, excepting in its somewhat stouter form, hardly differs from the male of the preceding species.

Egg.—The eggs are pearly white, never amethystine, 0.2^{mm} ($\frac{8}{1000}$ inch) long, elongate oval, often somewhat distorted in shape by crowding. They are laid usually in four rows, but the eggs at the outer end are

THE PURPLE SCALE OF THE ORANGE. 27

irregularly disposed, and sometimes the whole arrangement is confused. The number laid by a single female greatly exceeds that of the Long Scale; it varies from twenty-five to seventy, with a probable average of forty-five.

Young Larva.—The newly-hatched young is irregularly oval in shape, 0.3^{mm} ($\frac{12}{1000}$ inch) in length, and of a transparent white color, with a tinge of yellow at the extremities. The antennæ are stout, six-jointed. The eyes are minute, and of so fiery red a color that they resemble grains of cayenne pepper. The two bristles at the end of the body are almost invisible by reason of their fineness.

Life-history.—The metamorphoses of this species are exactly paralleled by those of the Long Scale, and are undergone in about the same periods of time. The broods of one species are sometimes in advance and at other times slightly behind those of the other.

Habitat.—Like the Long Scale, this species is found upon the twigs and branches, but has a somewhat stronger tendency to overrun the leaves and fruit. It is apt to infest the Lemon, Citron, and those varieties of Orange which have large oil cells (Tangerine, etc.). Although it is most at home upon the Orange and its kind, this scale is not exclusively confined to plants of this family, but is probably a general feeder upon plants of the order *Rosaceæ*, which includes nearly all of our fruit trees.

Origin and Spread.—The Purple Scale must be a common pest in most countries where the Orange is grown, for it is very frequently seen upon imported plants and upon foreign fruit in the northern markets. In Florida it is fortunately not as common as the Long Scale. It is, however, more abundant in the northern than in the southern portions of the orange belt. It is frequently associated with the Long Scale, and orange-growers do not readily distinguish the two species.

The introduction of the species into this country probably took place at an early date, but no certain knowledge of its first appearance exists. Mr. Ashmead (Orange Insects, p. 26) and Professor Comstock (Report Commissioner of Agriculture for 1880, p. 323) both give Glover as authority for the statement that this scale was imported into Jacksonville, Fla., in 1855, on some lemons sent from Bermuda, but in the citation given Glover refers to an entirely different scale, less than half the size of *Mytilaspis citricola*, of a different shape and habit, and which from his imperfect description appears to be the Chaff Scale, *Purlatoria pergandii* Comstock.

Parasites.—The parasites of *Mytilaspis citricola* and *M. gloverii* are identical, and the mode of attack is in both cases the same.

Descriptions of several species will be found in the Report of the Commissioner of Agriculture for 1880.

RED SCALE OF FLORIDA.

(*Aspidiotus ficus*, Ashmead.)

[Figs. 4 and 5.]

The following account of this species is given in the Report of the Commissioner of Agriculture for 1880, page 296:

"*Scale of Female.*—The scale of the female is circular, with the exuviae nearly central; the position of the first skin is indicated by a nipple-like prominence, which in fresh specimens is white, and is the remains of a mass of cottony excretion, beneath which the first skin is shed. The part of the scale covering the second skin is light reddish-brown; the remainder of the scale is much darker, varying from a dark reddish-brown to black, excepting the thin part of the margin, which is gray. When fully grown the scale measures 2^{mm} (.08 inch) in diameter. In some specimens the part covering the exuviae is depressed, and when the scale is removed from the leaf and viewed under a microscope with transmitted light, the exuviae, which are bright yellow, show through this part, causing it to appear as described by Mr. Ashmead. This scale is represented in Fig. 5, natural size; Fig. 5a, enlarged. * * *

"*Egg.*—The eggs are pale yellow.

"*Scale of Male.*—The scale of the male is about one-fourth as large as that of the female; the posterior side is prolonged into a thin flap, which is gray in color; in other respects the scale appears like that of the female. (Fig. 5b, enlarged.)

"*Male.*—(Fig. 4.) The male is light orange-yellow in color, with the thoracic band dark brown and the eyes purplish-black. It very closely resembles the males of *A. aurantii*, but differs from that species in being

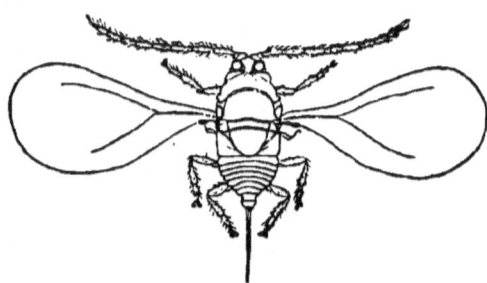

Fig. 4.—*Aspidiotus ficus* (Ashm.), male. (After Comstock.)

a smaller insect, with shorter antennæ, longer style, wider thoracic band, and with the pockets of the wings for the insertion of the hair of the poisers farther from the body.

"*Development of the Insect and formation of the Scale.*—The development of this insect from the egg to the adult state was followed through five generations. I give, however, only the substance of a part of the notes taken on a single brood—the second one observed—as that will be sufficient for our purpose. The observations were made upon specimens which were colonized on small orange trees in pots in my office in Washington. The rate of the development of the insects was probably slower than would have been the case in the open air in Florida.

"April 12, 1880, specimens of orange leaves infested by this scale were received from Mr. G. W. Holmes, Orlando, Fla. At this date males were found both in the pupa and adult state. The females also varied in size, and some of them were ovipositing. Eggs were placed on an orange tree for special study.

"April 13, the eggs began to hatch. The newly-hatched larva (Fig.

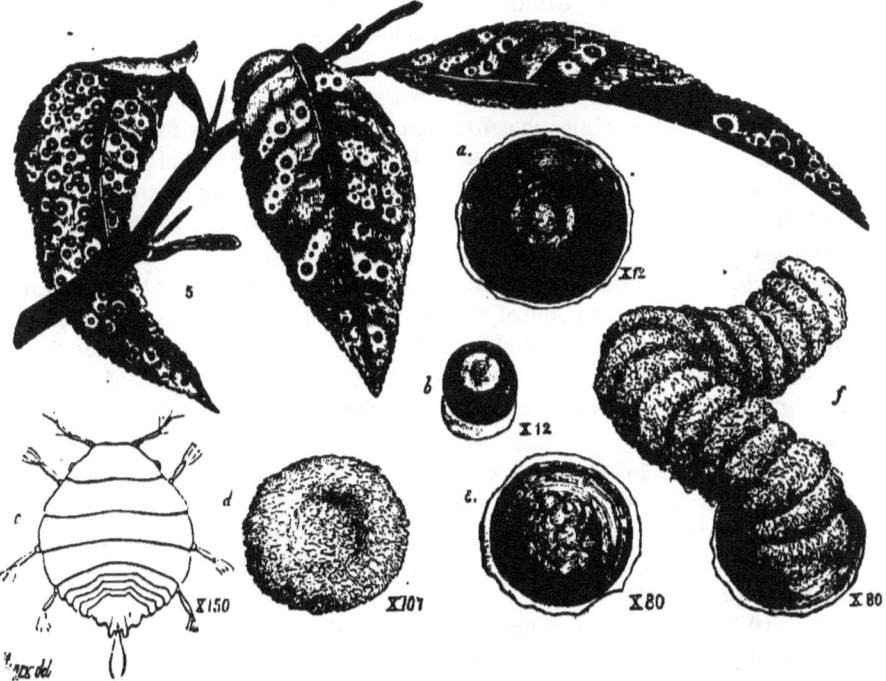

Fig. 5.—*Aspidiotus ficus* (Ashm.). 5, scales on leaves of orange, natural size; *a*, scale of female enlarged; *b*, scale of male, enlarged; *c*, young larva; *d*, *e*, and *f*, different stages in the formation of the scale. (After Comstock.)

5c) is broadly oval in outline and yellow in color. The antennæ are five-jointed; the three basal joints are very short and nearly equal in length; the fourth and fifth joints are each longer than the three basal joints together. The fifth joint is strongly tuberculated at tip so as to appear bifurcated. The eyes are prominent and of the same color as the body. The young larvæ are quite active, but they settle soon after hatching. Some settled the same day that they hatched.

"April 14, it was found that the young lice, although only twenty-four hours old, had formed scales which completely concealed them from sight. These scales resembled in appearance the fruiting organs of certain minute fungi. They were white, circular, convex, with a slightly depressed ring round the central portion (Fig. 5d); their texture was quite dense, and they were not firmly attached to either the insects or the leaf, a slight touch being sufficient to remove them without disturbing the larvæ. The larvæ had not changed in appearance, and were able to move their legs and antennæ.

"April 15, the lice had not changed perceptibly. The scales had become higher and more rounded.

"April 16, the lice had contracted considerably, being now nearly circular, at least as broad as long; in other respects there was no apparent change. The scales were found to vary somewhat; those most advanced having the central portion covered with a loose mass of curled white threads. (Fig. 5e.)

"April 17, there was apparent no further change in the larva; but the mass of threads covering the central part of the scale was found in some specimens to have greatly increased in size, equaling in height three or four times the width of the scale. This mass is cottony in appearance, and in those specimens where it is largest is more or less in the form of a plate twisted into a close spiral (Fig. 5f).

"April 19, not much change was apparent in the larva, but the mass of cottony excretion upon some of the scales had increased enormously; so that in some cases it extended in a curve from the scale to a point five times the width of the scale above the leaf and down to the leaf.

"April 20, no important change was observed either in the larvæ or scales.

"April 21, it was observed that the larvæ had become more or less transparent, and marked with large irregular yellow spots near the lateral margin of the head and thorax, and with a transverse row of similar spots across the base of the abdomen; the tip of the abdomen is very faintly yellow.

"April 22, no important change was noted.

"April 23, it was observed that the scales appeared faintly reddish in color with the center white; the reddish color, however, was due in part to the body of the larva, which is now orange-red, showing through the scale. It should be noted that in only a part of the specimens did the cottony mass become enlarged as represented in Fig. 5f. The greater part of the scales remained until this date of the form shown in Fig. 5e, and the cottony spirals have now disappeared, probably having been blown away.

"April 24, some of the larvæ had become deep orange in color.

"April 26, most of the scales had become deep orange in color with the central part white; some had at the center a small nipple-like protuberance; others still preserved a short tuft of a cottony excretion. This tuft is either removed by wind or otherwise, or it becomes compact, melted, as it were, to form the nipple-like projection referred to above.

"April 28, the insects appeared as they did two days ago; the scales had become very tough, and it was with difficulty that they could be removed from the insect.

"April 30, the insects still remained apparently unchanged. Some of the scales were only about one-half as large as others, and still remained perfectly white; these proved to be male scales. All the scales at this date had an elevated ring on the disk with a central nipple.

"May 3, many of the larvæ began to show that they were about to molt, the form of the next stage being visible through the skin of the insect.

"May 5, nearly all of the larvæ had molted; they were now orange-yellow, with the end of the body colorless. The last abdominal segment now presents the excretory pores which are represented in the drawing of the corresponding segment of the adult female. (Fig. 5.)* The molted skin adheres to the inside of the little scale, and therefore cannot be seen from the outside. The scales are now pink, or rose colored, with the center white.

"May 14, the insects had become a somewhat paler yellow, with the anal segment slightly darker. Most of the scales were now dark purple. On removing an insect a very delicate round white plate was observed adhering to the leaf where the mouth parts were inserted.

"May 18, the male scales were fully grown. At this stage they were dark reddish brown in color, with the center white, and the posterior side, which is elongated, gray. At this date some of the males had transformed to pupæ; others were still in the larva state; these larvæ were covered with roundish, more or less confluent yellow spots, leaving only the margin colorless; the end of the body was pale orange. The newly-transformed pupæ resembled in markings the larvæ just described. None of the females had yet molted the second time; their color was deep orange.

"May 21, nearly all of the males had changed to pupæ. It was observed that the last larval skin is pushed backwards from under the scale, to the edge of which it frequently adheres.

"May 24, none of the male pupæ had transformed to the adult state.

"May 29, it was found that during the five days previous more than one-half of the males had issued, and the remainder, though still under the scales, were in the adult state. It was now forty-seven days from the time the larvæ hatched.

"June 2, no males could be found; the females were about one-half grown, and were whitish with irregular yellow spots.

"June 9, eggs were observed within the body of a female.

"June 17, it was found that one of the females had deposited nine eggs, of which six had hatched. This is sixty-six days from the hatching of

---

* This figure reference is to the original report and not to Fig. 5 of this report.

the egg, and probably about twenty days after impregnation of the female.

"The insects of this brood continued to oviposit until July 1.

"*Number of generations per year.*—This insect, living on orange trees in a room on the north side of a building in Washington, passed through five generations in less than one year; the average time occupied by a single generation was a little less than seventy days. It is probable that in the open air in Orange County, Florida, there are at least six generations each year.

"*Habitat.*—Although I have carefully explored many orange groves in Florida and California, and have had an extensive correspondence with orange-growers, I have been unable to find this species in the last-named State, and have found it only in a single grove in Florida. This is the grove of Messrs. Holmes and Robinson, near Orlando, in Orange County. The insects were first observed here in the spring of 1879 on a sour-orange tree which was brought from Havana, Cuba, in 1874. On learning these facts I sent specimens to a friend at Havana in order to ascertain if the species occurred there. He at once returned me other specimens with the information that it is a very common pest in public gardens of that city.

"This species infests the limbs, leaves, and fruit indiscriminately. In the grove of Messrs. Holmes and Robinson it has spread slowly. The large trees which are infested do not seem to suffer much from it, but the young trees are greatly injured by it. Mr. Holmes considers the disfiguring of the fruit as the worst feature of the pest. The insect has multiplied to such an extent upon the trees upon which I colonized it in my breeding-room, that nearly all of them have been destroyed. The species is certainly one that is greatly to be feared, and there is no doubt that it would be a good investment for the orange-growers of Florida to eradicate the pest, even if in doing so it is found necessary to purchase and destroy all infested trees. This could be done now easily, but if delayed a few years the species will doubtless become permanently established."

Since the publication of the above by Professor Comstock, the Red Scale of Florida has made its appearance at San Mateo upon the St. Johns River. Its transportation was accomplished in 1881 or 1882 by means of infested fruit (Lemons), sent from Orlando, and packed for shipment at San Mateo. From the packing-house the pest escaped to orange trees in the vicinity, and soon obtained a foothold in the surrounding groves.

RED SCALE OF CALIFORNIA.

(*Aspidiotus aurantiæ* Maskell.)

[Fig. 6.]

This very destructive pest of the Orange is known as yet only from California; its introduction into Florida upon imported plants is how-

THE RED SCALE OF CALIFORNIA.

ever greatly to be feared. The following discussion of the species is found in the Report of the Commissioner of Agriculture for 1880, p. 293:

"*Scale of Female.*—This scale resembles that of *Aspidiotus ficus* in shape, size, and the presence of the nipple-like prominence, which indicates the position of the first larval skin; but it can be readily distinguished from the scale of that species as follows: It is light gray, and quite translucent; its apparent color depending on the color of the insect beneath, and varying from a light greenish yellow to a bright reddish brown; the central third (that part which covers the second skin) is as dark, and usually darker than the remainder of the scale; and when the female is fully grown the peculiar reniform body is discernible through the scale, causing the darker part of the outer two-thirds of the scale to appear as a broken ring. (Fig. 6b.) * * *

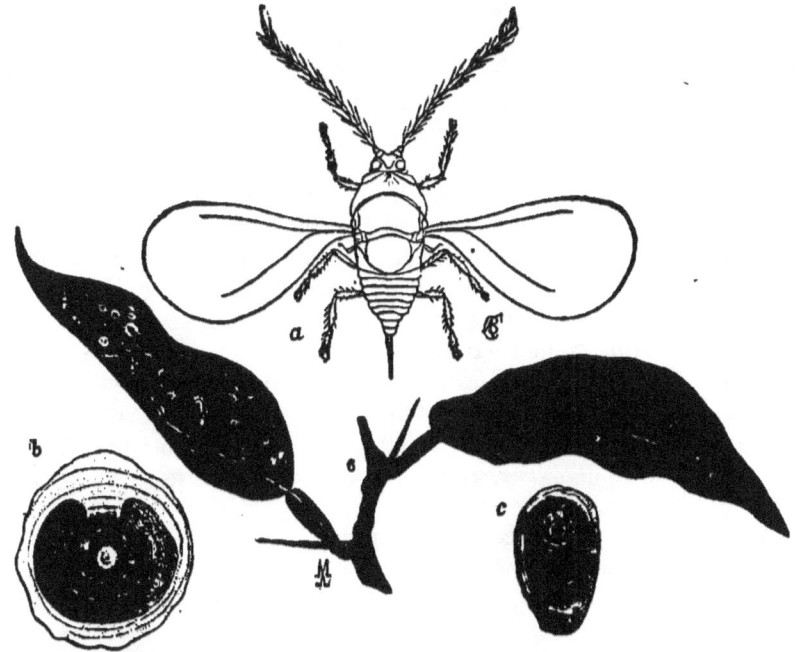

FIG. 6—*Aspidiotus aurantii* Maskell. 6, scales on leaves of orange, natural size; a, adult male, much enlarged; b, scales of female, enlarged; c, scale of male, enlarged. (After Comstock.)

"*Egg.*—I have not seen the eggs of this species, excepting those taken from the body of the female. And as I have repeatedly found young larvæ under the scales I am led to believe that the species is viviparous.

"*Scale of Male.*—The scale of the male resembles that of the female, excepting that it is only one-fourth as large; the posterior side is prolonged into a flap, which is quite thin; and the part which covers the larval skin is often lighter than the remainder of the scale.

"*Male.*—The male is light yellow, with the thoracic band brown, and

6521 O I——3

the eyes purplish black. The outline drawing, Fig. 6a, represents the shape of the various organs.

"*Habitat.*—I have observed this species in several groves at San Gabriel and Los Angeles, Cal. At the first-named place, where it is very abundant, it is said to have first appeared on a budded orange tree which was purchased by Mr. L. J. Rose, at one of the hot-houses in San Francisco. At Los Angeles it appears to have spread from six lemon trees which were brought from Australia by Don Mateo Keller.

"At first I considered this an undescribed species, as I could find no description of it either in American or European entomological publications. I therefore described it in the Canadian Entomologist under the name of *Aspidiotus citri*. Afterwards I obtained copies of the papers "On some Coccidæ in New Zealand," by W. M. Maskell, published in the Transactions and Proceedings of the New Zealand Institute, and found that he had described an insect infesting oranges and lemons imported into New Zealand from Sydney which was either identical with or very closely allied to the red scale of California. I at once sent to Mr. Maskell for specimens of the species described by him. These have just been received and prove to be specifically identical with those infesting citrus trees in California. Thus the question as to source from which we derived this pest is settled beyond a doubt.

"I have found *Aspidiotus aurantii* only on citrus trees. It infests the trunk, limbs, leaves, and fruit. The infested leaves turn yellow, and when badly infested they drop from the tree. This species spreads quite rapidly; and from what I have seen of it, I believe that it is more to be feared than any other scale insect infesting citrus fruits in this country. As illustrating the extent of its ravages in Australia, Dr. Bleasdale told me of a grove of thirty-three acres which nine years ago rented for £1,800 per year, and for which three years ago only £120 rent could be obtained.

"Specimens of this insect colonized on orange trees in the breeding room of the Department passed through their entire existence in a little more than two months; hence it is probable that in the open air in Southern California there are at least five generations each year, and possibly six. The mode of the formation of the scale in this species very closely resembles that of *A. ficus*, described at length in this report. The ventral scale, however, reaches a greater degree of development in *A. aurantii* than in *A. ficus*. At first it consists of a very delicate film upon the leaf; when the second molt occurs it is strengthened by the ventral half of the cast skin, the skin splitting about the margin of the insect, the dorsal half adhering to the dorsal scale and the ventral half to the ventral scale. Later, after the impregnation of the female, the ventral scale becomes firmly attached to the dorsal scale and to the insect; so that it is almost impossible to remove an adult female from her scale."

THE WHITE SCALE.
(*Aspidiotus nerii* Bouché.)
[Fig. 7.]

Although this species has not yet been reported from orange groves in Florida, it is known to occur upon various plants, within the limits of the State. Professor Comstock, in the Report of the Commissioner of Agriculture for 1880, p. 301, gives the following account of its appearance and habits:

"*Scale of the Female.*—The scale of the female is flat, whitish, or light gray in color, and with the exuviae central or nearly so (Fig. 7c). Exuviae dull orange yellow; the first skin usually showing the segmentation distinctly, the second skin more or less covered with secretion, often appearing only as an orange-colored circle surrounding the first skin. Ventral scale a mere film applied to bark of plant. Diameter of fully-formed scale, 2^{mm} (.08 inch). * * *

"*Eggs.*—The eggs are very light yellow in color.

"*Scale of Male.*—The scale of the male is slightly elongated, with the larval skin nearly central; it is snowy white with the larval skin light yellow; longest diameter, 1^{mm} (.04 inch) (Fig. 7 *b*).

"*Male.*—The adult male is yellow, mottled with reddish brown, central part of thoracic band reddish. Other characters represented in Fig. 7*a*.

"*Habitat.*—This is a very common European species which infests many different plants, and it is spread throughout our country from the

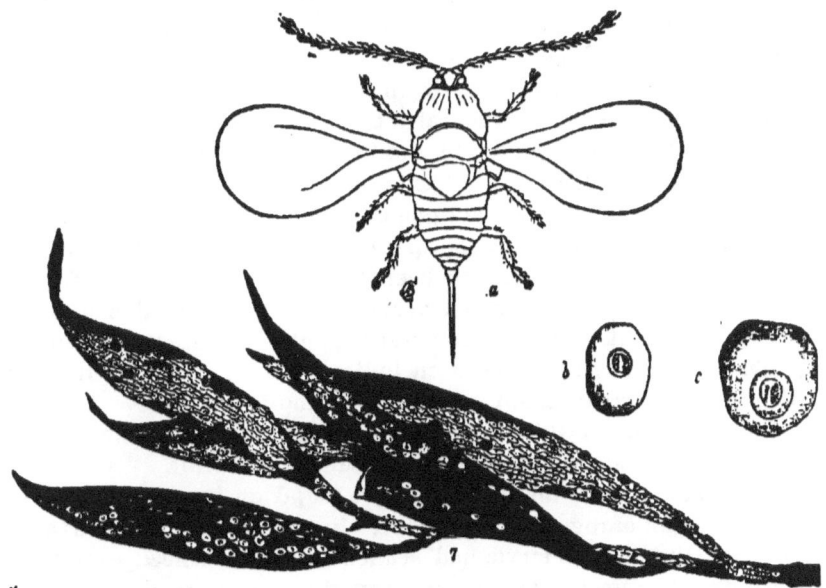

FIG. 7.—*Aspidiotus nerii* Bouché. 7, scales on leaves of acacia, natural size; *a*, adult male, enlarged; *b*, scale of male, enlarged; *c*, scale of female, enlarged. (After Comstock.)

Atlantic to the Pacific, and from the Great Lakes to the Gulf of Mexico. I have found it more abundant on acacias in California than elsewhere, and for a time believed that it had been introduced from Australia with this tree. Many trees were found the leaves of which were completely covered with the scales, appearing as if they had been coated with whitewash. Leaves of magnolia were received from Mr. C. H. Dwinelle, Berkeley, Cal., which were infested to a similar extent. The following is a list of the plants upon which I have studied this species: Acacia, Magnolia, oleander, maple, Yucca, plum, cherry, currant, and Melia (*Melia azederach*) in California; oleander in Utah; English ivy in a conservatory at Ithaca, N. Y.; ivy and "China tree" from Dr. R. S. Turner, Fort George, Fla.; grass and clover growing in pots with orange trees upon which I was rearing the scale at this Department; lemons imported from the Mediterranean by a San Francisco dealer; and lemons forwarded to me by Mr. Alex. Craw from the grove of Mr. Wolfkill, at Los Angeles, Cal.

"The scales upon magnolia from Berkeley, Cal., and upon oleander from Salt Lake City appear somewhat different from those on acacia and other plants. But after a very careful study of the different forms from each plant, I am unable to point out any character which will distinguish those on magnolia and oleander from others.

"Specimens of infested lemons from Europe were forwarded to me at Washington by the editor of the Riverside Press and Horticulturist, who had received them from a correspondent in San Francisco, who had imported them from the Mediterranean. Notwithstanding the great distance (once across the Atlantic and twice across the continent) which this fruit had been transported, the insects infesting it were alive and in a healthy condition. This illustrates the ease with which these insects may spread from one country to another, and the dangers attending the introduction of foreign fruit and nursery stock.

"The appearance of this pest upon citrus fruits in Southern California is greatly to be regretted, for the species is already so common on other plants that it may be difficult to keep the orange groves free from it. The fact, however, that it infests acacia, oleander, and other plants to such a great extent, and has been observed but few times in this country on citrus fruits, may be taken as an indication that it is not liable to multiply to any great extent upon oranges and lemons.

"In the specimens which I have seen the leaves of the lemon were not infested, but the scales were very abundant on the fruit.

"The young of this insect which were found on ivy in Florida were colonized on an orange tree in the breeding-room of the Department. When one day old the larvæ had settled and commenced excreting a covering; when four days old this covering was quite dense; on the twentieth day some larvæ molted, and on the twenty-eighth day the second molt occurred. It was observed that this molt was accomplished by a splitting of the skin at the sides of the body, so that the dorsal half of the skin became attached to the scale and the ventral half to the leaf. Soon after this molt all the specimens died. This was an indication that this species could not mature upon the orange. But a very

...has failed to reveal any character ...living on lemon in California. ...time occupied by a single genera- ...there are at least two each year, ...April, 1880, specimens of magnolia ..., Cal., infested by this insect. The ...ill 27th April. During this time (22d ...from Florida, upon which were scales ...s species. On the 21st of May other ...lorida; of these the females were about ...were in the pupa state. ...observed again at Los Angeles, Cal., the-
...s emerged in my breeding-cages from both the ...Florida specimens. And during August the ...t Los Angeles, Cal.
...e is apparently no regularity in the periods of ...is of all stages, from the egg to the adult, may ...e time."

CHAFF SCALE.

...rlatoria pergandii Comstock.)
[Plate V, and Figs. 8 and 9.]
—This is a thin, light colored ...lf as long as either of the Myti- ...is more or less circular, usually ...d, and less curved upon one side ...her. The first larval skin is a little ...than the rest of the scale; it is dis- ...is a circular shield, placed near the ...he side opposite the point. Beyond ...underneath the first larval skin may be distinguished the ...ess distinctly visible shield of the second molt. In well de- ...ales several faintly elevated lines or ridges are marked upon ...surface, which radiate from the point of beginning of the ...d are partly obliterated where they are covered by the molted ...A structure somewhat similar to this of the Chaff Scale is seen ...y sea shells, such as the limpet and the oyster.
...female scale is light straw color, 1.4^{mm} to 1.6^{mm} (0 06 inch) long.
...ale of Male.—The male scale is slender and of nearly equal width ...ughout. The material of which it is composed is very thin and ...ite in color; the larva skin at one end covers about one-third of the ...rface, is darker than the rest of the scale, and has a greenish tinge, ...r a dark green center. Length, 1^{mm} (0.04 inch).

Female.—The female has the form of a thickened disk, nearly circular in outline. The edges of the last four or five joints are serrate, with minute tooth-like lobes and plates. The color, at first waxy white,

Fig. 8.—*Parlatoria pergandii* Coms. *a*, scale of female, enlarged; *b*, scale of male, enlarged. (After Comstock.)

[Torn flap text:]
l margin is thin
When gravid reduced in cir. h a nearly com-)2 inch).
e Long Scale, r 0.2mm (0.008
and mottled ly in minute
on as it be- t scale, the nguishable e elongate dark pur- he second mouth or ter shed- becomes e color,
which, of the than what ip of
ons few ld, of p. t.

becomes dark purple at maturity. The serrated hin
and tinged with yellow.

The mature females do not entirely fill their scales
with eggs, their bodies, although much thickened, are
cumference, and in laying they surround themselves wi
plete circle of eggs. Length of mature female 0.6ᵐᵐ (0.

Eggs.—The eggs are as large or larger than those of t
and resemble them in shape and color. They are near
inch) in length, and are more or less amethystine in color

Young Larva.—The migrating larva is very broadly ova
with purple. It differs from the larva of related species o
details.

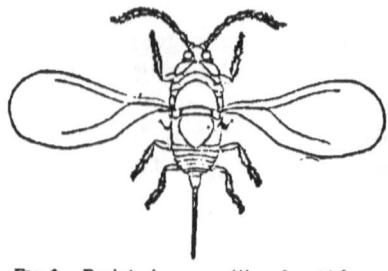

Fig. 9.—*Parlatoria pergandii*, male. (After Comstock.)

Male. (Fig. 9.)—As s
gins to form its permane
male insect becomes dist
from the female by its mo
form, and it soon turns to a
ple-red color. The skin of
molt is pushed toward the
thrown out of the scale. A
ding this skin the male insect
a pupa of dark red or purp
and has the form of the fly with members folded or abbreviate

The perfect insect emerges from the thin outer end of its scale
however, has no hinge or flap. The fly is very similar to those
genus *Aspidiotus*, but is shorter and stouter, and has larger eye
the species of *Mytilaspis*. The color is purple, mottled, and som
paler upon the large shield of the upper surface. Length to the
the stylet about equal to that of its scale, 0.6ᵐᵐ (0.02 inch).

Life history.—The young Chaff Scale repeats with slight varia
the history of the species already mentioned. After wandering a
hours, it chooses a fixed position, very often underneath a pile of
dead scales, and in a few days covers itself with a circular shiel
white tissue, so thin as to be quite transparent. This covering di
pears before the time of the first molt. After the molt the females c
struct a circular and the males a linear scale.

The number of eggs laid is variable. Professor Comstock records
one instance twenty-seven eggs. The average number is sixteen.

Number of Generations.—The earlier metamorphoses take place
about the usual intervals of twenty days, but the later periods var
with the seasons, and are greatly accelerated by hot weather.

The Chaff Scale appears to have one more brood than the Long Scale.
There are four summer generations, but these broods are so greatly
confused by unequal development in the females that the limits of each
cannot be exactly defined. The first brood in spring and the last brood

THE CHAFF SCALE OF THE ORANGE.

in fall may be assumed to be approximately contemporaneous with those of the Long Scale. They occur in March or April and in September or October. These months are therefore the proper ones for treatment with remedies.

Habitat.—The Chaff Scale infests by preference the trunk and larger branches, and to these it generally confines itself until every portion of their surface is thickly coated, and the young Bark-lice can no longer find places to plant themselves. It is also frequently seen upon the fruit, occupying the pit-like depressions of the rind. This habit, combined with its light color, renders it inconspicuous upon the fruit. Upon the trunks of trees, also, its resemblance to the bark causes it to escape notice, so that many persons whose groves are suffering from the attacks of this scale are unaware of its presence.

Food-plants and Origin.—It has been found upon various plants growing near infested orange trees. Japonicas and similar thick-leaved plants sometimes suffer severely from its attacks. It is not known to infest any native wild plants, and is not found upon the Wild Orange, except in the immediate vicinity of cultivated plantations. It cannot, therefore, be considered a native insect, nor is anything known with certainty concerning its introduction.

Professor Glover, in his report to the Commissioner of Patents for the year 1855, mentions the introduction in that year of a Scale-insect, which he says was imported into Jacksonville, Fla., on some lemons sent from Bermuda. This Scale-insect has been stated to be *Mytilaspis citricola*. From the brief description given by Glover, it is not possible to determine with certainty the species referred to, but the small size and shape of the female and the white color of the male scales agree closely with the species now under consideration, and render it probable that the Chaff Scale, and not the Purple Scale, was the insect in question.

Parasites.—In addition to many external enemies, a single Hymenopterous parasite attacks this scale, and is a very efficient destroyer of the species. It is a larger insect than those found in the scales of Mytilaspis, and its larva does not live within the body of the Coccid, as is usual with these minute parasites, but originates from an egg deposited beneath the scale and among the eggs of the Scale-insect, which is always of adult size when attacked. The grub of the parasite makes room for itself as it grows by eating first the eggs of its host and then her body. Sometimes, indeed, the eggs alone of the Coccid appear to suffice for its support and the mother Bark-louse is not molested.

The pupa of the parasite is formed under the scale, and although without cocoon or coverings of its own, is surrounded by the dry skin and egg-shells of the Bark-louse.

The fly issues through a round hole which it eats in the top of the scale.

The perfect insect is a four-winged fly, 1.2^{mm} (0.05 inch) long, honey-yellow in color, and with dark brown eyes. The antennæ have apparently six joints, but the last three joints are closely united into an elongate club, and the real number of joints is therefore eight. The abdomen is rather broadly oval, and in the female bears on the middle of her under side the sharply-pointed egg-drill.

The larva is a yellowish-white, naked grub, so thick and short as to be almost spherical. It is without visible members, even the head being withdrawn out of sight into the body. The body is plainly ringed, indicating the joints, and the dark intestinal contents are seen as a red or brown cloud through its walls. Length 0.5^{mm} (0.02 inch).

The pupa is twice as long as wide, flattened, oval, and has a tinge of yellow color. It shows the form of the perfect insect through the transparent envelope.*

THE ORANGE CHIONASPIS.

(Chionaspis citri Comstock.)

A new Bark-louse of the Orange has been described by Professor Comstock, in the Second Entomological Report of Cornell University, as follows: "In the Report of the Department of Agriculture for 1880 I described a species of Chionaspis which differed from all other species of that genus known at that time by the color of the scale of the female, which is black. This species was found on *Euonymus latifolia* at Norfolk, Va. I stated in my account of this insect that it occurred also on orange trees in Louisiana and Cuba. A re-examination of the specimens on orange has convinced me that they are specifically distinct from those on euonymus. I therefore propose for that form the specific name of *citri*. The species can be recognized by the following characters:

"*Scale of Female.*—The scale of the female is of a dirty blackish brown color with a gray margin; the exuviae are brownish yellow. There is a central ridge from which the sides of the scale slope like the roof of a house. The greater prominence of this ridge, and the more elongated form of the scale are the principal differences between this scale and that of the female of *Ch. euonymi*. There is no danger of its being mistaken for any other known species.

"*Female.*— * * * This species may readily be distinguished from *Ch. euonymi* by the following characters: There are no groups of spinnerets; the mesal lobes are larger and more distinctly serrate than in *Ch. euonymi*; and in the last-named species the plates are in twos, while in *Ch. citri* they occur singly."

According to observations made by Mr. L. O. Howard, the Orange Chionaspis is the especial pest of orange groves in Louisiana. It has been found by him at Pattersonville, Saint Mary's Parish; at Woodville, 50

---

* This parasite is evidently an *Aphelinus*, but the only specimen in Mr. Hubbard's collection is too poor for specific determination. —C. V. R.

THE ORANGE CHIONASPIS.

miles below New Orleans; on the Mississippi River above Algiers, and on the east side of the river in the New Orleans cemeteries.

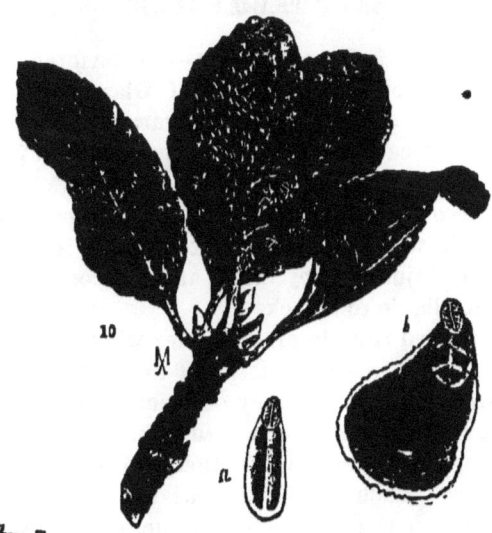

FIG. 10.— *Chionaspis euonymi* Comstock. 10, scales on Euonymus, natural size; *a*, scale of male, enlarged; *b*, scale of female, enlarged. (After Comstock.)

Fig. 10 represents *Chionaspis euonymi* Comstock, to which the above species is very closely allied.

CHAPTER III.

DIASPINÆ—Continued.

RAVAGES OF THE ARMORED SCALES.

Bark-lice omnipresent in Orange Groves.—In the foregoing pages an account has been given of all the species of Diaspinæ known to attack citrus plants in this country. The appearance, distinguishing characters and habits of each have been set forth with sufficient clearness, it is hoped, to render recognizable by orange-growers the different members of this group of insect pests, the most destructive and formidable with which they have to contend. It remains to consider the nature and extent of the injuries they inflict and the conditions under which the plant becomes liable to attack.

It may be premised that in all countries where the Orange is extensively cultivated Scale-insects exist, and not seldom make their presence known through the losses they occasion the fruit grower. From time to time there may be sudden irruptions of Scale-insects, which, like an epidemic, are wide-spread in their effects, and overrun a great extent of territory. Such an invasion, as has already been shown, occurred in Florida upon the supposed introduction of the Long Scale. In southern Europe also, where the Orange and the Lemon have been cultivated for centuries, the occurrences of scale epidemics have been recorded, one of which, in the first decade of the present century, prevailed throughout the entire district along the shores of the Mediterranean, from Italy to Spain, and spread consternation among the inhabitants, who were dependent upon the produce of their lemon and orange groves for support.

At the present day, however, owing to a better knowledge of these pests, the use of cheap and effective insecticides, and of effective instruments for applying them, such wide-spread devastation by Scale-insects need not be feared. The omnipresence of the pest, however, compels the orange-grower to be ever upon the alert if he would avoid loss of growth in the young or of productiveness in the older trees.

In Florida the greater part of these losses are caused by three Diaspinous scales: *Mytilaspis gloverii*, the Long Scale; *Mytilaspis citricola*, the Purple Scale, and *Parlatoria pergandii*, the Chaff Scale. These three insects are so universally distributed that it is safe to say no bearing orange tree exists in southern and eastern Florida upon which one or the other cannot be found.

The Long Scale is the most destructive, while it is the most readily destroyed. Few if any localities in the State are free from its presence. The Purple Scale, being stouter and thicker than the Long Scale, is more difficult to kill. It is not less injurious to the trees which it infests, but is less widely distributed.

The Chaff Scale is hardly less common than the Long Scale, and is very frequently associated with it. Of the three it is decidedly the most difficult to exterminate, owing, in part at least, to its habit of piling or lapping one over the other. Except upon very young trees it seldom does permanent injury, and is much less to be feared than the other two species. Its thinner scale renders it liable to the attacks of enemies to a greater extent than the Mytilaspis scales, and they sometimes cause its complete disappearance from a tree.

A fourth scale of this group, *Aspidiotus ficus* Ashm. has been mentioned as recently introduced, and there are still others awaiting importation from California and elsewhere.

Agencies which assist their Distribution.—During the migratory age the restless habit of the young Bark-lice impels them to crawl actively about, turning aside for no obstacles, but mounting every object met with in their path. The instinct of self-protection being entirely wanting in these degraded creatures, they make no distinction between dead and living objects, and crawl without hesitation upon the bodies of other and larger insects. The latter, impelled by the annoying presence of the intruders, fly away, bearing with them the scale larvæ, and thus assist in distributing them upon surrounding plants.

Some insects, however, do not notice, or at least do not resent, the liberties taken by the crawling lice.

Thus the Lady-bird beetles (Coccinellidæ) are frequently seen quietly feeding while several young Bark-lice, evidently attracted by their shining backs, are coursing in all directions over their bodies. It cannot be doubted that even these enemies of the Scale-insect bear with them in their flights this seed of the destroyer and scatter the pest from tree to tree. Doubtless very many flying insects, and also birds, with their sweeping tail-feathers, aid in disseminating Scale-insects.

But spiders, more than any other animals, must be considered efficient instruments in this mischievous work. Not only do they transport the lice—and it is an observed fact that the movements of the latter upon their hairy backs do not incommode the spiders—but they also harbor them under their webs in folded leaves, etc., where, safe from the attacks of parasites and enemies, they increase and multiply inordinately.

The nest web of a spider will most frequently be found the starting point from which the lice swarm forth as from a hive and cover the surrounding parts. Other webs, at a distance from the infected one, will be occupied in time, but only as the tide of scales reaches their vicinity, for it is not the habit of the migrating Bark-lice to wander far in search of such lurking places, however readily they accept the protection when found.

The observed fact that Scale-insects spread most rapidly in the direction of prevailing winds has often been verified, and has led to the belief in direct transportation by the winds, as the most important agency in their dissemination. This popular theory is thus stated by a writer: "Now, in the spring and fall, just when the insects are hatching and most numerous, we have our heaviest storms. * * * During one of these storms I have often seen leaves, twigs, and sometimes whole branches taken up and carried whirling through the air for a quarter of a mile or further. How easy, then, would it be for these microscopical insects, but a few atoms in weight, to be carried for miles."*

The gentle southeast trade-winds of Florida and the storms which are occasional, and, fortunately, somewhat rare visitants, are very different phenomena. While the influence of the former is sometimes seen in the more rapid spread of the Scale-insects towards the northwest it has never been observed that a sudden extension of the pest has followed any of the violent or long-continued wind storms on record.

That tempest-borne branches and leaves might carry the infection to a distance cannot of course be denied, but the dissemination of Scale-insects, continues without interruption at all seasons and in all parts of the State, a process of such constancy and regularity, cannot be attributed in any great measure to the fitful agency of occasional storms.

Nor can it be by direct transportation that the trade-winds assist in spreading Scale-insects, for winds of moderate force are not competent to dislodge the young lice from the plants. Of this any one may be convinced by trial with a bellows or with the breath. Minute and insignificant in weight though they are, they cling with tenacity to the bark, and the pressure of air upon their thin bodies only serves to press them into closer contact with the surface.

It is rather to the indirect action of the wind, to the influence which it exerts upon the flight of insects and other winged animals which transport Scale-insects, that we must look for an explanation of the observed phenomena.

And particularly is this influence of the wind felt in the case of spiders, most of the species of which are dependent upon the wind in their migrations. For, although wingless, they are enabled by means of the buoyancy of their web and the power which they possess of reeling it out upon the wind to bridge long gaps from tree to tree, and even to copy the flight of winged animals.

The gossamer spider makes its aerial voyages by clinging to a light tangle of web, on which, as by a parachute, it is borne to great distances by the wind.

Many species have this habit of the gossamer. Some, however, use, instead of a tangle, long lines of web which are cast out upon the wind to a distance of several hundred feet, until their buoyancy becomes

---

* Ashmead, Orange Insects, page 3.

sufficient to sustain the weight of the little aeronaut, or until in its sweep it becomes entangled in the branches of a distant tree or shrub, and forms a bridge upon which the spider readily crosses.

The warm ascending currents of spring, the southeast trade-winds in Florida, excite multitudes of spiders to set out upon their travels, speeding them on their way and directing their course. At this season of the year, when the migrations of insects are at their height, and all nature is in restless activity, Scale-insects also are most abundantly productive, and the leaves and branches of infested trees swarm with their young. Thus it is that in spring especially the spiders, aided by the winds, carry the Bark-lice in numbers and to great distances.

Conditions favorable to their Increase.—There is good reason to believe that Bark-lice, like many other destructive insects, do not, as a rule, originate the disorders which follow their attacks. An enfeebled condition of the plant, from whatsoever cause it arises, is generally necessary to provoke an invasion. Thoroughly healthy trees, even when infected, may remain uninjured for years. The Scale-insects upon them thrive only upon the lower or inside branches, and are held in check by their natural enemies and parasites. An unfavorable atmospheric condition, such as long-continued drought, the impoverishment of the soil, neglect of cultivation, and the many obscure or utterly unknown causes which produce "die-back," yellow and streaked foliage, or other indications of vegetable indigestion, if such it may be called, all tend to foster Scale-insects and favor their rapid increase.

In explanation of these facts, it may be conjectured, although it is not, perhaps, susceptible of proof, that peculiar conditions of the sap are especially favorable to the development of Scale-insects, and affect the reproductive functions, stimulating the females to greater productiveness. Observations show that the number of eggs deposited varies considerably, and that the maximum number is produced, not by solitary females upon vigorous plants, but by individuals of the advancing brood taken from portions of the plant plainly affected by their attacks.

Usual course of the Pest.—If it be true that outbursts of Scale-insects commonly owe their origin to some disturbance in the condition of the plant, it is no less a fact that their ravages not only aggravate the original trouble, but entail others, it may be, far more serious in their consequences. The countless throng of Bark-lice not only weaken the plant by sapping and diverting its vital juices and depriving it of nourishment, but they also strangle the parts which they infest by coating the surface and clogging its pores with their myriad bodies. Their long, hair-like sucking beaks penetrate and thread the cellular tissues of the growing bark, breaking through and altering its structure so that the tender bark of the twigs and younger shoots is destroyed, while the thicker bark of the trunk and larger limbs hardens and becomes, as it is popularly termed, "hide-bound."

In this condition healthy growth is impossible. If neglected and allowed to be overrun by the pest, the growth of the tree is checked;

the infested twigs and branches die; often the entire top is lost. The roots and trunk, however, survive, and the tree endeavors to repair the injury by throwing out shoots from below.

When the tree reaches this impoverished condition matters usually begin to mend. The Bark-lice upon the dead or dying branches perish by starvation, the parasites reassert their sway, and slowly the tree regains its health and vigor, but seldom its pristine beauty.

The opinion is often expressed that the tree will "throw off the scales," or that they will "disappear in time at the ends of the branches." The facts upon which this belief is founded are simply that the young lice, when the branches become crowded, wander off and on to new growth; their course is, therefore, naturally upward and outward. When the advancing army reaches the ultimate branches, the insects crowd upon the smaller twigs and leaves, killing them rapidly and involving themselves in the common destruction. The tide of scales is then checked, while the enemies thrive and multiply, feeding upon the dead and starving Coccids. There then occurs one of those sudden oscillations of the balance which are familiar enough to entomologists; the unseen enemies increase and the scales visibly diminish. The tree meantime has rest and may under favorable circumstances recover its vigor, in which case the trouble for the time being is over, and the lost branches are quickly replaced.

More frequently, however, the new growth, which always pushes out rapidly in such cases, will, as soon as it hardens, be overrun by the crawling scale-larvæ, newly hatched from eggs which were not involved in the destruction of the mother insects, and after an interval a new brood will be found again in possession. This process may be repeated many times in the tops of full-grown trees, and the orange-grower at each ebb in the tide will perhaps flatter himself with the delusion that the scales have in some mysterious manner disappeared at the ends of the destroyed branches. Well-grown trees may submit again and again to these vicissitudes. They may even permanently recover without the aid of applied remedies, but very young orange trees do not possess the powers of resistance of adult trees; their tops being small and their branches short, they are usually entirely overrun in a single season, and, if not attended to, sustain irreparable injury, resulting, in the case of budded trees, in the destruction of the budded portion.

Influence of Climate.—The retarding action of cold weather upon the development of Scale-insects, and the acceleration produced by the higher temperature of the summer months, has already been mentioned. The influence of a warm climate is shown in the increased number of annual generations. The species of Diaspinæ found in the Northern States have all, or nearly all of them, a single generation, occupying the summer months. The same species have in the warmer portions of the United States at least two broods, and in the extreme South those species with which orange-growers have to contend produce not less than three and some of them more than four generations.

The long-continued heat of summer acts as a check upon the advance southward of those species which inhabit the North, and is probably a more important factor in determining the geographical distribution of many species than the frosts of the northern winter.

Indeed the notion that Scale-insects are destroyed by frosts is entirely erroneous. Their eggs withstand any ordinary degree of cold, and the insects themselves survive a freezing temperature that kills the plants upon which they feed. The winter climate of a land in which the open culture of the Orange is possible cannot be sufficiently rigorous to kill even the young of Bark-lice. In Florida the coldest weather merely serves to retard their development.*

Natural Checks.—The parasites of Bark-lice, some of which have already been mentioned, and the numerous enemies to be considered hereafter, are similarly affected by climatic conditions. Their broods increase in number as they extend southwards, and in the main their activity keeps pace with that of their prey. Ordinarily, therefore, the various checks upon their increase are sufficient to prevent the spreading of Bark-lice to an injurious extent, and, as we have seen, it is only at times that they increase so rapidly as to entirely outstrip their enemies and overrun the plant.

---

* Mr. Joseph Voyle, in a report made to Professor Riley, and published in Bulletin No. 4, United States Department of Agriculture, Division of Entomology, gives the results of an elaborate series of experiments made by subjecting Scale-insects, with their young and eggs, to the action of low temperatures for varying lengths of time. In these experiments the Coccids were placed in a small tin cylinder and surrounded with a freezing mixture of ice and salt. The time of exposure was never less than one nor more than sixteen hours, and the temperatures ranged from 16° to 36° F. Eggs were killed when the minimum fell below 25° and were not killed at higher temperatures; the young Bark-lice were killed in every experiment. It is to be remarked, however, that an average time of nine days was allowed to elapse before the results obtained were considered final. As Mr. Voyle himself suggests, "Sometimes larvæ retain for several days an apparently natural appearance, leaving it doubtful whether their final death is the result of the temperature or want of food."

In regard to the eggs also it is probable that certain conditions not noted and not taken into account in these experiments vitiated the results, since they do not correspond with what takes place in the open air during severe frosts.

On this point Mr. Voyle himself gives evidence when he says: "During the past winter, 1882-'83, by some special observations, positive evidence was obtained that often very little damage was done to scale insects by cold that killed the tender orange shoots. On the morning of December 16, 1882, the thermometer was reported at various figures, from 19° to 25° F. My own lowest reading was 25°. On this morning I cut orange branches incrusted with scale insects, and found young migratory larvæ of *Mytilaspis* running about quite lively."

This discrepancy is remarked by Mr. Voyle, and the following explanation is suggested: "There are conditions practically unattainable artificially, where the coccids are protected from the effects of such temperature as under favorable conditions would be fatal to them. The leaves of the tree, the warm current rising from the ground around the trunk of the tree, and the initial heat of the tree itself perform an important part in modifying temperature for these insects. In a still atmosphere this might become a perfect protection against a temperature much lower than would prove fatal in other conditions."

CHAPTER IV

LECANINÆ—THE NAKED OR WAXY SCALES.

General Characters and Life-history.—The Bark-lice of this subfamily make no true scale. They are either naked or possess waxy coats adhering more or less closely to the body of the insect, but not fastened permanently to the bark. The development from the larva to the adult female is apparently one of simple growth, and no molts have been observed. The change in form takes place gradually and is due to the swelling of the body as it becomes filled with eggs or young, or to the accumulation of the covering of wax. Eggs are deposited in a cavity beneath the body of the mother, or are retained within her body until hatched, in those species which bring forth their young living.

The young change their position upon the plant at will, and this freedom of movement is retained until near the end of their lives. The insects, however, become more sluggish as they grow older, and at last, in the incubating period, the legs and other external members of the larva wither and the body becomes adherent to the surface of the plant. No males have been discovered in any of the species of the group which come within the scope of this treatise.

The newly-hatched young of the Lecaninæ closely resemble those of the Diaspinæ. They are active, six-legged creatures, with thin bodies, oval in form. They feed in the same manner, by plunging their sucking beaks into the cellular tissues of the plant, but the beak never grows very long, and while active life remains the insect has power to remove it and to reinsert it in a fresh place.

Two genera of Lecaninæ fall within the scope of this work.

In the genus *Lecanium* the insect makes no covering for itself or its eggs, but the skin becomes more or less toughened with age, and finally presents the appearance of a parchment-like scale. The species belonging to the genus *Ceroplastes* excrete a thick coating of wax, which wraps the body of the insect above, but is easily removed from its surface. Underneath the wax the skin of the Coccid is thin and tender.

THE TURTLE-BACK SCALE—BROAD SCALE.

(*Lecanium hesperidum*, Linn.)

[Fig. 11.]

Descriptive.—The full-grown Coccid is 3^{mm} to 4^{mm} (0.12 to 0.16 inch) long, broadly oval, more or less swollen, and convex upon the disk, surrounded by a thin, flat margin with two shallow notches on each side

THE TURTLE-BACK SCALE. 49

and one deeper indentation behind. The color changes with age from transparent yellow in the young to deepening shades of brown in the adult. Individuals attacked by parasites turn black. Until it becomes gravid and swollen with young, the insect is exceedingly thin and transparent, the green color of the leaf or bark showing through the body so that the very young Coccid is well nigh invisible. The surface is smooth and shining, with faint, scattered punctures on the disk. The six slender legs are concealed beneath the dilated margins of the body. The male, although for many years diligently sought, both in this country and abroad, still remains undiscovered.

Young Larva.—The new-born insect has the usual oval form of young Bark-lice. It is yellowish in color, and has a pair of six-jointed antennæ, and two long bristles at the anal extremity.

Metamorphoses.—The metamorphoses which take place in this species are very simple, and consist in a flattening and broadening of the form of the larva, and in the gradual loss of external organs by disuse. The first to disappear are the antennæ and the anal bristles; lastly, but not until the body becomes swollen with young, the legs become useless, and are imbedded in the excretions, which finally cement the insect to the surface of the plant. The body of the mother in this last stage of her existence becomes a casket filled with the young lice. These in due time swarm forth together and distribute themselves over the plant.

Fig. 11.—*Lecanium hesperidum* (Linn.) Adult females, on Orange, natural size. (After Comstock.)

Restriction to young Growth.—The young lice invariably settle upon the bark and leaves of tender growth. Even the adult insects do not appear able to pierce with their beaks the tissues of the plant when hardened by age, and only the gravid and incubating females are found upon parts which have completed a season's growth.

Gregarious Habits.—There is a tendency in the young to keep together, and at seasons when the Orange is in active growth, when the p'ant is pushing out an abundance of shoots, the swarming larvæ do not need to wander far in search of food. The progeny of each female then settle down together, and extensive colonies are formed. These colonies

6521 O I——4

never long outlast the growing season. If not sooner exterminated by the attacks of enemies and parasites, the hardening of the tissues of the bark and leaves gradually puts an end to their existence, and the young of later generations must seek elsewhere for their support.

Brood Periods.—Thus, in spring and early summer, when the Orange renews its foliage and new growth is abundant, the increase of this insect is most rapid, and the number and extent of its colonies often become alarming. The month of June is generally the time of greatest activity in this species. Later in the season the colonies dwindle and become reduced to a few gravid individuals. The young are obliged to wander far in search of bark sufficiently tender to be penetrated by their beaks. This can be found only upon the solitary shoots and vigorous leaders, which the tree in summer sends upwards from the trunk or main branches below. It is not surprising, therefore, that very many of the young lice hatched in summer perish from hunger, being unable to find a spot penetrable by their beaks, or they fall a prey to numerous enemies in their wanderings over the plant, and in fall and winter, as a rule, only solitary individuals are met with.

Excretion of Honey.—From minute pores upon the sides of the bodies of these insects exudes a colorless nectar. This liquid may also be ejected by them with considerable force, so that it falls upon the leaves and parts of the plant at some distance away, and forms a sticky coating; but it is never in sufficient quantity to form drops, as sometimes happens in the case of other sucking-bugs which produce honey-dew. If not lapped up by other insects, the nectar attracts a black sugar fungus (*Capnodium citri*), and the plant becomes coated with "smut."

Attended by Ants.—Like all sluggish nectar-producing insects, the *Lecanium hesperidum* is attended by troops of ants, which feed upon the sweet excretions, and not only clean the surface of the leaves about the Bark-lice, but also lick the insects themselves, and with caressing strokes of their antennæ induce them to give out the liquid more freely. Ants, therefore, are not enemies of this Bark-louse; on the contrary they are its friends, and afford it more or less protection from the attacks of certain enemies. The extent of their services to the Bark-lice has been greatly exaggerated, however, and they cannot prevent their destruction by internal parasites.

As indicators of the presence of this Bark-louse, ants become useful to the observing cultivator, for if a tree is in the slightest degree infested, and long before the colonies of Lecanium become destructive or even noticeable, the tell-tale stream of ants ascending and descending its trunk gives an infallible indication of the impending evil and guides the eye to the secret lurking places of the pest.

PARASITES.—Colonies of the Turtle-back Scale are, however, seldom allowed to dwindle and dissipate themselves solely by the action of their own laws of growth and existence; they are subject to the attacks of internal parasites which greatly hasten their dissolution. These para-

THE TURTLE-BACK SCALE.

sites are, as usual, minute Hymenopterous flies belonging to the family of the *Chalcididæ*. The destruction which they work upon colonies of the Bark-louse is so great that frequently it appears an accident due to oversight on the part of the parasites if among the throng an occasional individual Coccid escapes. Among scattered and solitary individuals of Lecanium the destruction by parasites is less complete and many escape. If it were to remain strictly gregarious at all seasons of the year this now common Bark louse would no doubt speedily become a rarity. The following four species of these parasites have been observed to prey upon *Lecanium hesperidum*:

Coccophagus lecanii (Fitch).—In this species the general color of the body is black, the crescent-shaped shield on the back between the wings is lemon-yellow in the female and brown in the male; eyes dark-red brown; antennæ light brown, with the tip of the club darker; wings clear, with dark-brown veins; thighs brown, yellow at the extremities, the remainder of the legs light yellow, with the last joint of the tarsi brown. The length varies from 1^{mm} (0.04 inch) in the female to 0.5^{mm} (0.02 inch) in the male.

This parasite lives upon several species of Bark-lice, and is found in all parts of the United States. In Florida it is the most common parasite of *Lecanium hesperidum*, and is seldom absent from its colonies. With rare exceptions a solitary specimen of Coccophagus occupies the body of each parasitized Lecanium. The Coccids are always attacked before they attain full growth. In dying they turn black and adhere firmly to the bark. The bloated and hardened skin of the Bark-louse forms a casket in which the parasite undergoes its transformation to a pupa of dark color, and from which it emerges in time as a perfect fly through a round hole eaten in the shell. If there are any distinct broods they coincide with those of the Bark-louse, and with the colonies of the latter the numbers of the parasite increase or diminish.

Coccophagus cognatus Howard (Fig. 12) is a somewhat larger species than the preceding, rather lighter (dark brown) in color. In the female the shield upon the back is orange-yellow; in the male the corresponding parts are tipped with light yellowish-brown. The front legs are fuscous, the middle and hind pairs darker; all the tarsi are whitish, with the last two joints dusky. Length of female 1.2^{mm} (0.05 inch), of male 0.6^{mm} (0.02 inch). This species, first noted and described by Mr. Howard (Report of Commissioner of Agriculture for 1880, p. 359), was bred from *Lecanium hesperidum* on orange trees in the orange house of the Department of Agriculture at Washington.

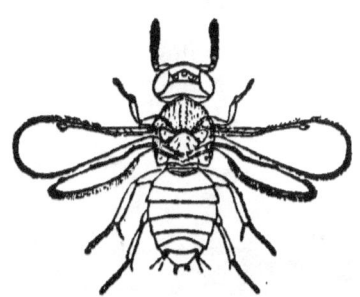

FIG. 12.—*Coccophagus cognatus*. (After Howard.)

The foregoing parasites, belonging to the genus *Coccophagus*, have eight-jointed antennæ. In the genus *Comys* the antennæ are eleven-jointed, the shield upon the back (*scutellum*) terminates in a tuft of long, stiff hairs, and the fore wings are clouded with brown.

Comys bicolor Howard (Fig. 13) is the largest parasite of *Lecanium hesperidum*. It has dark-brown eyes, head and face yellowish-brown, collar shining black, remainder of thorax yellowish-brown, with black hairs; abdomen shining black. The first and second pairs of legs are respectively dark and light brown, with the thighs white below, fuscous

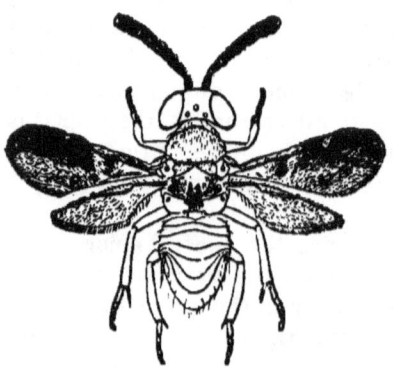

FIG. 13.—*Comys bicolor*. (After Howard.)

above; the hind legs dark, with silvery white tarsi; length 1.75^{mm} (0.07 inch). This parasite is found in company with *Coccophagus lecanii*.

Being larger it inhabits the full-grown scales, while the *Coccophagus* attacks only those which are partly grown. The Bark-lice which contain pupæ of this parasite turn black as with the preceding species.

Encyrtus flavus Howard (Figs. 14 and 15).—In this species the antennæ are eleven-jointed, but the scutellum is lustrous and without the tuft of hairs. The sexes are very dissimilar. *Female*, general color ocher-yellow; eyes brownish; eyelets carmine; antennæ brownish, or yellowish at base, three intermediate joints brilliant white, club at the end black; the fore-wings dusky, clear at base, with a clear band across the middle, and two triangular clear spaces on the outer third. Length, 1.2^{mm} (0.05 inch). *Male*, color shining metallic green, with bronze tinge on the back; legs light yellow, dusky at tips; antennæ dusky, yellow at base, the joints covered with long hairs. Length, 0.85^{mm} (0.03 inch).

FIG. 14.—*Encyrtus flavus*, male. (After Howard.)

FIG. 15.—*Encyrtus flavus*, female. (After Howard.)

Geographical Distribution and Food Plants.—*Lecanium hesperidum*

THE BLACK SCALE OF CALIFORNIA. 53.

(Linn.) is one of the best known and most widely distributed species of Bark-louse. For centuries it has been transported from one country to another, until it has become thoroughly cosmopolitan and a common pest in green-houses throughout the world. In mild climates, like those of southern Europe and the southern United States, it thrives in the open air. It is a general feeder, and although found most constantly upon plants of the citrus family, others in great variety are attacked. Marked preference is shown for plants with smooth bark and thick or glossy leaves; thus the Ivy, Oleander, and Japonica suffer equally with the Orange from the depredations of this Bark-louse.

THE BLACK SCALE OF CALIFORNIA.

(*Lecanium oleæ* Bernard.)

[Fig. 16.]

The following account of this scale is found in the Report of the Commissioner of Agriculture for 1880, p. 336:

"*Adult Female.*—Dark brown, nearly black in color; nearly hemispheri-

FIG. 16.—*Lecanium oleæ* Bernard. 16. adult females on Olive, natural size; *a*, female, enlarged. (After Comstock.)

cal in form, often, however, quite a little longer than broad; average length from 4^{mm} to 5^{mm}; average height 3^{mm}. Dorsum with a median longitudinal carina and two transverse carinæ, the latter dividing the body into three subequal portions; frequently the longitudinal ridge is more prominent between the transverse ridges than elsewhere, thus forming with them a raised surface of the form of a capital H. The body is slightly margined; outer part of the disk with many (18-30) small ridges which extend from the margin half way up to center of dorsum. Viewed with the microscope, the skin is seen to be filled with oval or round cells each with a clear nucleus; the average size of the cells being from .05^{mm} to .06^{mm} in length, while the nuclei average .02^{mm} in diameter. The antennæ are long and 8 jointed, the two basal joints short; joint 3 longest, joints 4 and 5 equal and shorter, joints 6 and 7 equal and still shorter, joint 8 with a notched margin and almost as long as joint 3. Legs rather long and stout, the tibiæ being about one fifth longer than the tarsi. The anal ring seems to bear six long hairs.

"*The Egg.*—Long oval in shape, 0.4^{mm} in length, yellowish in color.

"*Newly-hatched Larvæ.*—There is nothing very characteristic about the young larvæ; they are flat, and their antennæ are only 6 jointed.

"The black scale is stated by Signoret to be properly in France an olive scale, sometimes, however, becoming so common as to occur on all neighboring plants also. In California we find it infesting the greatest variety of plants, and becoming a very serious enemy to orange and other citrus trees. I have found it at Los Angeles on orange and all other citrus plants, on olive, pear, apricot, plum, pomegranate, Oregon ash, bitter sweet, apple, eucalyptus, sabal palm, California coffee, rose, cape jessamine, *Habrothmus elegans*; and elsewhere upon an Australian plant known as *Brachacton*, and also upon a heath. It preferably attacks the smaller twigs of these plants, and the young usually settle upon the leaves.

"The development of this species is very slow; and it seems probable that there is only one brood in a year. Specimens observed by Mr. Alexander Craw at Los Angeles, which hatched in June or July, began to show the characteristic ridges only in November. Mr. Craw has seen the lice, even when quite well grown, move from twigs which had become dry and take up their quarters on fresh ones.

"Although carefully looked for, the males, like those of so many other lecanides, have never been found.

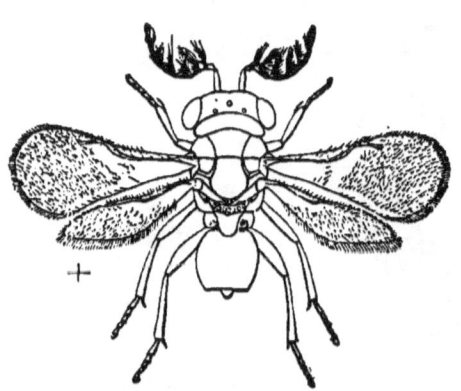

FIG. 17.—*Tomocera californica*, male. (After Howard.)

" A dark brown bark-louse has been sent me from Florida, on live oak, holly, oleander, orange, and one or two unknown plants, by Dr. R. S. Turner, of Fort George, which appears to be identical with *Lecanium oleæ.* It is, however, by no means as abundant or injurious in that State as in California.

"*Natural Enemies.*—Enormous quantities of the eggs of the black scales are destroyed by the chalcid parasite *Tomocera californica,* described on p. ——[368] of this report. [Fig. 17, male; Fig. 18, female.] Particulars as to the work of this parasite are given at the same place. Upon one occasion (August 25, 1880), I found within the body of a full-grown female a lepidopterous larva, which was very similar in appearance to the larvæ of the species of *Dakruma* described in my last report as destroying bark-lice. The specimen, however, was lost, and no more have been found since.

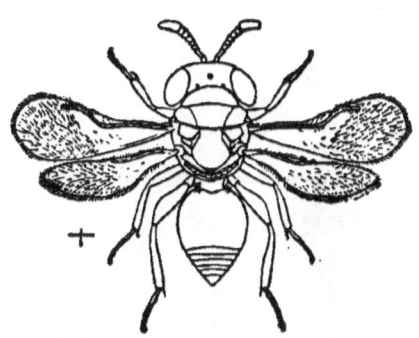

Fig. 18.—*Tomocera californica,* female. (After Howard.)

"A number of beetles of the genus *Latridius* were found under scales which had been punctured by the *Tomocera*, but probably would not destroy the live insect. Many mites were found feeding upon the eggs and young. The infested trees were also swarming with the different species of lady-bugs (*Coccinellidæ*)."

THE HEMISPHERICAL SCALE.

(*Lecanium hemisphæricum* Targioni.)

[Fig. 19.]

Professor Comstock, in the Report of the Commissioner of Agriculture for 1880, p. 334, thus treats of this Bark-louse:

"*Adult Female.*—Shape approaching hemispherical with the edges flattened. Average length, 3.5^{mm}; width, 3^{mm}; height, 2^{mm}. The shape and proportions vary somewhat according as the scale is formed upon a leaf or a twig. Upon the rounded twig it loses something of its hemispherical form, becomes more elongated, and its flattened edges are bent downwards, clasping the twig. In such cases, of course, its height becomes greater and its width less. The color varies from a very light brown when young to a dark brown, occasionally slightly tinged with reddish when old. The oval cells of the skin vary in length from .01^{mm} to .04^{mm}, and each cell contains a large granular nucleus. The antennæ are 8-jointed with joints 1 and 2 short and thick; joint 3 is the longest, and the succeeding joints decrease gradually in length to joint 8, which is longer than the preceding. Occasionally a specimen is found in which joint 5 is longer than 4, and I have seen individuals in which this was the case with one of the antennæ while the other was normal. The legs are long and rather slender; the bristle on the trochanter is long; the articulation of the tarsi is very well marked. (This fact has suggested to Signoret that the insects of this series are less fixed than their congeners.) The tarsal digitules are, as usual, two long and two short, those of the claws spreading widely at summit, and very stout at the base. The anal-genital ring (more easily seen than in the other species we describe) is furnished with eight long hairs. The anal plates are triangular with rounded corners, and are furnished with two long hairs upon the disk, and three much shorter ones at the tip.

"*The Egg.*—The egg is ellipsoidal in form, and 0.15^{mm} in length. In color it is whitish with a yellowish tinge, and is smooth and shining.

"*The newly-hatched Larva.*—The antennæ are only 7-jointed, and the tarso-tibial articulation is hardly marked.

"This bark-louse was first noticed in the orangery of the Department upon the leaves and twigs. It was also noticed upon various greenhouse plants, Disipyrus, Chrysophyllum, sago palm, and *Croton variegatum*. Shortly after being found here it was received from correspondents in California as infesting orange and oleander. During my visit to California I found it upon a single orange tree in the yard of Mr. Elwood Cooper, near Santa Barbara.

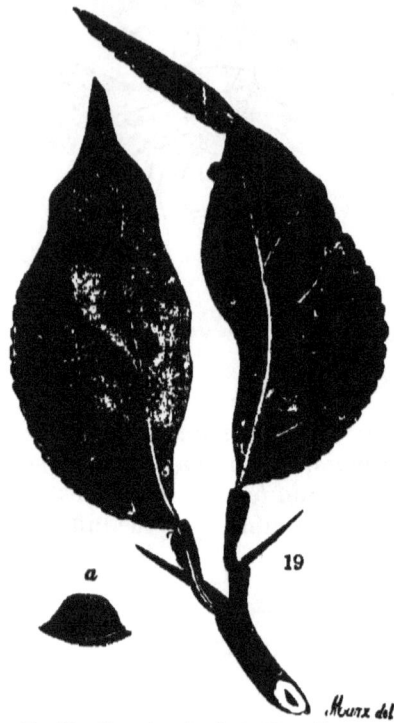

FIG. 19.—*Lecanium hemisphæricum* Targ. 19, adult females on Orange, natural size; *a*, adult female, enlarged. (After Comstock.)

"Actual observation shows the surmise of Signoret as to the locomotive powers of this insect to have been correct. We have seen the adult insects when removed from their positions crawl back with apparent ease."

THE WAX SCALE—WHITE SCALE.

(*Ceroplastes floridensis* Comstock.)

[Fig. 20.]

Descriptive.—The adult insect with its covering is from 2^{mm} to 3^{mm} (0.08 to 0.12 inch) in length; oval in form, convex above, flattened or concave beneath. The upper surface presents a rounded central prominence, and on the margins six or eight smaller prominences surrounding the central one, and separated from it by a well-marked depression. Near the posterior extremity, at the bottom of a deep pit, is seen the open end of a tube projecting from the body of the insect. The excreted

THE WAX SCALE OR WHITE SCALE.

covering is a soft wax, very similar to the white wax of commerce. The color is white, rendered impure by surface accumulations of dust and dirt. A faint tinge of pink is sometimes given to the semi-transparent wax by the red color of the insect beneath.

When the covering of wax is removed the naked body of the insect is disclosed to view. This has the form of an almost globular sack, with thin and delicate walls, inclosing dark red liquid contents, or eggs of similar color. The upper surface of the body bears six prominent tubercles, three on each side, and a short anal tube, the end of which, as has been seen, penetrates the covering of wax. Beneath the flattened ventral surface may be discovered the disused, but not wholly discarded, legs and antennæ of the larva. The under surface also usually shows the marginal notches, more plainly seen in Lecanium, and which indicates the three structural divisions of the body. From these notches radiate streaks of chalky white exudation, which at a hasty glance have the appearance of legs, but probably serve as a cement attaching the scale more firmly to the bark.

FIG. 20.— *Ceroplastes floridensis* Comstock. 20, adult and young females on Ilex, natural size; *a*, young female, enlarged; *b*, adult female, enlarged. (After Comstock.)

Larva. — The newly-hatched louse has the usual oval, flattened form. Color pale ruddy brown, with the members yellowish; antennæ 6 jointed, tipped with long hairs. The caudal bristles are very long.

Eggs 0.25^{mm} long, elliptical, having the color of sherry wine.

Life-history.—The eggs, to the number of seventy-five or one hundred, are deposited under the covering of the mother, and are simply transferred from the inside to the outside of her body, which becomes excavated below, and is more and more depleted as the process of laying goes on. At last, entirely collapsed, it forms a mere lining to the walls of the waxen casket, beneath which the eggs are brought to maturity and hatched.

The young, escaping from beneath the scale, scatter in all directions over the tree, and soon attach themselves, by their beaks, to the surfaces of the leaves. After they have begun to feed and to excrete wax, they are rarely seen to move by day, but at night they frequently change their position. Finally they desert the leaves, and at maturity the greater number will be found upon the bark of the twigs and smaller branches.

The excretions of wax exude from minute orifices called spinnerets, placed in groups upon various parts of the body, but chiefly upon the margins. At first the wax forms in ridges, which unite and form a crown around a central tuft. Smaller tufts to the number of a dozen or fifteen arise about the central elevation, and the young louse, when about a week old, appears as an oval white star upon the leaf. The wax gradually spreads over the surface of the insect, and for a time forms distinct plates; six of these, three upon each side, are large and distinct; the three remaining plates are small; they are situate one at each end and one in the center. After the insect has attained two-thirds its adult size, the plates are found to have coalesced, and form a thick, continuous sheet of wax, from which arise at least as many tufts as there were plates. The tufts, which are merely exfoliations of wax, marking the spots where the material is most abundantly given off, slowly but constantly melt into the surrounding mass. At full maturity, when the production of wax entirely ceases, these eruptive centers become obliterated, or are marked by a few projecting fragments which gather dust and dirt and cause discolorations and spots which have been variously described by different authors.

The honey-dew produced and given off by these insects attracts ants and other insects, and, as in the case of Lecanium, these lap the nectar from the bodies of the Coccids and from surrounding objects.

Broods.—The development of this insect is not very rapid, and extends over three or four months. The principal broods are in spring (April and May) and in midsummer (July and August). A third brood occurs in October or November.

Habitat and Food Plants.—This Bark-louse is found in all parts of the peninsula of Florida, but is not known to occur elsewhere. Its principal food plant is the Gall-berry (*Ilex glabra*), a plant which grows abundantly in the sterile "flat woods" and in low ground about ponds. In these waste places, often far removed from cultivated plantations, the insect may be found in such abundance that the stems of the gall-berry bushes are loaded with them in dense clusters, while the leaves and all surrounding objects are coated with the black smut which always accompanies crowded colonies of this and other nectar-yielding Coccids. Such infested patches of Gall-berry sometimes cover acres in extent.

Although the insect lives and thrives upon many other plants, and particularly upon such fruit trees as the Quince, Apple, and Pear, which in Florida do not find suitable climatic conditions, and are not thrifty, yet in cultivated orchards it is seldom destructive. Upon the Orange it occurs everywhere in numbers usually insignificant, but at times sufficient to excite apprehension. The white color and striking stellate form of the young, dotted over the glossy surfaces of the leaves, frequently attract attention, but their numbers are always so greatly reduced during growth that only three or four per cent. reach the adult age.

The thinning-out is not alone the work of enemies and parasites, but is also due to the fact that the lice, when they become gravid, cannot maintain their hold upon the smooth surface of the leaves. They fall to the ground and perish, being in the latter portion of their lives incapable of free movement and, therefore, unable to reascend the trees. The Orange is not, therefore, adapted to this species of Scale-insect, and is never subject to long-continued or very damaging attacks by it.

The occurrence of this Bark-louse upon wild plants, in portions of Florida very remote from cultivation, seems to indicate that it is indigenous, and not imported as supposed by Mr. Ashmead, who, however, considers it identical with *Ceroplastes rusci* (Linn.), a common European species. Professor Comstock, who has carefully compared the Old World species with our own, remarks that *C. floridensis* "presents several marked differences; the most easily noticeable being the small size of the central plate, and its entire disappearance so early in the life of the insect."

Parasites.—A small Hymenopterous fly has been bred from *Ceroplastes floridensis*. It is similar in appearance and habits to *Encyrtus flavus* Howard, previously mentioned as preying upon *Lecanium hesperidum*.* In his paper on parasites of the Coccidæ (Report Comm. Agric. for 1880, p. 369), Mr. Howard notices the occurrence of an allied parasite, a species of the genus *Tetrastichus*, which also remains undescribed.[1]

THE BARNACLE SCALE.

(*Ceroplastes cirripediformis* Comstock.)

[Fig. 21.]

The following account of this somewhat uncommon scale is given by Professor Comstock (Report Commissioner of Agriculture for 1880, p. 333):

"*Adult Female.*—Average length 5^{mm}; width, 4^{mm}; height, 4^{mm}. When naked the color is dark reddish brown; the shape sub-globular, with a strong spine-like projection at the anal end of the body. The waxy covering is dirty white, mottled with several shades of grayish or light brown, and even in the oldest specimens retains the division into plates, although the form is more rounded and the dividing lines by no means as distinct as at an earlier age. There are visible a large convex dorsal plate, and apparently six lateral, each with a central nucleus; the anal

---

* This may be *Aphycus ceroplastis* Howard, described in Bulletin 5, Bureau of Entomology, as bred from *Ceroplastes artemesiæ* Riley MSS., from Silver City, N. Mex.

plate, however, is larger, and shows two nuclei, and is evidently two plates joined together. Antennæ 6-jointed, and proportioned as with *C. Floridensis*. Legs long; tibiæ nearly twice as long as tarsi; digitules of the claw very large. The other tarsal pair very long and slender, but with a very large button. The skin is seen in places to be furnished with many minute, round, transparent cellules, probably *spinnerets* (indicated and so called by Signoret in his description of *C. Vinsonii*), and along the border are small groups of the constricted arrow-shaped tubercles mentioned in the last species; but the bristle-shaped *spinnerets* seem to be wanting, as in *C. Fairmairii* Targ.

"*The Eggs.*—Length, 0.35^{mm}, rather slender, little more than a third as thick as long. Color light reddish brown, rather darker than the egg of *C. Floridensis*.

"*Young Larva.*—Very slender; dark brown in color; legs and antennæ as with *C. Floridensis*.

"*Growth of the Insect.*—The growth of the insect and the formation of the waxy covering seems to be very similar to that of the last species. Soon after the larva settles the same two dorsal ridges of white secretion make their appearance, but soon split up into transverse bands. Examined on the fifth day after hatching, a larva showed seven distinct transverse bands, the anterior one being in the shape of a horseshoe. At the same time the lateral margin of the body was observed to be fringed with stiff spines, seventeen to a side. At nine days the small horse-shoe-like mass had extended so as to nearly cover the thorax, and the transverse bands had lengthened and widened until they presented the appearance of a nearly complete shield to the abdomen, serrate at the edges. Fifteen lateral tufts, such as were noticed in *C. Floridensis*, and such as Targioni figures in the larva of *C. rusci* (Stud. Sulle cocciniglie, Plate 1, Fig. 6) had appeared, though still small.

"At this stage of growth, as with the last species, all development seemed to stop, although the specimens lived on for months, the temperature in the breeding-room probably not being favorable to the formation of the plates.

"The smallest specimen in the collection with the plates already formed measures 2^{mm} long by 2^{mm} wide and 1^{mm} high. The color is light brown, and the wax has a somewhat translucent appearance. The dorsal plate

FIG. 21.—*Ceroplastes cirripediformis* Comstock. Adult female, natural size; *a*, female, enlarged. (After Comstock.)

is seven-sided; it is truncate anteriorly and pointed posteriorly. From each angle radiates a suture to the lateral edge, thus forming seven lateral plates, of which a single one is above the head, while above the anus is the suture between two. Through this suture projects the anal spur. Each plate has a dark brown patch in its center, and in the center of each brown patch is a bit of the white secretion.

"*Habitat and Food-plants.*—Found at Jacksonville and in Volusia County, Florida, on orange, quince, and on a species of *Eupatorium*, often in company with with *C. Floridensis*, although it was by no means so common a species."

GENERAL REMARKS UPON THE LECANINÆ.

Extent of Injuries.—The Bark-lice of this group are less injurious to trees and woody plants than their hard-shelled relations, the Diaspinæ. Of the five species of Lecaninæ which have been known to attack citrus plants, the widely-distributed *Lecanium hesperidum* (Linn.) is most common in Florida, and is generally recognized and somewhat feared by orange-growers. It is known to occur also in the orange districts of California, where, however, it does not appear to be destructive. The decimation which this unprotected scale suffers through the attacks of parasites and enemies, and the consequent short life of its colonies, effectively limits its destructive powers. Very frequently the orange-grower will become aware of its presence only to find it in its decadence and the life of the colony virtually extinguished through the activity of his invisible friends. This fortunate condition will be sufficiently indicated by the black color of the scales which are blasted by the presence of parasites.

Extensive invasions of *Lecanium hesperidum* have never been known to occur, in this country at least. The injuries which it inflicts in orange groves are confined for the most part to nurseries or young trees before they have become fully established. Upon older trees only limited portions, and particularly shoots in process of hardening, are usually found to be infested. Rarely indeed does this scale occupy the entire top of a grown orange tree. Still more rarely is an entire orchard overrun by it.

The species of this group having soft bodies, which dry up and shrivel after death, become loosened or washed by rains from their attachment to the bark, and soon disappear from trees. They do not, as in the case of the Diaspinæ, remain and form a permanent coating upon the bark, clogging its pores and exercising a baleful influence upon the health of the tree long after life in the insects themselves has become extinct.

The Black Scale of California, *Lecanium oleæ* Bernard, is, as its name indicates, an olive scale. In California, however, it is quite injurious to the Orange and its kindred, and is said to be spreading upon deciduous orchard trees in the more northern portions of the State. It is not distributed in Florida, but has certainly been introduced and is occasionally seen upon imported plants, particularly upon the Olive.

Lecanium hemisphæricum Targioni, according to Professor Comstock, has been found upon the Orange in California. It is not known in Florida.

Of the two species of wax scales, both of which are confined to Florida, *Ceroplastes floridensis* Comstock is by far the more abundant. *C. cirripediformis* is found in certain localities, but is rare or unknown throughout a large part of the orange district. Serious injuries rarely, if ever, result from the attacks of the wax scales on orange trees, although the young of the first named species are frequently sufficiently numerous to attract attention and excite alarm. They invariably disappear, however, or become reduced to a few solitary individuals, whose numbers barely suffice to perpetuate their race.

Smut.—The attacks of the various species of Lecanium or Ceroplastes are frequently accompanied by the appearance of the sugar fungus, *Capnodium citri* Berk. and Des., of which mention has been made in the introductory chapter of this work. The soot-like coating of the fungus covers leaves and bark, and even the Coccids themselves, feeding evidently upon the nectar which these insects have the power to eject to a considerable distance, and not upon the juices of the plant. In proof of this fact it may be mentioned that a similar black coating appears at times upon objects when smeared with the nectar produced by flowers, and it is always found upon sugar-cane, where the joints are not too much exposed to the light.

Not only does smut mask the operations of Scale-insects, so that it is not unfrequently mistaken for the cause of the ruin which they work, but it can hardly be doubted that it is itself directly injurious in clogging the pores and stifling the vital action of the growing parts of the plant. A coating of soot, to which this fungus bears so strong a resemblance, would, it may well be supposed, have an equally deleterious effect, particularly if, like the smut, it were applied to the plant with a coating of some viscid liquid.

CHAPTER V.

COCCINÆ: THE MEALY-BUGS.

General Characters and Habits.—Bark-lice, belonging to the subfamily Coccinæ, cover themselves and their eggs with masses of downy wax of white color, and hence they receive the name Mealy-bugs. Beneath the flocculent covering the Bark-louse lies concealed, sometimes nestling beside a mass of eggs so large as to quite overshadow the insect itself, sometimes surrounded by a crowd of young lice, whose successive generations in a short time cover the surface of an infested plant with incrustations of dirty-white color resembling mildew.

The Mealy-bugs retain their legs, antennæ, and other organs of the larva, and to a great extent their freedom of motion throughout their lives.

As in the last subfamily, development in the female is very simple, and there is but slight change of form from the larva to the adult. The males of this group form a pupa, and develop into two winged flies, like those of the armored scales, and while undergoing these changes they encase themselves in little sacks of flocculent wax.

Compared with other Coccids occurring on the Orange, the Mealy-bugs are of large size. In destructiveness they rival any of the preceding species. They secrete and eject honey-dew, and this, falling upon the leaves and upon the insects themselves, gives rise to the black smut fungus (*Capnodium citri*). The incrustation formed by the mealy bodies of the insects, befouled with smut, presents a very unsightly appearance, and trees smitten with these pests become conspicuous objects, visible at long distances.

Food Plants.—The Common Mealy-bug, *Dactylopius adonidum* (Linn.), is a well-known pest of the garden and greenhouse, attacking nearly all plants, even pines and evergreens, and undoubtedly including the Orange and its kind, at least in the gardens of southern Europe. In the United States, however, this species has not been known to infest orange groves, but its place is supplied by a very closely-related form, which is considered by Professor Comstock a new species of the same genus, and has been described by him under the name *D. destructor*. The habits of this and the following species, *Icerya purchasi* Mask., are similar, and, like the common garden insect, they attack, with disastrous results, almost all varieties of fruit and shade trees, as well as shrubs and herbaceous plants of the most widely different sorts.

THE DESTRUCTIVE MEALY-BUG.

(*Dactylopius destructor*, Comstock.

[Figs. 22 and 23.]

This species has been for several years very destructive to orange trees in groves and gardens in the neighborhood of Jacksonville, Fla., but although this, or some other species with difficulty distinguished from it, attacks the pineapple, Banana, Guava, and other tropical plants, no species of Mealy-bug has hitherto been reported as a pest in orange groves in the more southern portions of the State.*

Prof. J. H. Comstock gives the following account of this insect: †

"*Adult Female.*—Length, 3.5^{mm} to 4^{mm}; width, 2^{mm}. Color, dull brownish yellow, somewhat darker than with *D. longifilis*; legs and antennæ concolorous with body. The lateral appendages (seventeen on each side) are short and inconspicuous and are subequal in length. Upon the surface of the body the powdery secretion is very slight. In spite of the small size of the filaments, the *spinnerets* and the supporting hairs are as numerous and as prominent, or nearly so, as in *D. longifilis*; those upon the anal lobes being especially long. Antennæ 8 jointed; joint 8 is the longest and is twice as long as the next in length, joint 3. After 3, joints 2 and 7, subequal, then 5 and 6, joint 4 being the shortest. The tarsi are a little more than half the length of the tibiæ and the digitules are as in the preceding species (*D. adonidum*); claws strong.

FIG. 22.—*Dactylopius destructor* Comstock; female, enlarged. (After Comstock.)

"*Egg.*—Length, 0.25^{mm}; shape, rather long, ellipsoidal; color, light straw yellow.

"*Young Larva.*—Rather brighter colored than the egg. Antennæ 6-jointed with the female, with the same relative proportions as in the preceding species. Tarsi considerably longer than the tibiæ. The lower lip is large, conical, and reaches almost to the posterior coxæ.

"*Male.*—Length, 0.87^{mm}; expanse of wings, 2.5^{mm}. Color light olive-brown, lighter than in following species (*D. longifilis*); legs concolorous with body; antennæ reddish; eyes dark red; bands darker brown than the general color; anterior edge of mesoscutum and posterior edge of scutellum darker brown. Body, as will be seen from measurements, rather small and delicate compared with the size of the wings; head small, with almost no hair; antennæ 10-jointed, joints 3 and 10 longest and equal; joints 2, 6, 7, 8, and 9 nearly equal and considerably shorter

---

* Local outbreaks of the Mealy-bug are from time to time reported in the central portions of the peninsula. (See Appendix I.)

† Report of the Commissioner of Agriculture for 1880, p. 342.

than 3 and 10; joints 3 and 4 subequal and a trifle shorter than the following joints. The lateral ocelli are each just laterad of the center of the eye, and not at its posterior border, as in the following species. (This, however, is a character which will not hold with specimens long mounted.)

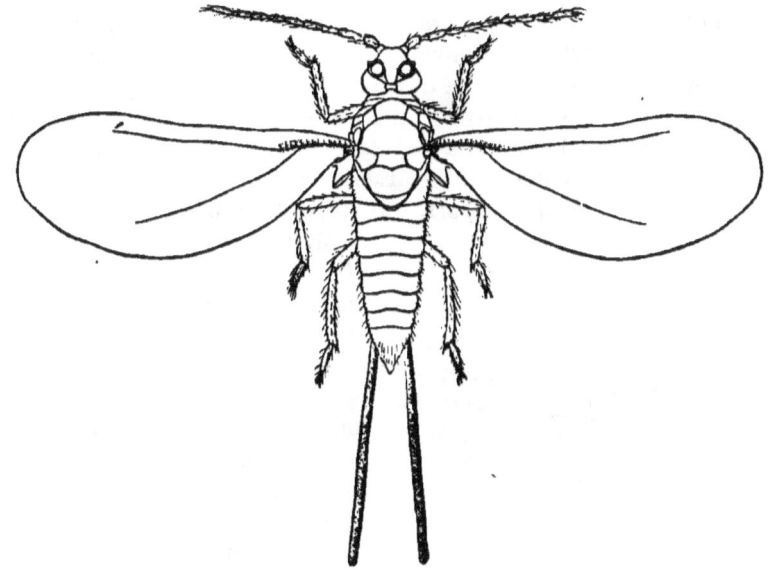

FIG. 23.—*Dactylopius destructor* Comstock, male. (After Comstock.)

Prothorax short; legs sparsely covered with hairs; tarsal digitules extremely delicate, and the button is very difficult to distinguish; we have been unable to discover a trace of the pair belonging to the claw. The anal filaments and the supporting hairs are similar to those of the following species.

"This species is readily distinguished from *D. longifilis* by the shortness of the lateral and anal filaments in the female. Indeed, for convenience's sake, we have been in the habit of distinguishing them as the mealy bug with short threads and the one with long. The life-history of this species differs quite decidedly from that of *D. longifilis*, in that true eggs, which occupy quite a long time in hatching, are deposited. The female begins laying her eggs in a cottony mass at the extremity of her abdomen, some time before attaining full growth, and the egg-mass increases with her own increase, gradually forcing the posterior end of the body upwards until she frequently seems to be almost standing on her head. The young larvæ soon after hatching spread in all directions and settle—preferably along the mid-rib on the under side of the leaves, or in the forks of the young twigs, where they form large colonies, closely packed together. As mentioned in the description, they are only slightly covered with the white powder, and many seem to be entirely bare, with the exception of the lateral threads.

"*Habitat.*—This species is very abundant upon almost every variety of house-plant in the Department green-houses, but especially so upon the Arabian and Liberian coffee-plants. On these plants they were found, curiously enough, in small pits or glands on the under side of the leaf, along the mid-rib. Almost every pit, of which there is one at the origin of each main vein, contained one or more young mealy bugs, and the larger ones whole colonies. The name *destructor* is, however, proposed for this insect from the damage done by it to orange trees in Florida, especially at Jacksonville and Micanopy, where it is the most serious insect pest of the orange.

"*Natural enemies.*—The Chalcid parasite, *Encyrtus inquisitor* Howard [Fig. 24], described in this report, was bred from a specimen of this mealy bug collected at Jacksonville, Fla. A small red bug was observed by myself and several of our correspondents to prey upon the mealy bug. The larvæ of another species have been found, but the mature form has not been obtained. These last have the faculty of changing color quickly from red to brown.

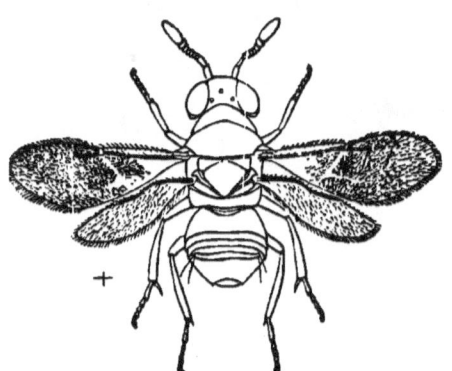

FIG. 24.—*Encyrtus inquisitor.* (After Howard.)

"The very curious larvæ of a lady-bird beetle, known as *Scymnus bioculatus*, were found feeding upon the eggs of the mealy bug at Orange Lake. These larvæ mimic the Dactylopii so closely that they might easily be taken for them. They are covered by a white secretion, and from each segment exudes a white substance which forms long filaments like those of the mealy bug. Removing the powder the larvæ are seen to be yellow in color, with two roundish dusky spots on the dorsum of each thoracic segment. Each segment of the body is furnished laterally with one long bristle and a number of small ones."

Two other parasites on *Dactylopius destructor* have recently been described by Mr. Howard (Bulletin 5, Bureau of Entomology, U. S. Dept. Agric.) as *Leptomastix dactylopii* and *Chiloneurus dactylopii*.

THE COTTONY CUSHION SCALE.

(*Icerya purchasi*, Maskell.)

[Fig. 25.]

This insect has not yet been introduced into Florida. The following excellent account of it is from the pen of Dr. S. F. Chapin, State Horticultural Officer of California:*

---

* Pacific Rural Press, October 28, 1882.

"This scale has been, it is asserted, known to be on the acacia for seven years in San José, but it is only during the past and present seasons that it has attracted attention. Its great prolificness and its destructive abilities have called widespread attention to it. This pest attacks everything in the way of tree, vine or shrub; all the evergreens as well as deciduous trees that fall in its way are attacked, and every ornamental shrub on the lawns of some portion of our cities will show its presence. The ivy, even, is not proof against it. In San Rafael, San Mateo, Santa Barbara and Los Angeles it is well established. While in San José it has not this season caused so great damage as last, yet in the citrus-growing regions it is becoming one of the most serious pests they have to encounter, and it is even stated that, should its ravages not be checked, orange and lemon culture will have to be abandoned.

"From the rapid destruction which follows the presence of this scale, it is well that it should be widely recognized, and its first invasion noticed and checked. In San José, in 1881, it was first noticed in May as the fully developed female, from which the first brood of young then appeared.

"This present season of 1882 the first young appeared May 25th, the mother insect having gradually matured her eggs from the opening of spring until the young were hatched. The egg of the *Icerya* is small, pale or orange red, elongated and ovoid. The young just hatched out are very active, and are very minute, perhaps the twenty-fifth of an inch in length. The body is pale red; the six legs and two antennæ are black. The antennæ are long and club-shaped, and have from six to nine joints, as they are further matured. The antennæ are covered with long hairs, which bristle forth prominently. The eyes are small and black. Between the pair of forelegs on the under side of the body is to be seen the beak or sucker, by which the insect secures its nourishment.

"The females partly grown are of a variety of colors, orange red mostly, and spotted over with white and green; some are nearly entirely a dirty white, and many are a pea green. It seems that the coloring matter of the plant they are upon colors them to some extent. Their body is ovoid and elongated and flattened, the back being ridged up with several segments quite prominent. Around the rim of the body are a multitude of hairs, standing out prominently. Around the rear half of the body on its rim are a row of tubercles or spinarets, from which a white secretion issues, forming a cottony cord, and these placed side by side and the interspace filled up by the same material running lengthwise the body and projecting from it, gives the whole a ribbed, satin-like appearance whitish in color. Gradually as the insect matures these projecting ridges approach each other at the ends, and are joined together and curved under slightly at the point, while the sides are at the same time curved under the whole length, and the edges joined together like a flat ribbon-like band, the whole forming, when complete, a soft elastic white sack, the size, and somewhat the shape of a medium sized white bean. The length, when mature, is about three-eighths of an inch; the width one-fifth of an inch.

"Inside the sack are deposited the eggs of the female, among the interstices of a mass of cotton-like fiber, which under a high magnifying power is shown to be round, and not more than one-sixth part the thickness of pure cotton fiber, with which it was compared in the same field. This mass of cottony fiber is filled with a great amount of granular matter, for the purpose, it may be, of affording sustenance to the young insects within the sack. The young hatch out in this sack, and make their way out into the world through a rent in the soft and tender underside of the sack.

"The female, after finding her home and during maturity, does not move, although she does not lose her legs, but clings tenaciously with her feet to her support, leaving the body tipped up in the rear and the cottony mass movable in any direction. The male insect was only found during a period of about two weeks from Sept. 25th. This was the observation of 1881, when I found them in great numbers. I have failed to find the male insect this season. It has a long red body, six legs and one pair of very long, dark and transparent wings, prominent eyes and antennæ very long and covered with hairs, arranged very much as the feathers of a peacock. (The antennæ are 16 or 17 jointed.)

FIG. 25.—*Icerya purchasi* Maskell. Females, adult and young, on Orange. (After Comstock.)

"The winged male is easily seen and easily caught, as it moves slowly about, and is not readily disturbed so as to fly away. The female insect lives upon the trunk of the tree and large limbs and down to the smallest twigs, around which it may be seen clinging in clusters sufficiently great to completely hide the branch; also upon the leaf, along the stem and ribs of which it is fixed, both above and below, although more abundant on the underside of the leaf.

"There are three broods of this insect in the season; the first appearing in May, the second in August and the third in October, or about three months apart. I have just observed, October 15th, the mature female with eggs fully grown and with the young hatched out and crawling in the same sack. In 1881 they rapidly increased from about the first of August, and were continually appearing, and still hatching out in December.

"Every female, it is estimated, produces from 200 to 500 young. The young will mature and produce a new brood in about three months."

CHAPTER VI.

INSECTS PREYING UPON BARK-LICE.

[Plate VI.]

Numerous enemies prey upon Bark-lice in all their stages, and always greatly reduce their numbers. Besides occasional enemies, such as the sucking-bugs and other predatory insects, which are general feeders, there are others which live almost or quite exclusively upon the Coccidæ. Some of these confine their attacks to particular kinds of Scale-insects. Several very common beetles of the family *Coccinellidæ*, the "Lady-birds," are useful destroyers of Bark-lice. One of the smallest of this family, *Hyperaspidius coccidivorus*, is found to colonize upon the trunks of orange trees thickly infested with Chaff Scale, and entirely free them of the pest. The young of a Lace-wing fly (*Chrysopa*) feeds upon the Bark-lice in all stages, and frequently makes its case of scales torn from the bark and often still containing living occupants. The Orange Basket-worm (*Platœceticus gloveri*) has the same habit, and the caterpillars of at least two moths are Bark-louse eaters. One of these (an unknown Tineid)[2] inhabits silken galleries, which it covers with half eaten fragments of scales, and performs such efficient service that every scale in its path is removed from the bark and suspended in the investing web.

The most important external enemies of the Scale-insect are certain mites, which are omnipresent upon trees infested with scale, and which feed upon the eggs and young lice. They breed rapidly and lurk in great numbers under old deserted scales, where their eggs are extremely well protected from the action of insecticides. For this reason, when an effective application has been made by spraying infested trees, the trunks should not be scraped for some time after, but the dead scales should be allowed to remain upon the bark for several weeks, in order that the mites which they harbor may be given time to complete the work of the remedy used. In this they may be confidently relied upon as powerful auxiliaries. When large numbers of the scales have been killed by spraying with oils, &c., the mites are often observed to increase suddenly, as they are much less affected by the application than the Scale-insects themselves. It seems probable that they feed upon the dead and dying Coccids as well as upon the living, and the loosening of the scales and abundance of food at such times stimulates them to rapid increase. They soon swarm in such numbers as completely to exterminate the remnant of the Coccids left alive by the wash.

Of all its enemies, the most efficient destroyers of the Scale-insect are its hymenopterous parasites; several species of which have already been noticed, each under the head of the particular Coccid with whose life history it is closely connected. Fig. 1 on Plate VI represents the common parasite (*Aphelinus mytilaspidis*) of the Apple Scale. These minute four-winged flies bore through the scale and deposit within a single egg. The little grub hatching from this egg feeds upon and destroys the occupant of the scale and completes its own transformations in its place. When fully adult the parasite emerges through a round hole eaten in the shell, leaving behind an empty domicile to serve as a shelter for the mites.

· The numerous species of these parasites, although not invariably confined in each case to a single species of Bark-louse, have distinct methods of attack from which they do not vary. Thus the Long and the Purple Scales are parasitized at about the time of impregnation of the females, or when they are not more than one-half their adult size, and the young Hymenopteron is developed entirely within the body of the Coccid. The skin of the latter hardens when life is extinct, and doubly protects the parasite during the latter part of its larval and in its pupa stage. The parasite of the Chaff Scale makes its attack at a later stage, often when the scale is full of eggs, and its larva does not enter the body of the Coccid, but feeds upon it and the eggs indiscriminately, occasionally devouring the eggs alone and leaving the mother Coccid untouched. Its pupa is formed naked within the scale, and has only such protection as this affords the Coccid and its eggs. In individual numbers these hymenopterous parasites abound to such an extent that rarely less than 25 per cent. and often more than 75 per cent. of the scales are attacked by them, and the work of destruction accomplished through their agency alone equals if it does not excel that of all other enemies combined. Doubtless without their aid the culture of the Orange and related trees would, in Florida at least, become impracticable.

INSECTS OF THE ORDER HYMENOPTERA.

ANTS.—No species of field-ant, in Florida at least, is in any sense predatory upon Scale-insects. With the hard-shelled Diaspinæ ants do not concern themselves, except that most of the carnivorous kinds will feed upon the contents of a scale which they chance to find torn from the bark. Many of the softer Coccidæ are attended by ants and to some extent protected by them, for the honey which they produce, and upon which the ants feed greedily without in the slightest degree harming or even disturbing the Coccids themselves.

The Chinese, it is said, have an ant which is really predatory upon Scale-insects, and which they colonize in some manner about their trees for the purpose of clearing them of these pests. If such a species exists, its importation to this country would be a great boon and could undoubtedly be accomplished. There is in fact nothing impracticable in the idea of domesticating ants and in keeping them with their nests in movable hives, as we do bees.

We have in Florida a minute yellow ant, very common, and very troublesome in houses, which might perhaps be employed in this way. This species seeks the shelter of buildings and hollow tree-trunks; it has not as yet been found possible to induce them to remain domiciled in exposed situations, and to attack the Scale-insects upon living trees in the open air; but when branches covered with scale are brought into the house, they are voraciously attacked, the scales eaten into or torn from the bark and their contents devoured. The nests of this ant are found in very dry and sheltered situations. It is not difficult to establish a colony in a box filled with shavings, paper, or other loose material. In order to accomplish this, one or more of the large queens must be obtained and confined with a sufficient number of the workers to act as attendants. If the box is kept in a suitable place, the ants will accept their new quarters, and may be allowed to roam at large and forage for themselves and their young, but the slightest exposure to light or dampness will cause them to desert the hive never to return. It is this dislike of exposure that has hitherto baffled every endeavor to colonize this ant upon orange trees and use it as a destroyer of the Scale-insect. Further experiments with this and other species are necessary to determine whether any of them can be effectively employed against Scale-insects.

INSECTS OF THE ORDER COLEOPTERA.

LADY-BIRDS—*Coccinellidæ.*

The beetles of this family are among the most efficient destroyers of Bark-lice and also of Plant-lice. Formerly they were supposed to feed exclusively upon small insects of various kinds. Although it is now known, through the investigations of Prof. S. A. Forbes and others, that the spores of fungi and other vegetable matter constitute a large part of the food of our common species, they are not on that account the less valuable in the orange grove.

The family contains numerous genera and species which fall into two divisions; the first, containing the species of larger size, includes the common insects, which are popularly recognized as "Lady-birds"; the second division embraces nearly all the smaller kinds, many of them insects of minute size, but very voracious and active destroyers of plant-eating insects and their eggs.

THE TWICE-STABBED LADY-BIRD (*Chilocorus bivulnerus*, Muls.). [Fig. 26, beetle; Fig. 27, larva.]—This species is 5^{mm} ($\frac{2}{10}$ inch) long, nearly hemispherical in shape, shining black, with a red spot on each wing-case.

The larva is rather broadly oval, the color bluish-black, with the first body-joint whitish. The body bristles with black spines, which are in turn covered with spinules and give to the insect a mossy appearance. The spines are arranged in six longitudinal rows.

Fig. 26.— *Chilocorus birulnerus.* (After Riley.)

The larva, when full grown, attaches itself firmly by the false legs at the end of the body, and becomes wedge-shaped; the skin of the back splits and gapes open, partly disclosing the pupa, which, however, remains within the skin of the larva. This mode of pupating is characteristic of the entire family.

The pupa is short and thick, tapering suddenly behind, in color black, mottled with dusky brown. The stout spines of the larva are replaced by patches of spiny hairs.

Fig. 27.— *Chilocorus birulnerus,* larva. (After Comstock.)

The Twice-stabbed Lady-bird is as abundant in Florida as in all parts of the eastern and southern United States, and, with its larva, is frequently seen upon the orange trees, feeding upon Scale-insects and also upon Aphis. It is rather fond of cool, damp situations, and is most abundant in old groves, upon the trunks of trees infested with Chaff Scale and fungi. It tears up the scales and devours the Coccids and their eggs. Several broods occur during the year. The larvæ appear to be somewhat gregarious, and frequently when they form their pupæ suspend themselves in clusters to shreds of Spanish moss or in patches upon the bark when it is coated with lichens.

EXOCHOMUS CONTRISTATUS Muls. (Fig. 28, beetle; Fig. 29, larva.)— This is a much smaller species than the preceding. The beetle is 3.3^{mm} (0.13 inch) long. The head, thorax, and body beneath are black, but the wing-cases are red, with a black spot near the tip of each.

Fig. 28.—*Exochomus contristatus.* (Original.)

The larva has the oval form and spiny appearance of *Chilocorus birulnerus,* but is handsomely marked with black and white. The spines of the latter become in this species prominent spiny tubercles.

The pupa is not provided with spiny hairs, but is smooth and marbled with black and yellowish brown, in a manner recalling the shell of the tortoise.

In habits this Lady-bird hardly differs from its larger relative, *Chilocorus birulnerus.* It however shows no preference for the shade, and is found feeding in exposed situations upon the branches infested with Scale-insects, or upon shoots covered with Plant-lice. It is exclusively a southern species. In Florida it occurs everywhere upon the Oak, and frequently becomes abundant in the orange grove, where it does good service in ridding the trees of insect pests, devouring the eggs and the young of the larger kinds, and tearing up the scales of Bark-lice in order to feed upon their contents. contents. It is also an active destroyer of the Orange Aphis.

Fig. 29.—*Exochomus contristatus,* larva. (Original.)

THE BLOOD-RED LADY-BIRD (*Cycloneda sanguinea*, Linn.). [Fig. 30, larva; Fig. 31, pupa; Fig. 32, adult beetle, enlarged and natural size.]—

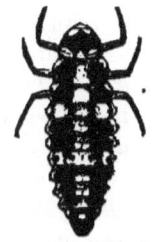

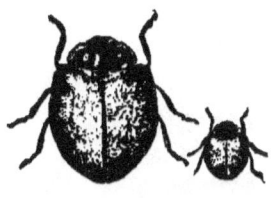

Fig. 30.—*Cycloneda*, larva — enlarged. (After Comstock.)

Fig. 31. — *Cycloneda sanguinea*, pupa—enlarged. (After Comstock.)

Fig. 32.—*Cycloneda sanguinea* — natural size and enlarged. (After Comstock.)

As its name indicates, the color of this species is orange-red or blood-red, varying somewhat in individuals. The head and thorax are black, each with a pair of yellowish spots; the thorax is also bordered with yellow. Length 5^{mm} ($\frac{2}{10}$ inch). The larva is of a more elongate form than the preceding species; the body not armed with spines, but with rows of small tubercles bearing tufts of short hairs. The colors are bluish-black spotted with orange.

The pupa is orange yellow, clouded and spotted with dusky brown or black.

This is a most common and widely-distributed species, extending even to California, where, however, it is said to be less abundant than in the East. Like most of the species, it is not connected with any particular plant, but is found wherever Plant-lice occur, feeding upon their honey-dew in preference to Bark-lice or other insects, but not seldom attacking the Orange Scale-insects when the Aphis is not at hand. It is a sun-loving species, and is most active and voracious in the hottest weather.

HIPPODAMIA CONVERGENS Guér. (Fig. 33, larva, pupa, and adult; Fig. 34, beetle, enlarged.)—This species is also common from the Atlantic to the Pacific, and everywhere feeds voraciously upon the various species of Aphis and Bark-lice. Its wing-cases are orange-red, with five or six rather small black spots on each, but the remainder of the body is black. The head has a white crown and the thorax is edged with white and has two converging dashes or short lines of white upon the disk.

Fig. 33.—*Hippodamia convergens*. (After Riley.)

The pupa is orange-red, of the same shade as the wing-cases of the adult, and has upon its surface a varying number of black spots. The spots are in some individuals entirely wanting, but three spots upon each wing-pad and at least one pair upon the first abdominal joint are very rarely absent. The surface of the pupa is without spines or hairs.

74   INSECTS AFFECTING THE ORANGE.

The larva has the same general colors as the perfect beetle, but is mottled, the brighter red appearing as spots surrounded by dusky areas; the prominences upon the back of each body-joint are clothed with downy hairs; the single pair upon each of the first three joints forms raised shields of black color; the head and legs are dark.

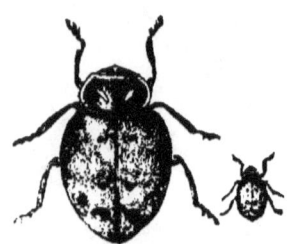

FIG. 34.—*Hippodamia convergens*—natural size and enlarged. (After Comstock.)

The larva of this, as well as that of some other species, is attacked by an internal parasite which causes its death soon after it has become adult. The Lady-bird larva attaches itself to the plant in the manner usual to it when about to change into pupa; the pupa, however, never appears, but the body of the larva becomes rigid and dry, and in shrinking sometimes discloses the outlines of the little oval cells formed by the parasites within. The number of parasites found in the body of a single Lady-bird varies from three to six, or even eight. Each parasite finally issues through a separate hole, eaten in the skin of its host, and appears as a little four-winged fly of black color and with banded wings (Fig. 35). It has been described by Mr. L. O. Howard

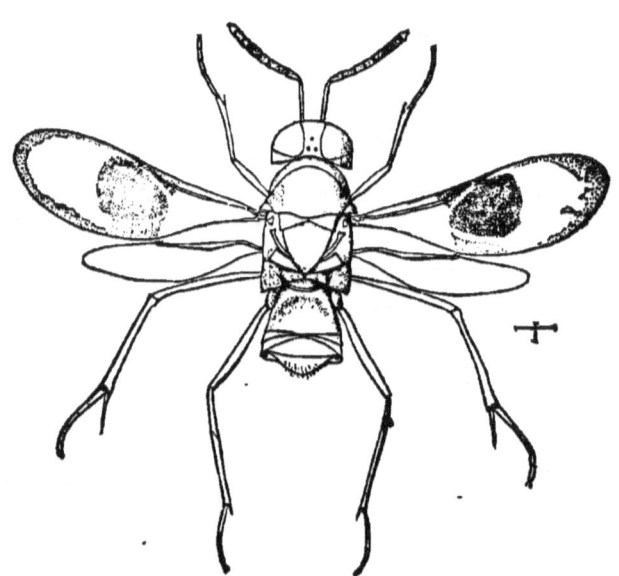

FIG. 35.—*Homalotylus obscurus*. (Original.)

(Bull. 5, Entom. Bureau, United States Department of Agriculture, 1885, p. 22) under the name of *Homalotylus obscurus*. Species of the same genus are known to attack the larvæ of Lady-birds in Europe.

THE SCALE-DEVOURING HYPERASPIDIUS (*Hyperaspidius coccidivorus* Ashmead; Plate V, Fig. 2; *a*, larva; *b*, head of larva much enlarged; *c*, part of side margin of the head, showing antenna and ocelli; *d*, beetle.)—Although on account of its small size this little beetle has been generally overlooked, it is probably the most useful of its family as a destroyer of Bark-lice. It attacks principally the Chaff Scale (*Parlatoria pergandii*), and lives in colonies upon the trunks and branches of orange trees infested with this scale. Both the perfect beetle and its larva busy themselves without ceasing in emptying the scales of their contents, and many instances have been observed of trees ultimately cleared of Chaff Scale through their persistent efforts.

The larva is 1.8^{mm} ($\frac{7}{100}$ inch) in length; body dark purple, covered with minute pubescence having a silver-gray reflection; the head and legs black.

The pupa has the color of the larva, and the form, in outline, of the perfect beetle.

The imago is broadly oval, shining black, with a badly-defined red spot upon each wing-case. Length, 1^{mm} ($\frac{1}{100}$ inch).

The strength of the little insect is apparently not sufficient to penetrate the hard scales of some of the Diaspinæ; it is not often seen to attack either the Long Scale (*M. gloverii*) or the Purple Scale (*M. citricola*), but appears most frequently upon trees infested with Chaff Scale (*P. pergandii*). Even here it does not seem able to bite through the upper shell, but inserts its thin, wedge-shaped head and jaws between the Scale-insect and the bark and eats into it from below. The perfect insect, and to some extent the larva also, devour the young of any species of Bark-louse, but have not been observed to attack Aphis or any other insect.

The young hatch in spring, from eggs laid in patches among the scales.

EPITRAGUS TOMENTOSUS; family *Tenebrionidæ*. (Fig. 36.)—This is about half an inch in length, regularly oval in form, and convex above. The body is dark brown, densely sprinkled with ash-gray pubescence. The habits of the perfect insect are similar to those of the Lady-birds, and it is very commonly found upon orange trees, engaged in feeding upon Scale-insects of all kinds. It tears the scale from the bark and devours the contents, and sometimes the substance of the scales also. Its early history is unknown, but the larva probably lives upon the ground among oak leaves. The beetle is also found abundantly upon scrubby oaks, where it feeds also upon Bark-lice.

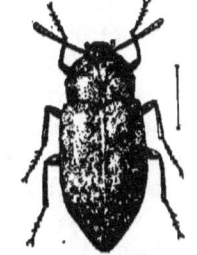

FIG. 36.—*Epitragus tomentosus*. (Original.)

Mulching the trees with oak leaves is very certain to attract these beetles, and they do good service in checking the increase of Scale-insects, although they are seldom present in sufficient numbers to effectually clean the trees.

PREDATORY LEPIDOPTERA.

The Coccid-eating Dakruma (*Dakruma coccidivora* Com. n.). [Plate VI, Fig. 3: *a*, egg; *b*, larva; *c*, pupa; *d*, moth; *e*, moth resting on a Barklouse.]—The predatory habits of this little moth were first made known by Professor Comstock (North American Entomologist, I, p. 25), who found its larva eating various species of Bark-lice. It is also very common in the spring of the year on orange trees infested by the soft bodied Coccids, *Lecanium, Ceroplastes*, &c., and does incalculable service in clearing them of these pests. It, however, does not attack the Dia pinæ unless compelled by hunger to do so, and seems to experience some difficulty in biting through their hard scales.

Several larvæ live together socially in silken galleries, with which they cover twigs and branches infested with Scale-insects. Underneath the covering of web the caterpillars of Dakruma move back and forth, actively engaged in removing the Bark-lice from the bark and suspending them in the investing web. Nothing could be more thorough than their work. Branches incrusted with Lecanium scales are very quickly cleared of the lice, and the Dakruma larvæ do not cease to extend their operations until every individual Coccid in the colony has been lifted from its place and securely fastened in the web above.

While constructing their galleries the caterpillars stop occasionally to feed upon the Coccids. At such times they seldom finish their repasts, but, like busy workmen, as they are, hastily snatch a bite or two by way of lunch, and suspend the half-devoured fragments in their web. When the entire scale colony has been secured within its net, the Dakruma larva rests from its labors and feeds at leisure upon the Coccids suspended in its larder. It devours not only the eggs and young and the softer parts of the Bark-lice, but even to some extent their harder skin or scale. The result of its operations upon Lecanium and Ceroplastes scales is to utterly annihilate the colonies of these insects which they attack.

Larva.—A rather slender caterpillar, nearly half an inch in length, very dark green, almost black in color; the body bears a few long hairs arising from pale brown spots.

Pupa.—The chrysalis is formed within the galleries of the larva, and is loosely wrapped in a cocoon of silk. It is slender, tapering to the anal extremity, of varying shades of brown, darkest on the back and lighter on the belly and wing-pads.

Imago.—A small, dark-colored moth, one-third of an inch in length. The body is dark-brown above and gray beneath; the forewings are light gray, with markings of brown and black; the eyes are black and distinctly faceted.

Egg.—White, oval, the surface covered with a network of raised lines, the meshes forming irregular hexagons.

History.—The eggs are laid singly among the Coccids; they hatch in five or six days; the caterpillars, if food is abundant, attain their full growth in ten or twelve days; their pupa stage lasts about the same length of time, unless belated in June or July, in which case they remain in pupa until the heat moderates in August or September. The caterpillars are first seen in March, but are not common until April or May. The moths are most abundant in June, but disappear in midsummer and appear again in the fall. There are at least two, and possibly three, broods in the spring and early summer, and one in the fall. The pupæ and a few belated larvæ may be found in winter at any time.

THE PALE DAKRUMA (*D. pallida* Comstock).—Another species, closely resembling the preceding and having similar habits, is described by Professor Comstock (Rept. Comm. Agric. for 1879, p. 243) from gall-like Coccids on Oak. From its similarity of habit this species may be expected to feed upon Orange Scale-insects, although it has not been actually observed to do so. It is known from the first species by its lighter color in both the adult and larval stages.

SCALE-EATING TINEID.[2] (Fig. 37.)—The caterpillars of a Tineid moth with habits very similar to Dakruma, are found eating various Coccids, and have also been observed to feed upon the common Long and Chaff Scales on Orange. Several specimens of the moth were bred in winter from larvæ inhabiting tightly-rolled dead leaves involved in the webs of a social leaf-eating caterpillar (*Anæglis*). The leaves thus occupied had been infested by Scale-insects, and the scales within the retreat of the larvæ were all gnawed and partially devoured.

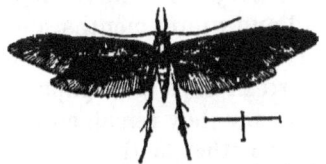

FIG. 37.—*Scale-eating Tineid.* (Original.)

In summer the same species is found forming silken galleries like those of Dakruma upon orange branches infested with Diaspinous scales.

The following observations of the habits were made upon several larvæ placed upon a twig of Orange covered with Long Scale (*Mytilaspis gloverii*). The larvæ began at once to make a tangle of web in a fork of the twig, which was afterwards extended into a gallery along the branch. From time to time a larva reached out and tore a scale from the bark. Sometimes it devoured the whole scale, with the contained insect; again it turned the scale over and ate the contents, eggs and mother Coccid, retreating finally to its gallery and taking with it the empty shell, which it fastened in its web. Occasionally the caterpillars detached from the bark and fastened in their web scales with their living contents untouched.* From the frequent additions made to it, the retreat of the caterpillars soon became entirely coated with fragments, and could with difficulty be distinguished from the surrounding bark.

---

* The contents of these scales were, however, sooner or later devoured. The larvæ also frequently gnawed into a scale at one end and pulled out and devoured the insect, leaving the empty scale still attached to the bark. They also ate sparingly the gummy exudations of the bark.

These fragments consisted in great part of half-eaten scales, from which the eggs and the Coccids had been extracted.

Larva.—The caterpillars are about one-fourth inch long, dark purple in color, with lines of lighter color in fine blotches along the sides.

Pupa.—The chrysalis is sometimes formed upon the branches within a cocoon of silk densely covered with scales, and sometimes concealed in a dead, rolled leaf, or otherwise protected under fragments lodged in spider-webs, &c. It is dark brown in color, and of the usual form, without striking peculiarities.

Imago.—The moth is less than one-third inch in length, with rather long wings; head and thorax are ashen gray; the upper wings are lustrous lead color, with silvery scales intermixed; they are marked each with a single distinct black spot near the base and a pair of faint dots near the tip. The under wings are silvery gray, with the membrane showing iridescent blue between the scales in the middle of the wing; the antenna in one sex has the third joint thickened and curiously excised, the excavation covered with a tuft of long scales.

History.—The larvæ of this species have been observed only in the fall and winter months, and the number of broods is not known. It may be assumed to have three or four broods. Moths appeared in thirteen or fourteen days from pupæ formed late in September. In December and January they remained twenty days in pupa.

Two other moths of this family (*Tineidæ*) have been noted* as feeding upon Coccids in Florida, but they were bred only from gall-like Bark-lice found upon Oak, and never occurring upon orange trees.

INSECTS OF THE ORDER HEMIPTERA.

THE SPIDER-LEGGED SOLDIER-BUG (*Leptocorisa tipuloides*, Latr.; Plate VI, Fig. 4.)—This is a slender, long-legged bug. The color of the body is orange-yellow, with a rounded spot of black upon the thorax; the legs, antennæ, and tip of the beak are black; the wings in the adult have a band of black across the middle and an oval spot of black covering the terminal half; the legs are covered with almost invisible, short, stiff hairs, which cause small light objects to adhere to them. The bodies of the young especially are covered with fragments, consisting in great part of the pellicles of insects which have been emptied of their contents by the bug. Length of the adult, $\frac{7}{10}$ inch.

The habits of this bug are sluggish, but it flies readily when adult. It is found, often in great numbers, upon the Orange and other plants when they are infested with the common Lecanium Scale (*Lecanium hesperidum*, Linn.). The bug sucks the juices of these soft-shelled Bark-lice, but has never been observed to puncture the hard scales of the Diaspinæ. Unfortunately the Leptocorisa does not discriminate between friends and foes, but destroys many predatory and useful insects.

---

* Rept. Comm. Agric. for 1879, p. 244.

It has been observed to capture and suck the juices of ants and of the larvæ of the Lace-wing flies, and also to empty of their contents the eggs of other insects.

Eggs.—The eggs are long, vial-shaped objects, brick-red in color; they are deposited upright, in small masses, aglutinated with a viscid, frothy substance, which dries very slowly and remains sticky long after the eggs have hatched. The eggs hatch in about one week after they are deposited.

Life-history.—The number of broods is indefinite; solitary individuals are found at all seasons, but become more numerous in spring and fall, upon plants infested with Lecanium Scale, which also breeds most rapidly at these seasons. The young suck the juices of plants for a short time after hatching, but afterward feed exclusively upon insects. They change their skins frequently, gradually acquiring fully-developed wings and other characters of the adult; the process occupying, according to the season and temperature, from three weeks to two months. This species is much more gregarious in its habits than most predatory Soldier-bugs. Not only the young, but also the adult insects are frequently found in large colonies.

Parasite.—The only enemy known to attack this bug is a minute Proctotrupid fly, belonging to the genus *Telenomus*,[3] which is bred within, and destroys its eggs. The parasite is black, with yellow legs. A single fly issues from each egg of the bug, leaving a round hole eaten in the side of the shell.

Two small bugs (*Hemiptera*) prey upon the Mealy-bug (*Dactylopius destructor*). Specimens of the young bugs were sent to the Department of Agriculture, from Florida, on leaves of Orange infested with Mealy-bugs, and were observed to suck the eggs and young lice of the Mealy-bug.

In the young of one species the color is deep red, with brown eyes; antennæ and legs pale reddish or yellowish white, with the thighs slightly dusky; the antennæ four-jointed, the fourth joint longest; the proboscis short, rather stout; from each side of the abdomen, near the tip, projects a pair of long bristles. Length, when adult, about 3^{mm} ($\frac{12}{100}$ inch).

The other species is a smaller insect than the preceding. The young bugs are coral-red, the shanks and tips of the legs white, the antennæ also parti-colored, having the third joint and tip of the terminal (fourth) joint white; the proboscis is white, and reaches beyond the middle of the body; the body and members are covered with short, pale hairs. The adult is purple-brown, with lighter eyes, and has parti-colored legs and antennæ; the wings are ornamented with a large chocolate-brown spot edged with white or pale red, and situate at the base of the membranous portion, near the tip of each wing-cover; the body and surface of the wings are thinly covered with silvery hairs, giving a hoary appearance to the insect. Length 2.2^{mm} ($\frac{8}{100}$ inch). The egg is long and slender, vase-shaped, pearly white, with a tinge of pink, and has a white rim; it is deposited singly, lying upon its side, in any situation where the female may find a lurking place.[4]

This little bug is one of a number of insects often associated with the Orange Web-worm, *Anæglis demissalis*. (See Chapter X.)

INSECTS OF THE ORDER NEUROPTERA.

LACE-WINGS.

CHRYSOPA. (Fig. 38, adult fly and eggs of *Chrysopa oculata*.)—There may frequently be seen, moving rapidly about upon the trunk and branches of the orange tree, little flocculent masses, grayish in color, nearly hemispherical, and of about the size of a split pea. When one of these mossy bunches is examined closely it is found to be an insect, whose back is covered with a nondescript collection of fragments, consisting chiefly of the dried skins and broken remains of insects. This is the young of a Chrysopa, or Lace-wing fly, and the covering with which its soft body is protected, and which renders it less conspicuous upon the bark, is formed from the accumulated remains of the victims whose juices have served the animal for food.

FIG. 38.—*Chrysopa oculata*.

The Lace-wing feeds to a great extent upon Bark-lice, tearing loose the scales from the bark, and after devouring the soft contents adding a portion of the *débris* to the load upon its back. Plant lice and many other small insects are also eaten. The activity and rapacity of the larva is remarkable; it wanders restlessly over all parts of the tree in search of food, and although insignificant as to numbers in comparison with the swarming millions of its prey, it yet exercises an appreciable influence in holding them in check.

Larva.—The body of the larva, divested of its extraneous covering, is somewhat broadly oval, divided into joints, from the sides of which arise branching spines. These spines serve to hold in place the loose, dry materials which are piled upon its back. The legs are quite long and slender, adapted to rapid movements, and the jaws are sickle-shaped, long and keenly pointed, projecting beyond the ambuscade under which the insect moves.

Pupa.—When prepared to pupate, the larva forms an almost globular cocoon by drawing together with strands of silk the loose materials it bears upon its back, and constructing beneath it a spherical cell of thin but strong parchment, pure white in color. Within this the pupa lies curved like an embryo. The pupa has the form of the perfect insect, barely masked by a transparent envelope, and with the wings and other members contracted and closely applied to the body. It gradually changes in color from white to pale green, and finally issues by pushing outward a circular cap which forms one end of its cell.

Imago.—The perfect insect is a four-winged fly, of a delicate pea-green color; eyes a resplendent copper bronze. The wings are large, closely-veined, hyaline with a violet reflection; when at rest they meet in a ridge like the peak of a roof. The antennæ are black, paler outwards. Head porcelain-white; the enlarged first joint of the antennæ, and also a triangular spot on the head at the base of each antenna purple red; a band of the same color on each side of the thorax.

Eggs.—The eggs are laid upon various parts of the tree, often near a colony of Plant-lice, in groups of five to fifteen, each supported on the end of an erect, bristle-like stalk, about 0.4 inch in length. The object of this device is said to be the preservation of the egg from the young of its own kind, for such is the rapacity of the larva that those first hatched would immediately devour the remaining eggs if they were deposited within reach upon the surface of the plant.

Life-history.—The development of Chrysopa is quite rapid in hot weather, and is greatly retarded by cold. There are apparently but two broods each year, in spring and fall. Eggs are seen as late as the middle of July, but the larvæ only are abundant in midsummer. In winter both larvæ and eggs are found, but the perfect insect is not common except in early summer and late in the fall. There are said to be several species of Chrysopa frequenting the Orange, which, however, are with difficulty distinguished from each other, and have identical habits. One of these has been described as new by Ashmead under the name *Chrysopa citri.*

Parasites (Perilitus sp.).[5]—A four-winged parasite destroys the Chrysopa, and issues from its cocoon. It is of slender form, with the abdomen stalked; color beneath light yellow, above black, with yellow markings; the legs yellow, the antennæ dark, the face yellow; eyes, vertex, and back of the head black; the rings of the hind-body are alternately black and yellow. Length, 3^{mm} ($\frac{12}{100}$ inch).

HEMEROBIUS.—Several species of this genus, which is closely allied to Chrysopa, exist upon orange trees and feed upon the young of Bark-lice, and to a still greater extent upon Plant-lice (*Aphis*). They have nearly the same habits as Chrysopa, but the larvæ do not protect themselves with a covering of fragments. The larvæ are mottled with gray, brown, and dull red, and are more slender than those of the preceding species.

The pupa is formed in a globular cocoon of white parchment, not covered with fragments.

The perfect insect is much smaller than Chrysopa; the wings are less transparent, and are covered with down of light-brown color.

MITES—ACARINA.

Next to their internal parasites, Mites constitute the most important enemies of Scale-insects, and exert a constant and very powerful influence in checking their increase. They are at all times present wherever Scale-insects exist, and in numbers limited only by the food supply. They cannot penetrate the hardened shells of mature Scale-insects, but they destroy great numbers of the young lice, as soon as the latter have fastened themselves to the bark, and while their scales are still soft and thin. They also creep into the open end of scales which have begun to hatch, and destroy a portion of the eggs. The scales vacated by parasites, in which have been left convenient open doorways, furnish the Mites with secure retreats and places of deposit for their eggs. Usually the dry and distended skin of the Coccid is left by the parasite, nearly filling the scale, and with a minute exit hole immediately opposite that in the outer shell. Thus the Mites or their young and eggs are provided with a double envelope separated by layers of confined air, and nearly impervious to liquids. It is, therefore, not astonishing that applications sufficiently penetrating to kill Scale-insects do not reach the Mites and their eggs thus protected. In fact the latter very frequently increase enormously after an effective application, because the loosening of the scales by the wash enables them to penetrate to and feed upon the dead or dying Bark-lice, and the supply of food is for a time largely increased.

To cause a marked increase in the number of the Mites, it is sometimes sufficient to loosen the scales here and there upon the trunk and branches which are most thickly encrusted with them, by scraping the bark with a stick or knife blade. This gives the Mites an increased supply of food, and stimulates them to active breeding. The result is often to effectively check the progress of the Scale-insects for the time being, although they cannot be exterminated in this way. The method is not advanced as a practicable remedy, and cannot be made to replace the proper application of insecticides, but from its simplicity it is frequently useful as a means of gaining time, when remedies are not at hand.

GLOVER'S ORANGE MITE (*Tyroglyphus ? gloverii* Ashmead). [Plate VI, Fig. 5.]—This is the commonest species found among Orange Scale-insects; it is also the smallest species and the most active and rapid in its movements; it is somewhat longer than broad, slightly flattened; in color it varies from pure white to yellowish, and often a pale pink or flesh-color. This color-variation is due to the varying nature of its intestinal contents, seen through the semi-transparent body. Length about 0.1^{mm} ($\frac{4}{1000}$ inch).*

The eggs are white, and are deposited either singly or in small groups, under a tangle of spider's web, among dead scales, &c.; lurking places in which the white, six-legged young congregate and undergo their transformations.

---

* The form in most soft-bodied Acarina is very changeable, depending upon the condition of the animal, whether full-fed, or depleted by fasting. The figure of this species on Plate VI represents the shape commonly seen. When emaciated, the sides of the body become deeply sinuate or lobed, deep pits are formed upon the upper surface in front, and several transverse folds in the skin appear to divide the abdominal portion into segments. In plethoric individuals, the distention of the body into an oval sack obliterates every trace of fold or depression upon its surface.

This species certainly feeds upon the eggs of Coccids, and probably also upon their young, and sucks the juices of the adult Bark-lice, whenever it can get at them.

THE HAIRY ORANGE MITE.[6]—Probably the next in point of abundance is a larger mite, dark red in color, covered with pale hairs, broadly oval in form, and with several irregular indentations upon the back. This mite is also very rapid in its movements, and is certainly predatory upon Scale-insects or their eggs.

The eggs are sherry-brown in color, quite large and globular, and are usually deposited singly upon the leaf among scales, or strung like amber beads upon strands of spider's web, which harbor the mites and their young.

The six-legged young are spindle-shaped, of a lighter, ruby-red color, the extremities pale, and have an eye-like prominence on each side of the anterior body. The length of the adult is 0.3^{mm} ($\frac{112}{1000}$ inch).

THE SPEAR-HEAD MITE.[7]—Another not uncommon Red Mite seems to be predatory upon Scale-insects. It is rather larger than the preceding; dull, opaque red, not hairy; the body is distinctly diamond or spear shaped, somewhat flattened, with a sharp median ridge upon the back, having on each side a longitudinal depression; a band of pale brown is sometimes seen across the middle of the back. Length, 0.35^{mm} ($\frac{144}{1000}$ inch).

This species is sluggish and solitary. The eggs are deep red, globular, and are deposited singly among scales.

There are numerous species of Mites found about and among Scale-insects, of which a few only appear to be dependent upon them for their subsistence, or peculiar to the orange tree and its kind. Some of these mites are undoubtedly merely scavengers, living about, if not upon, the dirt and *débris* that collect where the plant is fouled with Scale-insects, but never appearing to attack the insect itself in any stage. Possibly they feed upon the excrement or excretions of other insects, or upon molds that accompany such ejected matter.

The predatory Mites are usually active, running hither and thither restlessly, occasionally stopping to examine the sealed edge of a scale or to pry into a vacant and deserted shell.

The young of Mites frequently differ entirely from the adults in form and coloration; they have, moreover, but three pairs of legs, while the adults have four pairs. The life-history of many species is imperfectly known.

THE SPOTTED MITE.[8]—This is a rather large, egg-shaped or pear-shaped Mite, with a very plump, smooth, shining, and pellucid body, either white or honey-yellow in color, and provided with a few very long and fine bristle-hairs; the division of the body into two parts is barely indicated by a fine line; in adult specimens the body behind is more or less clouded with red-brown, forming sometimes a distinct spot; a large round spot on each side, upon the declivities of the hind-body, varies in color with the age and condition of the individual, from sulphur-yellow to brick-red and dull brown. Length, 0.38^{mm} ($\tfrac{15}{1000}$ inch).

The Mite is slow in movement, and gregarious. White, elongate eggs, and the six-legged young are found in groups of three or four to twenty upon scale-infested orange leaves.

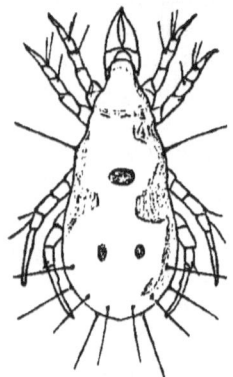

Fig. 39.—*Orange Mite.* (Original.)

While this Mite may with some probability be considered a scavenger, feeding upon dead vegetable and animal matter, it is almost certain that it does also suck the eggs of Scale-insects, with which it is very closely associated.

A species of *Rhizoglyphus* (?),[9] similar to but distinct from the preceding, was sent by Professor Comstock from Florida. It was found in all stages from egg to adult on orange leaves infested with the Long Scale and the Common Mealy-bug. Fig. 39 represents the mite, after a drawing by Mr. Th. Pergande; the following are his notes upon the species: "These Mites were especially numerous around the Mealy-bugs, and they were noticed to suck and destroy the eggs of that insect; the eggs of the Mite were deposited between the egg-masses of the Louse and also on the leaf itself; the eggs are white, perfectly oval; the Mites are white, almost transparent, the full-grown ones slightly yellow, with one or sometimes three pale brownish spots; when there is only one spot it is generally situated on the posterior portion of the abdomen, but when there are three spots they are arranged as shown in the figure—the front one is largest and the two posterior spots are small and rather indis-tinct. The male is shorter and stouter than the female."

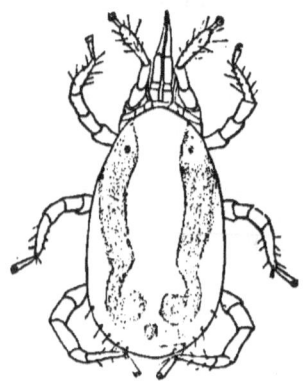

Fig. 40.—*Orange Mite.* (Original.)

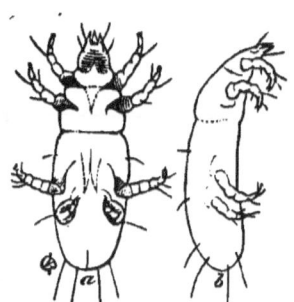

Fig. 41.—*Tyroglyphus mali.* (After Riley.)

Associated with the foregoing is a Mite [Fig. 40] with a more flattened form, concerning which the following notes are given, with the figure here produced:[10]

"A single specimen of a second species of Mite was also found on an orange leaf sent by Professor Comstock, from Sanford, Fla. This Mite is quite different from the preceding; it is smaller, more yellow, and there are small and very distinct eyes; the legs, especially the first pair, are quite differently formed. It is not as hairy and not as slender as the

MITES WHICH DESTROY SCALE-INSECTS. 85

other species. This Mite also evidently preys either on the Mytilaspis or the Dactylopius."

A very long-bodied Mite, without spots, is found occasionally in empty Mytilaspis scales; it has the same habits as the Spotted Mite. This species may be identical with *Tyroglyphus malus* Shimer, which preys upon the Oyster-shell Bark-louse of the Apple. The figures of the latter, from Riley's Fifth Missouri Report, are here reproduced. [Fig. 41.]

THE ORBICULAR MITE.—This is the largest Mite found among Scale-insects; it is nearly circular, or slightly oval, in outline; the body is thick and somewhat flattened, covered with a polished, horny shell of brown color, surmounted by a few fine bristles. The shell or carapace is turned under at the sides and ends, so that the short, stout legs are concealed beneath it as the animal walks, and only the tip of the head and beak project beyond the front margin. Length, about 0.4^{mm} ($\frac{16}{1000}$ inch).

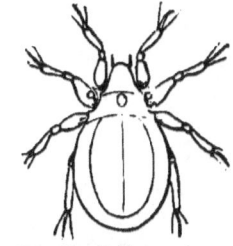

FIG. 42.—*Nothrus ovivorus*. (After Packard).

This is an active, wandering Mite, undoubtedly predatory upon Scale-insects, but found also sucking the eggs of many other insects. Its eggs are laid, and transformations undergone, under loose bark and in crevices, where the early forms are mingled with those of numerous other Mites, from which they have not been clearly distinguished.*

A variety of other Mites are found from time to time wandering over scale-infested leaves and branches, but the forms above indicated are believed to include those most closely connected with orange pests.

---

* This may be the *Nothrus ovivorus* of Packard, Fig. 42, which is found sucking the eggs of the Canker-worm.

CHAPTER VII.

MEANS OF DEFENSE AGAINST SCALE-INSECTS—REMEDIES.

INTRODUCTION OF SCALE-INSECTS ON IMPORTED PLANTS.

In the wide range of insect life few forms possess a greater vitality than is found among the Bark-lice, and none are more readily transported upon plants from place to place, and from one country to another. Whenever orange plants are imported from infested districts, Scale-insects will be brought with them, and their introduction and spread in regions where they were before unknown are inevitable.

Even the soft and unprotected Coccinæ sustain without injury an astonishing amount of rough handling, and exist for long periods of time without food or moisture.

During the winter of 1882-'83 living specimens of the Common Mealybug (*Dactylopius adonidum*, Linn.) were sent to the writer, through the mails, from Italy and also from Morocco, inclosed with a few orange leaves in common letter envelopes. Although the orange leaves were entirely dry, and some of the insects were crushed between their surfaces, many, even of the adults, were found to be uninjured, and young lice had even been produced in transit.

The scale-covered Diaspinæ, it may well be supposed, are even better able to sustain long voyages than their soft-bodied relatives, and their eggs are not affected by long-continued drought, nor by sudden changes of temperature.

It can hardly be doubted that all the common Bark-lice found upon the Orange in Europe have been many times imported into Florida upon living plants. In this way, in the year 1835, it is supposed, the common Long Scale (*Mytilaspis gloverii*) was introduced, first at Jacksonville, and subsequently at Saint Augustine, from whence it spread devastation over all the groves then in the State.

In 1855, according to Glover, a new scale, probably the Chaff Scale (*Parlatoria pergandii*), was introduced into Florida on some lemons sent from Bermuda. More recently a new and very destructive scale has made its appearance at Orlando, in Orange County, Florida, and is slowly but surely spreading to other parts of the State. This is the Red Scale of Florida (*Aspidiotus* [*Chrysomphalus*] *ficus* Ashmead). It was first observed in a grove near Orlando, in the spring of 1879, upon a sour-orange tree brought from Havana, Cuba, in 1874. Professor

Comstock received specimens from Havana, and learned that it was a very common pest in the public gardens of that city.

In California, owing to the very direct communication with China and Japan, and frequent importations of plants from these countries, many destructive species of Bark-lice have been introduced upon fruit and shade trees. Some of these are the most serious pests of their kind; many have a wide range of food-plants, including also the Orange, and one at least, the Red Scale of California, is peculiar to citrus plants. It was introduced into California from Australia. Professor Comstock believes this to be the most destructive species known to infest citrus plants in this country. Its introduction into Florida, together with others now ravaging the groves of California, is greatly to be feared, and is probably only a question of time, as the interchange of plants between these two States increases annually.

Not only plants of the citrus family, but many other trees and shrubs, and notably the Olive, may cause the introduction of Scale-insects, some of which have, besides the Orange and its kind, a great variety of food-plants.

It would be well for the horticultural interests of Florida if some system of inspection of imported fruit-trees could be adopted and vigorously enforced by the State. This would, no doubt, be difficult of accomplishment, and, perhaps, impracticable. Individual importers should, however, be made fully aware of the danger which exists of introducing other destroyers more serious than those already at hand, and should be on their guard. Living plants received from foreign countries ought to be carefully cleaned upon their arrival, and all insects found upon them destroyed.

It is not easy to estimate the extent of the damage that would be occasioned should any of the Aspidiotus scales now ravaging the groves and orchards of California be permitted to obtain a permanent foothold in Florida.

PRECAUTIONARY MEASURES.

Infection from nursery Stock.—What has been said as to the danger of introducing exotic Scale-insects by importations from abroad will apply as well to the spreading of domestic species by the exchange and sale of nursery stock.

It must be acknowledged that many of the leading nurserymen are fully alive to the necessity of establishing and maintaining a reputation for painstaking care, and rarely send out infested plants. Others exercise less care and frequently scatter insect pests by means of the befouled plants they distribute.

Close planting in the nursery is a most frequent cause of the appearance of Scale-insects in destructive numbers. Young orange trees are planted a few inches apart in rows, and are often left for years in close ranks, with their branches interlocking, and affording easy passage for the migrating young of Bark-lice, so that if they effect a lodgment upon any plant, the entire row, and even the whole nursery, is quickly overrun by them.

The crowding of the plants prevents free and vigorous growth; they are stunted, and for want of nourishment, as well as lack of light and air, they are thrown into a condition in which they are particularly liable to the attack of Scale-insect. In common parlance, "they breed scale."

In the existing almost universal distribution of the pest, those nurseries only can be kept from becoming foul in which a reasonable amount of space is allowed to each plant for its growth and cultivation. At least 18 inches should intervene between the plants, and the rows should be not less than 3 feet apart. Experience teaches that it is easier to keep clean and uninfested a large, well-ordered nursery than it is to remove the Scale-insect from a single orange tree of moderate size when once the pest has become fully established.

No part of the grove is so liable to suffer neglect as the nursery, and it is unfortunately a very common practice to allow seedling plants to grow up without attention in neglected corners, and frequently to become so foul with scale as to become a source of infection to the groves and nurseries in the vicinity.

To this neglect, undoubtedly, is due the fact that the advance of insect pests has fully kept pace with that of the orange industry in the recently occupied districts, both in Florida and California.

Protection afforded by Hedges and Forest Trees.—It is a serious evil, and one as yet hardly appreciated, that in Florida, in removing the forest to make way for the advancing orange groves, every tree is generally sacrificed. Not even in the lanes and roadways has the ax spared an occasional pine to serve as a wind-break against the sweep of storms. In many districts, once well clothed with timber, the naked land for many miles now lies exposed to the destructive force of gales, which, by whipping and thorning the fruit, will, when the groves begin to bear, occasion severe losses.

The pines of the original forest, from their great height, serve to break the force of upper currents, and a single giant tree extends its protecting influence over a wide area. If cut, the loss is well-nigh irreparable; many generations must elapse before its place can be satisfactorily supplied by the lower and more spreading oaks and pines of second growth. But a discussion of this subject, though of sufficient importance to horticulturists, would be out of place in the present treatise, were it not for the great value of wind-breaks as an aid in isolating and preventing the spread of Scale-insects and other pests of fruit-trees.

From the time of their first appearance it has been remarked that Scale-insects spread most rapidly in the direction of prevailing winds. This phenomenon is now known to be due to the influence of the wind in guiding the flight of other insects which transport the minute, crawling young of Bark-lice upon their bodies.

The feet and tail-feathers of birds are also invaded by the crawling lice, which are thus borne with them in their flights to be scattered over new plantations.

The leaves and branches of shrubs and trees standing to the windward of a grove protect it by receiving these pest-laden visitors, and detaining them long enough to relieve them of the scale-larvæ they bear upon their bodies.

It is, therefore, a great protection to leave narrow belts of timber between adjoining groves, allowing the undergrowth to spring up and form a natural screen, or else to replace this with cultivated plants. Fences may usefully be replaced by thorny hedges, which will aid in maintaining an effective quarantine against invasions of Scale-insect and other minute pests.

To be of value the screen or hedge should, of course, be composed of such plants as are not themselves subject to the attacks of orange insects; otherwise it may first become infested and afterward prove a source of danger, in place of a safeguard. For example, the Oleander is not desirable in the neighborhood of orange trees, because of its liability to the attacks of certain soft Scale-insects (*Lecanium*.) On the other hand, pines, cedars, and other coniferous plants, having very few insect enemies in common with other plants, are absolutely safe, and are also admirably adapted to form wind-breaks.

CLEANLINESS.

Beneficial action of Light.—It is with plants as with animals, a rule to be borne in mind that foulness breeds vermin. The growing bark as well as the leaves has its pores and its respiratory functions, for the proper performance of which it needs exposure to light and air. From the lack of these conditions for healthful growth, the inside branches of orange trees dwindle and lose vitality, becoming breeders of Scale-insects, which thrive best when the plant has lost its vigor.

Pruning and opening Tops to Light and Air.—Upon trees of considerable size and which have formed dense heads, Bark-lice usually make a start upon the devitalized inside branches, and from thence they may spread over a portion or the whole of the tops.

It may be doubted if any bearing orange tree entirely free from scale can be found in Florida. Somewhere under the canopy of leaves there will always be a twig or stifled branch upon which the enemy lurks in concealment, latent, but ever present, and waiting for favorable conditions to swarm forth in destructive numbers and possess the tree. The careful cultivator needs not to be warned of this source of danger, and will not allow dead and dying branches to remain and accumulate until they become a menace to the health of the tree and breeders of insect pests. He will frequently examine his bearing trees, and at least once each year remove the unfruitful and devitalized inside growth from their tops.

Clearing off Webs.—Young trees, while they require less pruning than the old, will well repay the time and care that may be expended in keeping them free from entangling moss and from the webs of insects. These not only befoul and injure the trees, but directly foster Scale-insects by sheltering and protecting them from the attacks of many very active enemies and parasites. The webs and lairs of spiders in particular may be regarded with suspicion, and will very frequently be found to harbor the foe when it can be found nowhere else.

Scrubbing the Trunks.—Accumulations of Scale-insect, living or dead, as well as of lichens and other fungi, upon their trunks affect most injuriously the health of trees, and their removal from the bark always causes a marked improvement in condition. The incrustations upon orange trees formed by Chaff Scale are particularly hurtful. This species continues to accumulate for many generations, piling its scales over each other as long as it is possible for the young to find a crevice through which to insert their sucking beaks. There results a dense crust, which remains for years, and becomes still further consolidated and converted into a tough, fibrous coating by the threads of the peculiar fungus, which, as has already been mentioned, feeds upon the *débris* of this Bark-louse.

To partially cleanse the trunks of orange trees, without entirely destroying the life that always remains in scale-crusts, no matter of how long standing, is to expose the plant to fresh incursions of Scale-insects by clearing away the obstructions to their spread. Therefore it is important not only that the clearing should not be neglected, but that, when undertaken, the work should be thorougly done.

For scrubbing the trunks properly a brush stiff enough to remove the scales is required, and to insure the destruction of any insects or eggs that may escape, hidden in unseen crevices, it should be dipped in cleansing liquids, such as the dilute kerosene and soap emulsions recommended in the following pages for spraying the trees, or very strong solutions of lye may be used, and will be more effectual in destroying fungi than the kerosene washes. Solutions of whale-oil soaps are very commonly employed and with good effect; but if the solutions are thick and strong, as indeed they need to be in order to kill the insects, the trunks should be rubbed down before they dry with clear water, to remove the film of soap, for this, if allowed to remain, has a tendency to harden the bark by clogging its pores.

Palmetto Brushes.—A better implement than the common domestic scrubbing-brush, usually employed in cleaning tree-trunks, may be made in a few moments out of a bit of saw-palmetto root (root-stalk) by pounding the ends until the fibers separate and form a brush. For the removal of scales and dead bark nothing better than this rude brush can be devised. In Florida the material is always at hand and costs nothing. In use the palmetto brush wears away slowly, but never wears out so long as any portion of it remains.

POPULAR METHODS AND REMEDIES.

Cutting back infested Trees.—The utter inadequacy of nearly all the washes hitherto used has led many fruit-growers to despair of obtaining permanent benefit from the application of remedies, and a common practice has been to cut back badly infested trees, leaving only the main trunks, or in the case of well-grown trees, a portion of the main branches, and to scrub thoroughly every part of these with solutions of soap or lye, using a stiff brush, and as far as possible removing every scale. This, however, involves great care and considerable labor, and the complete extermination of the pest is rarely accomplished in this way. The loss of branches is indeed replaced with extraordinary rapidity, but the Scale-insects reappear as if by magic, and in one or two years become as bad as before.

Fumigating.—Various plans have been proposed for destroying Scale-insects with pungent vapors of various kinds. The difficulties in the way of applying vapors to trees growing in the open air are very great, and appear to have been overlooked by the advocates of this method. Tobacco smoke has been very frequently tried in inclosed green-houses, but although it will destroy Plant-lice (Aphis), it is found to have no effect upon Scale-insects, which are far too well protected by their tightly sealed scales to be reached by vapors, except those of a corrosive nature.

Sulphur has been recommended, evidently on theoretical grounds only, as its fumes are not less destructive to vegetable than to animal life. The chlorophyl of the leaves and plants is bleached and the life of a plant destroyed by a short exposure to any gas containing sulphur. Actual trial of fumigation upon the Orange was made by covering a young and vigorous plant with a barrel and exposing it for ten minutes to the fumes produced by burning one ounce weight of sulphur. The leaves were completely bleached and the plant killed. The Scale-insects upon it (Long Scale) were uninjured by the sulphur vapor, and survived until the bark became entirely dead and dry, perishing finally from want of food and moisture.

Applications to the Roots.—No results of any value have been attained by attempts to kill Scale-insects through the juices of the plant by making applications to the soil with the expectation that they will be taken up by the roots. Many nostrums are advertised and sold as insecticides, which it is claimed act in this way. There are also in the market not a few combined fertilizers and insect-exterminators, so-called, to which is assigned a double action, beneficial in the case of the plant, but deadly to the insect life which it supports. These claims are based upon the assumed power of the plant to appropriate and mingle with its juices unchanged the substances which have insecticide properties—an assumption wholly at variance with the known laws of vegetable physiology. In fact an insecticide, if it could be introduced into the circulation through the roots of the plant, would be far more likely to injure the plant itself than the Bark-lice upon it.

Inoculating with Poisons.—For the same reason it has been found impossible to reach and destroy insect pests by inoculating the bark or wood of the trunk or branches.

The attempt has usually been made by boring into the trunk of the tree, introducing the article to be tested, and tightly closing the hole with a plug. Numerous experiments of this sort are recorded. Of the long list of substances which have been thus tried, and which includes many mineral and vegetable poisons, as well as sulphur and other substances possessing insecticide properties, none have proved effective.

Popular Fallacies.—There is a widespread and apparently well-founded opinion that vigorous trees are in little danger from attacks of Scale-insects, but if from any cause a tree becomes enfeebled, its investment is only a question of time. Many persons therefore reject the aid of insecticides, and when a tree becomes infested, rely upon a liberal use of fertilizers to restore its lost vitality and force it into vigorous growth, believing that in this way it will rid itself of the pest. It cannot be denied that this course of treatment is often successful, at least for a time, but the Scale-insect is never entirely eradicated, and its return at some future time may be expected. Indeed, overstimulation by means of fertilizers is apt to defeat its object, and reaction follows in unfavorable seasons.

In fighting Scale with fertilizers, therefore, success may be said to depend upon conditions unknown or beyond our control. When these are favorable, the system may be found to work well; otherwise failure is inevitable, and by adhering to it valuable time will be lost, and the pest will perhaps be allowed to spread until it can with difficulty be controlled.

EFFECTIVE REMEDIES.

Kerosene.—This is without doubt the most effective insecticide for use against Scale-insects, and it is almost the only substance known which will with certainty kill their eggs without at the same time destroying the plant. The difficulty of diluting it, and the danger to the plant of applying it undiluted, have long prevented its extensive use. Easy methods of emulsifying the oil and rendering it miscible with water are now known, and have recently been set forth by Professor Riley in his official reports.

Milk and Kerosene Emulsions.—The method of emulsifying kerosene with milk, as given in a preliminary report on Scale-insects in the Report of the Commissioner for the years 1881 and 1882, remains the best and simplest, where milk can be easily and cheaply obtained. The milk should first be heated nearly to the boiling point, and then mixed with kerosene in the proportions one part of milk to two parts of keroseue. The mixture requires to be very violently churned for a period, varying with the temperature, from five or ten minutes to half an hour. If the mixture is quite hot the emulsion is very easily and quickly formed. It is quite thin while warm, but thickens on cooling. If cold, the process is delayed, but after continued agitation the emulsion forms suddenly, as in butter making, and becomes at once an ivory-white glistening paste, or jelly.

To form a perfectly stable emulsion more violent agitation is required than can be effected by hand stirring, or by dashing in an ordinary churn. The particles of oil and milk are more readily driven into union by passing the mixture through the spray-nozzle of a force-pump.

The aquapult pump (Fig. 43), which is also one of the most effective instruments for spraying trees, may be satisfactorily used for this purpose. The pump is inserted in a pail or tub containing the mixture, and this is pumped back into the same receptacle through the flexible hose and spray-nozzle until the emulsion is formed. From 3 to 5 gallons of emulsion may be churned at one time by means of the ordinary hand form of this pump. For larger quantities a larger pump or some form of druggist's churn will be required.

The emulsion, if well made, is permanent, provided it is not exposed to the air, which causes in time a partial separation of the oil. The union of the ingredients is purely mechanical, and the presence of the kerosene does not prevent the fermentation of the milk, which will become sour and curdle without, however, separating from the oil.

FIG. 43.—The aquapult.

For fresh milk may be substituted an equivalent of condensed milk and water, or of sour milk. If sour milk is used no subsequent curdling of the emulsion takes place, and it is therefore preferable to sweet milk.

The milk emulsions may be diluted in water to any extent, and if cold require to be thinned at first with a small quantity of water. One part of emulsion to nine or ten parts of water will be found to make an effective wash.

Soap and Kerosene Emulsions.—The difficulty of obtaining fresh milk in Florida, and the cost of condensed milk, have made a cheaper substitute desirable. This is found in a solution of soap, which forms with kerosene an equally good emulsion. The quantity of soap used in solution need not exceed one-quarter of a pound to one gallon of water, but stronger soap solutions are required to form a permanent emulsion. The percentage of kerosene may also be varied greatly. But emulsions containing over 80 per cent. of the oil have too light a specific gravity and are not readily held in suspension in water. On the other hand, in the process of emulsification, kerosene loses a portion of its value as an insecticide, and emulsions containing less than 30 per cent. of the oil, although they do not at all, or only very slowly, rise to the surface when diluted with considerable quantities of water, are nevertheless too much weakened for effective use against Scale-insects.

The following formula is considered the best for general use. It gives a wash of sufficient strength to kill the eggs of those species of Scale-insect which are commonly found in Florida, although in dealing with some of the Aspidiotus scales a somewhat stronger emulsion may be required.

FORMULA:

    Kerosene .... 2 gallons = 67 per cent.
    Common soap or whale-oil soap . ½ pound ⎱ = 33 per cent.
    Water .... 1 gallon ⎰

Heat the solution of soap and add it boiling hot to the kerosene. Churn the mixture by means of a force-pump and spray-nozzle for five or ten minutes. The emulsion, if perfect, forms a cream, which thickens on cooling, and should adhere without oiliness to the surface of glass. Dilute before using, 1 part of the emulsion with 9 parts of cold water. The above formula gives 3 gallons of emulsion and makes when diluted 30 gallons of wash.

Necessary precautions in the use of Kerosene.—A reckless use of any penetrating oil upon plants cannot fail to prove detrimental. Kerosene is, however, much less injurious than the lighter oils, naphtha, benzine, &c., with which, in a crude state, it is associated. The refined oil, such as is commonly used for illuminating purposes, is safer, and should always be used in preference to the lower grades, which contain a large admixture of other oils exceedingly deadly to vegetation.

Effect of Kerosene upon the Orange.—Although the action of kerosene proves more injurious to some plants than to others, a healthy orange tree is but slightly affected by it, and will even support without serious injury applications of the undiluted oil if judiciously made, *i. e.*, applied in fine spray and avoiding exposure of the plant to hot sunshine or to frost before the oil has evaporated. Unhealthy trees and trees suffering from the attacks of Scale-insects receive a shock more or less severe, according as their vitality is more or less impaired. Young, tender shoots, budding leaves and blossoms, are not much affected by kerosene, and may even be dipped in the pure oil with impunity.

The heat of the sun increases to an injurious extent the action of kerosene, and applications of very strong solutions or undiluted kerosene, if used at all, should be made on cloudy days or at evening.

Milk or soap emulsions containing 60 or 70 per cent. of oil and diluted with water ten times are more nearly harmless to the Orange than any other insecticide capable of killing the Scale-insect. Nevertheless the plant receives a shock, imperceptible when the tree is in good condition, but sufficiently severe when it is infested and injured by Scale to cause the loss of the old, devitalized leaves. Complete defoliation and the death of moribund twigs and branches may be expected to occur in extreme cases. The shock is invariably followed by a reaction, and in ten to fifteen days new growth appears. This growth is healthy and natural, and if the application has been sufficiently thorough to destroy the Scale-insect, results in permanent benefit.

Enough has been said to show that kerosene is a powerful remedy, perfectly effective and safe if used in moderation, but hurtful in strong doses; that its use undiluted is attended with danger, is entirely unnecessary, and cannot be recommended. In Appendix II will be found an examination of results obtained in experimental applications of kerosene, together with other insecticides, arranged in tabular form for convenience of comparison.

The most favorable season for applying kerosene washes is undoubtedly early spring or as soon as all danger of frost is past. The shedding of the last year's leaves, which takes place naturally after the orange tree has renewed its foliage in spring, is often accelerated by the action of the oil, which is thus made to appear very severe. But the loss of old and devitalized leaves is of slight consequence, and in the case of badly infested trees is a positive advantage, as the leaves in falling carry with them the scales most difficult to reach with insecticides.

Whale-oil Soap.—This has long been considered one of the best insecticides known, and is extensively used as a remedy for Bark-lice. Experiments show that very strong solutions kill the Coccids but have little or no effect upon their eggs. Solutions of one pound of the soap to three gallons of water failed to kill the adult Bark-lice or their eggs, and did not destroy all the young. The strongest solution used, one pound of the soap to one gallon of water, killed all the Coccids and few or none of the eggs.

This solution solidifies on cooling, and must, therefore, be applied hot. The effect upon the trees is about equal to that of effective kerosene emulsions; badly infested trees are somewhat defoliated, but new growth and vigorous trees are not appreciably affected. As the eggs are not killed, several applications at intervals of four to six weeks will be required to clear a tree of scale. (See Appendix II, table 2.)

Whale-oil soap is sold in Eastern Florida at 10 to 12 cents per pound. The cost of an effective wash is therefore much greater than emulsions of kerosene. For scrubbing and cleansing the trunks of orange trees this soap may be recommended. A solution of 1 pound to 4 gallons will probably be sufficiently strong for this purpose.

Potash and Soda Lye.—These substances have been recommended as remedies for Scale-insect in California. According to reports promulgated by the State Horticultural Commission, solutions as strong as 1½ pounds to the gallon of water are deemed necessary to exterminate the pest, and are said to have been used with good results upon Peach, Pear, and other deciduous fruit-trees. Although these caustic solutions burn and partially destroy the bark, it is said to be soon restored, and no loss of fruit results if applied in winter while the trees are dormant.

Experiments made in Florida upon the Orange with caustic soda and potash lyes show that solutions of 1 pound to 2, 2½, and 3 gallons were of little or no practical benefit as regards the extermination of Scale-insects, while the effect upon the trees was more severe than with applications of pure kerosene. Unlike kerosene, lye is injurious to the tender portions of the plant, and new growth is destroyed at once by strong solutions. Solutions of 1 pound to the gallon severely cauterize the leaves and tender bark, and kill back the smaller branches, but fail to destroy all the Bark-lice, and have hardly an appreciable effect upon their eggs. (See Appendix II, table 3.)

Concentrated potash is somewhat stronger than soda lye, but the results attained with it are also unsatisfactory. In the strongest applications, made with a solution of two pounds of potash to one gallon of water, the trees were burned as by fire, the leaves were charred without falling from the branches, all the growth under two years old was destroyed, and the main trunks alone remained alive. The Scale-insects perished with the cauterized bark and foliage; nevertheless, a very large percentage of their eggs escaped destruction, and continued to hatch. A few days later the young were seen in abundance, crawling over the blackened trunk and branches. It is probable that they all perished, however, through inability to penetrate the cicatrized bark with their sucking beaks. The trees thus treated survived, indeed, but in a mutilated condition and with an entire loss of symmetry in their tops.

It would appear from careful experiments and observations with both soda and potash lyes, that these substances are inferior to kerosene in killing power as regards Scale-insects, and far more injurious to the tree when used in solutions strong enough to be effective as insecticides. Weaker solutions are, however, extremely useful in cleansing the trunks of orange trees with the scrubbing brush. For this purpose they are superior to solutions of soap, and have an advantage over dilute kerosene emulsions, in that they destroy the spores of lichens and fungi, which kerosene does not.

Crude Carbolic Acid or Oil of Creosote.—The crude oil, dissolved in strong alkalies or solutions of soap, forms a very effective remedy for Scale-insect. It may also be emulsified with milk in the same manner as kerosene. The undiluted oil is, however, exceedingly injurious to vegetation, and destroys the bark of Orange and other trees. It is, in fact, a more dangerous substance than kerosene, and requires to be used with great caution. Solutions, emulsions, and soaps containing it should be very carefully mixed, in order that no globules of free oil may be allowed to come in contact with the bark of the tree.

Its action upon the Scale-insect is even more powerful than kerosene, but it does not destroy as large a percentage of the eggs. The effect upon the Coccids is not immediate, as in the case of other insecticides, and for three or four days after an application very few of the insects die. At the end of a week, however, the Bark-lice are found to be affected and continue to perish in increasing numbers for a week longer. Even after the lapse of three weeks the destructive action of the oil is still appreciable. These facts lead one to suspect that the insects are killed, in part at least, by the poisoning of the sap upon which they feed.

The visible effect upon the plant appears to confirm this view. Leaves upon infested trees begin to drop after four or five days, and the defoliation reaches a maximum during the second week. As is the case with kerosene, the effect upon the tree depends upon its condition at the time of application; but carbolic acid is more severe in its action, and there is greater loss of leaves and infested branches. With care, however, an application may be made sufficiently strong to exterminate the scale without serious injury to the plant, and, as new or vigorous growth is very slightly affected, recovery is rapid.

The following solution of crude carbolic acid will be found nearly if not quite as effective as a 64 per cent. kerosene emulsion, and may be applied without danger to orange trees. Dilute the carbolic acid with twice its volume of soap solution (2 ounces common soap to 1 pint hot water). Mix thoroughly until all the oil is dissolved. Add, before using, to one part of the above solution twenty parts water, and apply in as fine spray as possible.

The most effective method of using oil of creosote is to saponify it with heavy oils and potash. In this way a solid soap containing about 12 per cent., by volume, of the oil may be obtained. The process of making the soap is, however, exceedingly tedious and difficult, and unless proper appliances be used the resulting product is imperfect and even dangerous to use, as it contains a large amount of free creosote. Manufacturers of carbolic soap could undoubtedly supply a better article and at a less cost than the consumer could make for himself.

(For detailed experiments see Appendix II, Table 4.)

SULPHURATED LIME.*—A combination of lime and sulphur, made by boiling the sublimate (flowers) of sulphur in milk of lime, is sometimes recommended as a "cure-all" for application to orange trees. The preparation contains a mixture of sulphides and sulphates of lime, together with varying quantities of the uncombined ingredients. By continued boiling the action of the sulphur is rendered more complete, and if an excess of lime is present the mixture becomes highly caustic, eating the skin from the hands and destroying the tender leaves and bark of plants. Its preparation is rendered unpleasant and even dangerous because of the sulphurous fumes that are given off.

One part sublimated sulphur, two parts lime, and ten parts water, boiled together half to three-quarters of an hour give the best results. After standing a short time the uncombined lime settles to the bottom, leaving a clear yellowish liquid, which, according to the United States Dispensatory, is "an impure aqueous solution of sulphide of calcium, necessarily containing hyposulphite of calcium."

Under varying conditions higher combinations are formed, and the chemical reactions are exceedingly complicated.¹¹ A large percentage of the yellowish-green mass consists of insoluble and inert sulphides, but with these are mingled other compounds of lime and sulphur, which give off sulphureted hydrogen gas (hydro-sulphuric acid), and are gradually altered by exposure to the air. When, therefore, the mixture is allowed to stand in open barrels, the sulphur compounds part with their active gases, and at length only the caustic action of the lime remains.

Use in the Orange Grove.—As an insecticide sulphurated lime has nearly the same value as potash or soda lye, and in like manner, by its caustic action, it kills the Bark-lice, but does not destroy their eggs, unless it is applied strong enough to injure the bark.

Its action upon the plant resembles very closely that of potash and other caustics, which are more injurious to the young growth than to the older and less vital parts of the tree.

The imperfect mixture formed by adding sulphur to lime in the act of slaking is deficient in strength, and has little value as an insecticide.

Sulphurated lime may prove useful to orange-growers as a destroyer of fungi, and it is advocated as a remedy for foot-rot or other diseases of a similar nature. But these claims, it is proper to state, have not as yet been substantiated by sufficient evidence.

---

* The term "sulphurated lime" is here used as a convenience, and is made to include the various compounds formed by the action of hot water on lime and sulphur. In strictness, the monosulphide (Ca S.) is not formed by the wet process here given. It is thus described:

"Sulphurated Lime is a grayish-white, or yellowish-white, powder, gradually altered by exposure to air, exhaling a faint odor of hydrosulphuric acid, having an offensive, alkaline taste, and an alkaline reaction. Very slightly soluble in water and insoluble in alcohol. On dissolving Sulphurated Lime with the aid of acetic acid, hydrosulphuric acid is abundantly given off, and a white precipitate (Sulphate of Calcium) is thrown down." (United States Dispensatory, 1883, page 326.)

If used in sufficient strength to kill Scale-insects, the hands and arms must be protected from the liquid by rubber gloves, and care must also be had to avoid inhaling the poisonous gases exhaled.

In its active state the preparation is a depilatory, and by applying it as a paste the hair upon any part of the body may be reduced to gelatine and removed.

Bisulphide of Carbon.—The few trials made of this substance have not given very satisfactory results, and additional experiments are needed to determine whether it can be safely and economically used as a remedy for Scale-insects. Although a powerful insecticide, the extreme severity of its action upon the trees and the cost of the materials detract greatly from its value. It is an exceedingly volatile and explosive liquid, which must be kept in tightly-sealed glass bottles, and the fumes cannot be inhaled by man or other animals without danger. The bisulphide may be emulsified with oils and milk or soap, but not more than three or four fluidounces should be contained in each gallon of the diluted wash.

Appendix II, table 5, gives the result of some experiments with bisulphide of Carbon.

Sulphuric Acid.—A single experiment with sulphuric acid, 4 fluidounces in 6 quarts of water, applied with a brush as far as possible to all parts of a young tree, killed nearly all the Scale-insects, and very nearly killed the tree. The bark was blackened but not destroyed, and nearly all the leaves dropped. The tree, however, slowly recovered.

Sulphate of Iron.—This substance is exceedingly injurious to vegetation, but is, nevertheless, a very common ingredient of patent and proprietary remedies. Its presence can be detected by the inky-black or brown stains which it forms in the substance of the leaves and the rind of the fruit.

It does not affect the Scale-insect except by destroying the vegetable tissues from which it gets its subsistence.

Ammonia.—With this in a pure state no experiments have been made, but to its presence in fermenting urine is probably due the insecticide properties of the latter. Applications of urine have often been recommended as a remedy for scale, and are certainly not without value, but if allowed to stand and ferment, and especially if soot or other absorbents of the ammonia are mixed with it, it becomes highly injurious to vegetation, and if applied at all should be greatly diluted. A mixture of soot and fermented urine applied undiluted to a small orange tree effectually cleared it of scales, but very nearly killed the tree.

Silicate of Soda.—This is a thick viscid liquid, sometimes sold as a solid. It is readily soluble in water. When sprayed upon orange trees it soon dries and forms a coating of gum which partially peels off, carrying with it many of the old dead scales and some living ones. When applied in sufficient strength it kills most of the Coccids, but does not destroy the eggs. It injures the plant more than kerosene, with which it cannot be compared in efficiency or cheapness. The preparation is inert and harmless to man, and acts mechanically by covering and stifling the Bark-lice or by removing them bodily from the tree. (See Appendix II, table 6.)

Very many substances used separately, or in various combinations, are recommended as remedies for Scale-insect. Among the number the following have been examined with more or less care and found to be of doubtful or of no value: sal-soda, muriate of potash, salt, lime, soot, and ashes.

Many otherwise valueless washes and applications have been rendered partially effective by the addition of a small quantity of free kerosene. The result in all such cases has been a very unequal distribution of the oil, some portions of the tree receiving a dangerous dose and other portions none at all. It seems hardly necessary to point out the uselessness of such half-way measures in combatting a pest which the most perfect remedy is powerless to eradicate unless applied with thoroughness and care.

THE APPLICATION OF INSECTICIDES.

Fineness and Force of Spray.—In dealing with an enemy so thoroughly protected as are many of the Bark-lice, liquid insecticides should be applied in as fine a spray as possible, or at least in moderately fine spray, driven with considerable force, in order to increase to the utmost their penetrating power. The aim should also be to reach and thoroughly wet every portion of an infested tree, so that no individual Scale-insect shall escape the action of the liquid. This result is not attainable by the old method of sending a jet from a distance into the tops of the trees. An ordinary garden syringe is practically useless. There is needed a force-pump and a nozzle giving a finely atomized spray. This nozzle should be attached to a sufficient length of flexible hose to allow it to be introduced into the top of the tree. The orifice of the nozzle should be directed at a right angle to the hose, and not in line with it. The jet of spray may thus by a turn of the wrist be directed upward or downward, and brought into contact with all parts of the foliage and branches, from beneath as well as from the upper side.

The Cyclone Nozzle. (Fig. 44: 1, profile; 2, plan; 3, section).—A nozzle which answers the above conditions and is easily attached to any force-pump by means of a rubber tube is described in the report of the Entomologist (Report of the Commissioner of Agriculture for 1881-'82, p. 162). It consists of a shallow, circular, metal chamber soldered to a short piece of metal tubing as an inlet. The inlet passage penetrates the wall of the chamber tangentially, admitting the fluid eccentrically, and causing it to rotate rapidly in the chamber. The outlet consists of a very small hole drilled in the exact center of one face of the chamber. The orifice should not be larger than will admit the shaft of an ordinary pin. Through this outlet the fluid is driven perpendicularly to the plane of rotation in the chamber. Its whirling motion disperses it broadly from the orifice, and produces a very fine spray, which may be converted into a cloud of mist by increasing the pressure in the pump. The perforated face of the nozzle-chamber is removable for convenience in clearing the orifice when it clogs. The diameter of the chamber inside need not exceed one-half inch and its depth one-quarter inch. A nozzle of these dimensions attached to the aquapult pump covers one and a half square yards of surface at a distance of 4 or 5 feet from the orifice. The amount of dispersion depends somewhat upon the thickness of the perforated face of the chamber. The diameter of the cone of spray may be increased by countersinking the exit hole and making its edges thin.

Three-eighths-inch gum tubing is sufficiently large to supply one or a gang of several nozzles. The tubing must be strengthened with one ply of cloth.

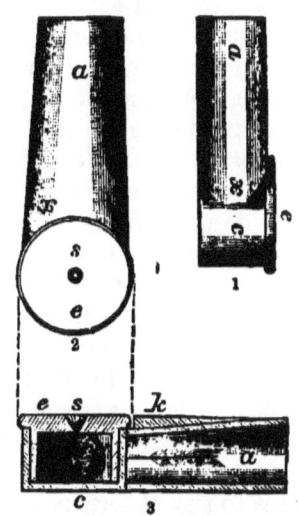

FIG. 44.—Cyclone or eddy-chamber nozzle. (After Barnard.)

In use, the end of the hose is supported by being fastened to a light rod of wood, which forms a handle, by means of which the nozzle may be applied to all parts of the tree. For full-sized trees a rod long enough to reach nearly to their tops must be used. For this purpose a convenient device may be made by passing the small rubber hose through a hollow bamboo rod of the required length. A three-sixteenth brass tube inserted in a bamboo rod has also been used.

Plate VII exhibits a complete outfit for treating orange groves with liquid insecticides, from a photograph taken during actual service in the field. This consists of a common pendulum pump inserted in a barrel and mounted upon a cart. The liquid is delivered through two lines of hose, each ending in a cyclone nozzle. The arrangement here shown permits the spraying of two rows of young trees at once, and thus effects a considerable saving in time. In the same plate is shown an aquapult pump fitted with a cyclone nozzle and a single length (12 feet) of three-eighths-inch hose. The pump is inserted in a pail, ready for use as a portable apparatus for one, or preferably for two men.

Several Applications necessary.—Unless exceptional care is exercised some portions of the bark or leaves will escape thorough wetting and isolated scales will be left alive. The eggs also to some extent will escape destruction and may hatch in sufficient numbers to restock the plant. As a rule, therefore, two, or even more, applications will be necessary. A second application should not follow too closely on the first. Sufficient time should be given for the hatching of all the eggs which may have been left alive. On the other hand, if delayed too long, a brood interval will have elapsed and fresh eggs will be deposited. Successive applications should, therefore, be made at intervals of not less than three and not exceeding six weeks.

Proper Seasons for applying Remedies.—If kerosene emulsions are used trees may be treated for Scale at any time during the growing season. Strong solutions of lye, whale-oil soap, and other applications which are injurious to tender growth do least harm to the trees when dormant. The brood periods of Scale-insects are quite irregular, and breeding is more or less continuous throughout the year. As a rule, however, in Florida new broods begin in March, June, and September, and in these months, or the month succeeding each, the application of insecticides gives the greatest advantage. The period immediately preceding the appearance of each brood is that in which the majority of scales are filled with eggs, upon which many insecticides have little or no effect. The months of February, May, and August, and the winter months from November to January, are, therefore, seasons in which the application of remedies is likely to prove least effective.

To apply washes in winter is somewhat hazardous, and exposes the trees to risk of serious injury, by causing them to put forth new growth at a time when there is danger from frost. For in Florida the Orange is never quite dormant even in the coldest winter, and the reaction that follows an application is liable to start the buds unless the weather remains uniformly cool.

When the air is charged with moisture, and the nights are cold, with heavy dews or frost, the evaporation, even of volatile oils, is checked, and they remain too long in contact with the plant. Applications made under such atmospheric conditions sometimes prove very severe, and cause the tree to shed all its leaves, or even kill the branches.

PART II.

MISCELLANEOUS INSECTS AFFECTING THE ORANGE.

CHAPTER VIII.

RUST OF THE ORANGE.

NATURE OF RUST.

Discoloration of the Fruit.—The brownish discoloration of the rind of oranges, familiarly known under the name of "rust," has, since the production of this fruit became an important industry in Florida, given great concern to the producers, and occasions annually serious loss by affecting injuriously the salableness of the fruit. In appearance the rust varies from a light or dark brown stain beneath the cuticle to a rough incrustation resembling an exudation of resinous gum upon the surface. In the former case the golden color of the ripe orange is more or less obscured, and in the latter entirely destroyed by the discoloration. When entirely coated with rust the surface becomes finely chapped and roughened, giving to the unripe fruit a likeness to russet apples.

The season during which rust makes its appearance includes nearly the entire period of growth of the fruit, beginning in early summer, when the fruit has attained less than one-third its full size, and continuing late into autumn. Its most rapid increase is, however, in August and September, as the orange approaches maturity. Rarely is there any real increase after the rind begins to ripen, although the discoloration usually attracts attention just at this time, and frequently occasions unnecessary alarm. On the contrary, there is always a perceptible brightening as the fruit attains its full color, and oranges slightly affected, or affected very early in the season, when fully ripe show but little trace of rust.

Is Rust a Fungus, or an exudation of Gum?—The term "rust" is very indefinitely applied to a great variety of plant diseases, some of which are clearly due to the presence of fungi, and others are considered pathological conditions of the plant, attributable to, for the most part, unknown or conjectural conditions of soil or climate.

A good example of the first class is found in the common and very destructive rust of the Fig. Any one who will take the trouble to examine with a good glass the brown discoloration upon the surface of the leaves may easily detect the sacks, or asci, of the fungus, filled to bursting with the spores, or pouring them out upon the surface.

Nothing of this kind is seen upon the leaves or rusted fruit of the Orange. A microscopic examination of the fruit-rind reveals no forms of fungus, but shows the oil-cells to be more or less completely emptied of their contents, and the outer layers, the epithelial cells, clogged with brownish resin, or entirely broken up and divided by fissures, which permit evaporation of the fluids from the underlying cells. **The rind of rusted fruit, therefore, shrinks and toughens, and loses by evaporation or oxidation the greater part of its essential oil.**

THE ORIGIN OF RUST.

Reasons for considering it the Work of a Mite.—If we examine critically with a hand lens of considerable magnifying power the surface of a rusted orange, we will find here and there in the depressions, groups of minute white filaments adhering closely to the rind. Carefully transferring one of these filaments to the stage of a compound microscope, and applying a power of several hundred diameters, the character of the object is clearly shown. It is the cast skin of an insect.

If the examination chance to be made in winter, when the fruit is ripe, the number of these exuviæ will not be strikingly great. But if made in autumn or late summer, the surface of every orange showing rust will be found thickly sprinkled with them, and we shall be forced to conclude that we have before us the relics of a numerous colony, which at some former period infested the fruit.

Extending the examination to fruit that as yet shows no indication of rust, we will, if the season is not too far advanced, obtain abundant confirmation of this conclusion, and find these colonies in the full tide of their existence. The former occupants of the cast skins prove to be elongate Mites, of honey-yellow color, too minute to be seen as individuals with the unassisted eye, but visible in the aggregate as a fine golden dust upon the surface of the fruit.

The Mite on the Leaves.—Having tracked the Mite by means of its telltale exuviæ, and detected it at work upon the fruit, if we turn our attention to the leaves it needs no prolonged search to discover it here also, and in even greater abundance. In fact, it is evidently upon the leaves that the Mites exist and propagate throughout the year; for not only are they found upon fruiting trees, but upon plants of all ages, in the nursery as well as in the grove.

Nothing resembling the rust of the fruit follows their attacks upon the leaves. Each puncture of the Mites gives rise to a minute pimple or elevation, until the surface of the leaf becomes finely corrugated, loses its gloss, and assumes a corroded and dusty appearance.

This tarnished appearance of the foliage is very characteristic, and remains, a permanent indication of their depredations, after the Mites themselves have disappeared.

First appearance of Mites on the Fruit.—From the time when the cellular structure of the rind has completely developed, and the oil-cells have begun to fill, until the fruit is far advanced in the process of ripening; in other words, from early spring until late in autumn, it is liable to attacks of the Mites, but it is in the intermediate period of its growth that the fruit offers conditions most favorable to their increase.

Attacks of the Mite always followed by Rust.—The evidence that rust follows as a sequence upon the depredations of this Mite is circumstantial rather than direct, but it is also cumulative. Oranges marked and kept under observation, but allowed to remain upon the tree, have in all cases rusted after being overrun by the Mites. Those upon which no Mites made their appearance remained bright to maturity.

A very large number of observations show a close connection between the occurrence of Mites upon the foliage and rust on the fruit, so that it may be stated as a rule, when the foliage of a tree retains its gloss, the fruit also will be bright, and, conversely, when the condition of the leaves indicates the presence of Mites in great numbers, the fruit will be discolored.

This is found to be true, not only of the entire tree, but of restricted portions. Thus the upper, the lower branches, or one side of an orange tree may produce rusty fruit while that on the other parts of the tree remains bright. In such cases there will always be a marked difference in the condition of the foliage upon the two portions, and the leaves surrounding the affected fruit will indicate more or less clearly the work of the Mites.

Other and perhaps more conclusive reasons for considering the Mite responsible for rust will be better understood when the habits of the Mite itself have been considered.

Interval between the Disappearance of the Mites and the Appearance of Rust.—As has been already indicated, the Mites do not permanently infest either the surface of the leaf or the rind of the fruit, but wander off to fresh feeding-ground when, through their combined attacks, all the accessible oil-cells have been emptied of their contents, or the tissues have been too much hardened by advancing maturity to be easily penetrated by their beaks.

The effects of their punctures upon the cellular structure of the plant, however, continue after their departure, and upon the fruit, rust develops with a varying interval, depending possibly upon the relative humidity of the air. Usually the discoloration is very apparent after the lapse of a week, and the rind continues to harden indefinitely, or as long as it is exposed to the air.

THE RUST-MITE.

(*Typhlodromus oleivorus* Ashm.)

Description.—The so-called Rust Insect (Fig. 45, *a b*) is a four-legged Mite, honey-yellow in color, and about three times as long as broad. The body is cylindrical, widest near the anterior extremity, and tapers behind, terminating in two small lobes, which assist the animal in crawling and enable it to cling firmly to the surface upon which it rests. The front is prolonged in a conical protuberance, which appears to be composed of two closely-applied lobes. The upper surface at its widest part is marked on each side with shallow depressions, which are faintly prolonged on the sides and reach nearly to the terminal lobes. The abdomen consists of about thirty segments. The beak, a short, curved tube, is usually retracted between the organs of the mouth. The latter form a truncated cone, concealed from above by the projection of the front, and difficult to resolve into its component parts. Under high powers it can be seen to consist of at least two thick lobes, which in the living Mite have a reciprocal forward and back movement.

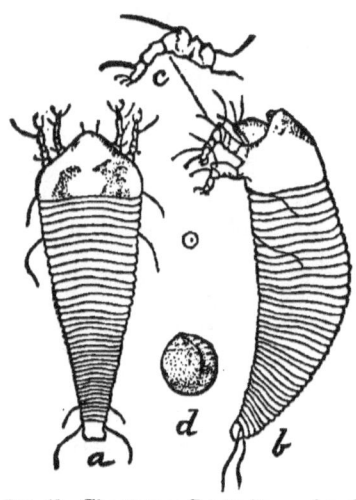

FIG. 45.—The Orange Rust-mite: *a*, dorsal view; *b*, lateral view—enlarged, the dot in circle indicating natural size; *c*, leg; *d*, egg, with embryo just about to hatch— more enlarged. (After Hubbard.)

The two pairs of legs are placed close together, at or very near the anterior extremity, and project forwards. They are four-jointed, and terminate in a curved spine, with opposing bristles. (Fig. 45, *c.*) The intermediate joints bear one or two very long, curved bristles. Several fine bristle-hairs, arising from the under surface of the body, curve upwards at the sides, and two very long bristles at the caudal extremity, curving downwards, are trailed after the Mite as it crawls.

The length of the adult Mite is 0.14^{mm} ($\frac{5}{1000}$ inch). The young do not differ essentially in structure from the adults, but are thick and short, almost cordiform, and the legs are very short.

The eggs, which are deposited singly or in little clusters upon the surface of the leaves, are spherical, transparent, with a yellow tinge. Their diameter is more than half that of the mother at its widest part, and they probably increase in size by the absorption of moisture after they are laid; otherwise the body of the Mite could not contain more than three or four fully-developed ova. The embryo is curved within the egg, its head slightly overlapping the tail. (Fig. 45, *d.*)

Life-history.—In hot weather the eggs hatch in four or five days, but in winter their development is more or less retarded by cold, although it is not entirely arrested even by frost, and the duration of the egg period seldom exceeds two weeks.

The young are bright, translucent yellow in color. Within a week or ten days they undergo a metamorphosis or molt, during which the animal remains dormant for about forty-eight hours. With its legs, which are placed close together, and stretched out in line with the body, and with its two-lobed anal proleg, it clings closely to the surface of the leaf. The form becomes more elongate and spindle-shaped. The body of the transforming Mite separates from the old skin, which becomes pellucid and empty at the extremities, and finally splits longitudinally, releasing the renovated Mite. The rejected pellicle is left firmly adhering to the surface on which it rests, but is in time removed by the action of the weather, and much sooner from the leaves than from the rind of fruit.

The adult Mite is slightly darker than the young in color, and becomes more opaque as it grows older. No sexual differences have been distinguished, nor has the act of coupling been observed.

Owing to the difficulty of confining the Mites without interfering with the conditions necessary to their existence, it has not been possible to determine the duration of their lives. It is, however, safe to conclude that they live several weeks after reaching the adult stage. The number of eggs deposited is also uncertain, but it is probably not abnormal, and the enormous populousness of their colonies must be attributed to rapid development, and comparative immunity from enemies and parasites, rather than to excessive fecundity.

Food.—This evidently consists of the essential oil which abounds in all succulent parts of the Orange and its congeners, and which the Mites obtain by penetrating with their sucking beaks the cells that lie immediately beneath the epidermis. That they do not feed upon the chlorophyl is shown by the color of their intestinal contents, which has no tinge of green, but a clear yellow, unmistakably indicating the source from which it came.

Wandering Habits.—While engaged in feeding, the mites remain quiescent for a length of time varying from a few minutes to half an hour. They then move on a short distance and again become motionless. If disturbed they have a habit of erecting themselves upon the leaf, clinging to its surface only by the anal proleg.

When dissatisfied with their surroundings, or when food becomes scarce, they wander restlessly about, and undoubtedly travel to considerable distances. Their rate of progress on a smooth surface is quite rapid, and amounts to 10 or 12 feet per hour. It is therefore not surprising to find them changing their position frequently; disappearing suddenly from one portion of a tree and appearing as suddenly in great numbers upon another and distant part of the same tree.

It is not to be understood that the Mites show any concert of action in moving their colonies, or that they are in any other sense gregarious than that they are usually found very thickly scattered over those parts of an infested plant which offer favorable conditions for their support. Thus the new growth of many orange trees becomes occupied or infested by them as rapidly as the leaves fully mature, and the number upon a single leaf may be estimated by many thousands.

Numerical Abundance.—The following examination, made in January, will give an idea of the extent of the brood during the coldest part of the Florida winter.

From a large number of leaves of late autumn growth one was selected which showed an even distribution of Mites upon its surface. An area of one square inch was accurately marked out with a needle, and subdivided into sixteen equal squares. The number of Mites and their eggs upon four of the small squares, taken at random, was counted, and found to aggregate 1,142.* This gives for the square inch under observation 4,568 mites. The leaf was then cut into squares and triangles, and was found to cover 15 square inches upon a sheet of paper.

On the supposition that the experimental square inch gives a fair average, the number of Mites upon the upper surface of this leaf was 68,520. Certain portions, not exceeding one-quarter of the whole, were, however, more or less thinly populated. Deducting, therefore, 27 per cent. from the above, we have 50,020 Mites, the approximate population of the upper surface. The under side of the leaf was less thickly infested, but the number of Mites may be estimated as one-half that of the upper face, or 25,000. Thus the number of Mites and their eggs, upon a single leaf, is found to reach even in midwinter the enormous sum of 75,000.

In early summer, when the breeding is active, these estimates will be greatly exceeded. At times an orange tree may be so completely infested with the Mites, that of its thousands of leaves very few can be found free from their presence. If, then, we attempt to calculate the number that may exist contemporaneously upon a bearing tree, we find it represented not by millions but by billions, and the figures obtained convey no definite impressions to the mind.

Preference shown for half Shade.—An examination made on a bright, sunny day shows that, while the Mites cannot long endure the direct light and heat of the sun, they also avoid dark shade. At midday they are more abundant upon the under side of exposed leaves, and although they at all times show a marked preference for light, they desert those parts of leaf or fruit upon which it falls brightest. On a leaf partially exposed to the sun the Mites congregate near one edge in the morning, and in the afternoon cross to the opposite side of the same surface, following the shifting shade, which, by reason of its curvature, the edges of the leaf throw upon one side or the other.†

Rings of Rust on Fruit.—On the fruit, this preference of the Mites for half shade causes a phenomenon which will be recognized as very com-

---

* The number of eggs exceeded that of the Mites, a phenomenon not often observed, and which may be attributed to unusually cold and unfavorable weather at the time of the examination and for several weeks previous.

† The conditions most favorable to their increase are afforded by luxuriant foliage when thoroughly penetrated by light, but dense shade effectually bars their progress. Vigorous young trees on which the foliage is illuminated from beneath by radiation from the surrounding soil are especially subject to attack, the succulence of their leaves serving only to increase enormously the numbers of the invading host. The same luxuriance in older trees, whose branches interlock in the grove and shade the ground, acts unfavorably upon the productiveness of the Mites and checks their increase. These are facts of importance, as will be seen when we come to consider the means of combating the pest.

mon on rusty oranges. This is the occurrence of rust in a well-defined ring, obliquely encircling the orange as the ecliptic does the earth. The rust ring is seen most plainly on fruit from the upper portion and south side of a tree when it stands with others in a grove, and will be found to mark the band of half shade between the portion of the orange most directly exposed to the sun's rays and that in densest shadow. The surface covered by this penumbra band is precisely that upon which the mites gather most thickly in the middle of the day. Here their attack upon the rind will be most severe and its after effects most noticeable. (Plate VIII.)

There is also observable in rusted fruit a marked difference in the amount of discoloration upon the opposite sides. Even where no plainly marked ring is visible, the side of the fruit which upon the tree was turned towards the sun frequently presents a bright spot, and the opposite side an area of lighter bronze, with less sharply defined boundaries.

These facts, taken in connection with the observed habits of the Mites, may be regarded as the strongest evidence showing a connection between rust and their attacks upon the fruit.

Influence of Weather.—It has been already observed that the hatching of the eggs, although retarded, does not cease in cold weather, and that the breeding continues throughout the year. Frost, which is sometimes severe enough to kill the adult Mites, does no injury to the eggs, and the severity of a winter has little, if any, effect upon their prevalence during the following summer. In droughts, however, there is some evidence that many of the eggs dry up and are exterminated. The extremely dry seasons of 1881 and 1882 were followed in the winter of 1882–'83 by the brightest crop of fruit that had been known for several years.

Agencies which assist in the Distribution of Mites.—The activity of the Mites and their readiness to climb upon anything they meet in their path renders it evident that any living creature which passes from one tree to another is competent to transport the Mites with it. The tail-feathers of birds must sweep thousands from the surfaces of the leaves, and spread them from tree to tree or from grove to grove.

So readily do they relinquish their hold when brought into contact with a moving body, that the point of a needle swept across the surface of an infested leaf will usually be found to have several Mites adhering to it.

The same agencies which assist in the spread of Scale-insects undoubtedly serve to scatter the Mites. Not only do they climb readily along the webs of spiders, but they may frequently be seen upon the bodies of the spiders themselves, which do not seem to be at all disturbed by the restless movements of their little attendants.

The wandering habit of spiders is well known. Their method of bridging great distances by casting out hundreds of feet of silken line, to be wafted by the winds and caught in distant trees, has often been noted. There is little doubt that of all other modes of dissemination, both of Scale-insect and Rust-mite, that of transportation by spiders is the most important, the most constant, and regular. The spiders bear with them upon their hairy bodies the young Bark-lice and the adult Mites, conveying them in their own migrations to distant points, and colonizing them under their protecting web whenever they chance to select the leaves of a citrus plant as their resting place.

And here is found the solution of that puzzling influence of the wind so often remarked in the case of Scale-insects, and which has led many to believe that they are disseminated directly by this agency, and therefore spread most rapidly in the direction of the prevailing currents.

Spiders of the web-making kinds are necessarily dependent upon the wind in making long voyages. The warm southeasterly winds of spring excite in them the migratory instinct, and at a time when the orange trees are swarming with the quickened life of Scale and Mite from a thousand projecting points of branch or leaf, the spiders are sending out their lines of rapid transit, and are bearing with them "on the wings of the wind" the seeds of mischief to the orange-grower.

RAVAGES OF THE RUST-MITE.

The Mite known only upon Plants of the Citrus Family.—The Rust-mite attacks indiscriminately the various species of Citrus in common cultivation, but has not been observed to feed upon plants of any other genus. It is found upon the Lime, Lemon, Citron, Shaddock, Bigarde, and Tangerine, and none of the varieties of the Orange are known to be in any degree exempt.

Upon the leaves and fruit of all these species of Citrus the effects of its attack are essentially the same, although the rust is most noticeable on the Sweet and Bitter Orange.

Effect of Attacks upon the Foliage.—Like certain internal animal parasites which feed only upon the fat of their hosts, and do not touch its vital organs, the Mite does not destroy the vital functions of the leaf. The chlorophyl is untouched, and the plant is robbed of a portion only of its essential oil. The leaves never drop, no matter how severely attacked, but there is loss of vitality, and the growth of the plant is checked. This is especially noticed in young trees, which are frequently overrun by the pest in early summer, and during the remainder of the year make little progress.

The foliage of affected trees wears a dry, dusty appearance, and loses color. The leaves are without gloss, and become slightly warped, as in droughts.

Rusted Fruit.—If severely attacked by rust before it has completed its growth, the orange does not attain its full size. Very rusty fruit is always small. Its quality is, however, improved rather than deteriorated. The toughened rind preserves it from injury and decay, prevents evaporation from within, and carries the ripening process to a higher point.

Rusty oranges can be shipped without loss to great distances. They keep longer, both on and off the tree, and when they reach the northern markets are superior to the bright fruit in flavor. Consumers not being aware of this fact, however, prefer the latter, and the reduced price of the bronzed fruit more than offsets to the producer its superior keeping and shipping qualities.

Introduction and Spread of the Mite.—Of the origin of the Rust-mite, whether native or introduced, we as yet know nothing. As far as has been observed, it is not found upon the wild orange trees in Florida, although it attacks them indiscriminately with others of the citrus family when transplanted to open ground, and it may exist upon them in small numbers in their native swamps.

It is said that a few years ago rust was entirely unknown; but the orange industry in this State is of such recent growth that attention has not long been directed to this matter. When but little fruit was produced, occasional discolorations of the rind would naturally pass unnoticed.

Periods of Increase.—As is the case with most invasions of insects, the pest, although increasing rapidly for a time, is likely to reach a maximum in a few years and afterward decline. This has been the experience in former years with Scale-insect, and is attributable to comparative immunity from enemies and parasites at the outset. As the number of their enemies increases, that of the destroyers diminishes, until in time a state of equilibrium is reached, which is disturbed only temporarily by the changing conditions of climate, or other and obscure causes.

It seems probable that the Rust-mite has reached or is already past the period of maximum destructiveness, and that succeeding years will witness its subsidence. The Mite has at present few enemies, and of these the most important are unfortunately not abundant. They give promise, however, of greater efficiency in future, as they belong to families many of whose members are as prolific as the Rust-mite itself.

Geographical Distribution.—Rust appears to be known upon the Orange only in Florida. Within the limits of the State, however, its presence is universal. No section, whatever claims may be made to the contrary, is exempt.

REMEDIES.

Influence of Soil and Methods of Cultivation.—The effect upon the prevalence of rust of various systems of cultivation and of applications to the soil, for the purpose of changing its nature or supplying assumed deficiencies in its composition, has been the subject of endless discussion, and of experiments affording negative or conflicting results, which cannot profitably be reviewed here.

Suffice it to say, no method of combating rust by the indirect action through the plant of chemical substances applied to the soil has been proven effective. By forcing with fertilizers or high cultivation, no improvement is effected in the color of the fruit. This depends, not upon the condition of the tree, but rather upon the number of the Mites, which is, in fact, increased by an abundant supply of new growth and a constant succession of fresh and vigorous leaves.

It seems, however, to be an established fact that the fruit is less liable to rust upon low than upon high lands. Groves planted upon moist, rich hammock or clay soils produce, as a rule, brighter fruit than those upon high, sandy pine lands.

This result is commonly attributed to the abundance of moisture in low ground; but it may be more directly due to the denser shade afforded by a more vigorous foliage and reduced radiation from a darker soil. In the native wild groves, which are always densely shaded by forest, neither rust nor Mites are found, and the same immunity is enjoyed by cultivated trees planted in similar situations.

Preventive Measures.—Any means which will enable us to produce on the light, sandy soil of the uplands those conditions of shade which appear natural and grateful to the Orange, and which we have seen are unfavorable to the increase of the Rust-mite, should, if the foregoing account is correct, give immunity from Rust. In point of fact, there is strong evidence to warrant the belief that with intelligent management almost any grove may in a few years be made to produce bright fruit, by reducing the radiation and darkening the soil, (1) with mulch, or, still better, with a liberal coating of muck, (2) by encouraging the branches to grow low and spreading, and especially avoiding the vicious practice of trimming young trees too high.

Other ways of shading the ground and promoting vigorous leafy growth will occur to every orange-grower.

Those who advocate forest culture for the Orange may justly claim for it the advantage of affording comparative immunity from rust; but a discussion of the merits and demerits of this and other systems of cultivation must be left to the horticulturist.

It may, however, be proper to suggest that where isolation is practicable much can be accomplished toward the exclusion of such pests as the Rust-mite and the Scale-insect by properly arranged natural screens. Narrow belts of original forest, with its undergrowth, may be left, at least on the southeast side of the grove or on high land; the tall pines may be supplemented by hedge-rows of the native Holly, the Jujube, or other evergreen shrubs, which thrive upon uplands in the South.

Such wind-breaks not only protect the bearing trees and fruit from the whipping action of southeasterly gales, but afford the best and only hindrance to the spread of Mites and Bark-lice, prohibiting their direct importation upon spiders and other insects, through whose aid they are disseminated.

Application of Insecticides.—As the Rust-mite lives exposed upon the surface of the plant, neither inhabiting a gall nor making any protective covering for itself or young, it is not a difficult matter to reach it with insecticides thoroughly applied. The adult Mites are very delicate, and readily succumb to applications of moderate strength, but the eggs possess much greater vitality, and require for their destruction solutions of great penetrating power. The immature Mites, while undergoing their transformations, are also difficult to kill, and appear to be specially protected by the old skin, within which their changes take place.

These three stages, the adult, the molting young, and the egg, exist simultaneously at all seasons of the year. The development of the Mite has been shown to be very rapid. The eggs hatch in four or five days, the time extending rarely, in winter, to two weeks. Molting takes place in seven to ten days, and lasts two days. Eggs are probably laid in a few days after the molt.

In applying remedies, it follows from these data that if the Mites alone are killed, and their eggs left alive, young Mites reappear immediately, adults are found in ten or twelve days, and fresh eggs are deposited within two weeks. If the molting Mites are also left alive, very little good can be accomplished, as a fresh crop of adult Mites and eggs will be produced in two or three days.

In combating Rust-mite the difficulty in killing the eggs compels us to adopt one of two alternatives. We must either use powerful insecticides, in solutions even stronger than are required for Scale-insects, or else make several applications, at short intervals, of washes competent to kill the Mites only. In this way the trees may be freed of Mites, by killing the young as they hatch, and not allowing any to reach the adult stage and produce a fresh crop of eggs.

The following substances have been tried and their effects noted upon the Mites and their eggs:

Whale oil soap.—The action of this substance upon the Mites is peculiar. A trace of it in solution causes them to relinquish at once their hold upon the leaf. All other liquids that have been tried, even if they kill the Mites, increase the tenacity with which they cling to its surface. All the free * mites are at once removed from leaves dipped in a solution of 1 pound to 100 gallons of water. Stronger solutions are, however, required to kill them or their eggs and the dormant (molting) young.

The following experiments made in the laboratory upon infested leaves, show the action of solutions of various strength. In order to retain the Mites upon the leaves, the liquids were beaten into foam, which was spread evenly upon both surfaces, care being taken to wet every part of the leaf.

(1.) Solution: 1 pound to 100 gallons. Free Mites washed from the

---

* This term includes adults and young not dormant, or undergoing transformation.

leaf with spray and collected upon blotting paper, began to crawl away as soon as dry, and showed no injury the following day. Eggs and molting young remained upon the leaf and were not affected.

(2.) Solution: 1 pound to 50 gallons. Applied in foam. Free Mites in great part killed. Molting young and eggs not killed.

(3.) Solution: 1 pound to 32 gallons. Adult Mites all killed. Molting young in part killed. Eggs not killed.

(4.) Solution: 1 pound to 16 gallons. Adult Mites all killed and shriveled, in two or three hours. Molting Mites, about 80 per cent. killed. Eggs, a large percentage killed.

(5.) Solution: 1 pound to 5 gallons. Adult Mites all killed. Molting Mites apparently all dead in two days. Eggs evidently affected, not all killed, but many collapsed by the second day.

(6.) Solution: 1 pound to 1 gallon. (This solution is nearly solid when cold.) Mites all killed. On the second day all the eggs appeared collapsed and dead.

The whale-oil soap usually supplied by dealers is inferior to that used in the above experiments. As an effective remedy for Rust-mite a solution of 1 pound to 5 gallons of water may be recommended. It should be applied in early spring, before the new growth begins. Two or three applications will be required, which should be made at intervals of one week. The cost of the wash, at the ordinary retail price for the soap (10 cents per pound), is 2 cents per gallon.

Very weak solutions may be made effective if used at frequent short intervals, but the labor and expense of making the numerous applications required will be very great.

A solution of 1 pound to 5 gallons will not injure the trees, but may cause the blossoms to drop. No directions can be given as to the greatest strength of solution that can be used upon blooming trees without loss of fruit, as this depends largely upon the condition of the tree. Solutions of 1 pound to 10 gallons can probably be safely used, in most cases, and will be effective if several applications are made at intervals of a few days.

Sulphur.—The Mites, both adult and young, are very sensitive to sulphur, and are readily killed by it in any form in which it can be made to act upon them. The eggs, however, are not readily affected, and even survive an exposure to the fumes, which will kill the plant. Fumigation cannot be resorted to without extreme danger to the life and health of the tree. The finely powdered (sublimed) flowers of sulphur does not affect the plant. It adheres more readily than might be supposed to the smooth surfaces of the leaves, and, especially when they are roughened by the Mites, it is not entirely washed away by heavy rains. Although it does not kill the eggs, it effectually exterminates the free Mites, which are sure to come in contact with it in their wanderings, and if it can be made to remain upon the plant, the young as they hatch are also destroyed.

RUST OF THE ORANGE—REMEDIES.

Flowers of sulphur must therefore be regarded as one of the cheapest and most effective remedies for Rust-mite, and it may be used to great advantage in connection with whale-oil soap or other insecticides. It may be suspended in water and applied in spray. With proper appliances the dry powder may be sifted or blown upon the foliage when wet with dew or rain. A little wheat flour added to the powder would increase its adhesiveness.

The pharmaceutical preparation known as milk of sulphur (precipitated), although a much more finely divided powder, proves milder in its effect upon the Mites, and its cost will prevent its extensive use.

EXPERIMENTS.

(1.) A small seedling Orange infested with Rust-mite was covered with a nail-keg and fumigated for ten minutes by burning one ounce of sulphur under the keg. All the Mites were destroyed, but the eggs remained alive ten days, and finally dried up with the leaves of the plant, which was entirely killed.

(2.) Flowers of sulphur dusted over infested leaves through a loosely woven cloth. Free Mites all dead in twenty-four hours. Molting young all dead in three or four days. Eggs not killed in nine days, but young Mites killed soon after hatching.

(3.) Experiment No. 2 repeated in the open air, and leaves allowed to remain on the tree. Heavy rains on the second day did not remove all the sulphur. Results the same as in No. 2. Mites all killed. Eggs not killed.

(4.) Milk of sulphur dusted upon the leaves through muslin. Effect less powerful than in Nos. 2 and 3, but Mites in the end all killed. Eggs not killed.

(5.) Milk of sulphur; two ounces, by measure, of the powder suspended in one gallon of water. Leaves dipped in the liquid, when dry were lightly coated with grains of sulphur. Adult Mites dead on the second day. Some molting Mites and numerous eggs alive on the second day.

(6.) Leaf with Mites confined in a tight box with another leaf on which sulphur had been dusted. No effect after twenty-four hours. On the third day, however, only one adult Mite appeared to be alive. In six days all the Mites were plainly killed. Eggs not killed.

This experiment was repeated with sulphur scattered in the bottom of the box, and precautions taken to prevent its contact with the Mites. Results precisely the same as before.

Note.—By confinement in very tight metal boxes, Mites may be kept alive between one and two weeks, or until the leaves dry up or mold. The destruction of the Mites in this experiment was therefore due entirely to the slow volatilization of the sulphur.

(7.) Sulphuretted hydrogen. Leaves dipped in water strongly impregnated with the gas. In twenty-four hours all adult Mites were dead or dying. In thirty-six hours all free Mites were dead. In the same time 40 to 50 per cent. of the molting Mites died. On the third day many molting Mites remained alive. Eggs not killed.

The above solution of sulphuretted hydrogen (sulphur water) was prepared by passing through two gallons of water, the gas given off by three ounces of sulphuret of iron, treated with dilute sulphuric acid.*

The remarkable results obtained with sulphur in these experiments, and especially the effect of the gas in solution upon the adult Mites, suggests the use of water from the sulphur springs which abound in various parts of Florida. Although it cannot be supposed that these natural waters contain a sufficiently high percentage of the mineral to render them powerful insecticides, their value cannot be determined without trial. Persistent applications may suffice to ultimately exterminate the Rust-mite or cause its disappearance from the trees. In view of its possible importance as a remedy, those who have access to natural springs or who now use flowing wells of sulphur water for the purpose of irrigation, should thoroughly test it by making repeated applications at short intervals.

Kerosene.—Emulsions containing 66 per cent. of kerosene oil, and diluted with water ten times, as in applications for Scale-insects, do not kill the eggs of the Rust-mite. The same emulsions, diluted one to twenty, kill nearly all the mites, but do not kill the eggs. With dilutions of one to forty, many adults escape destruction. In all the experiments made with kerosene upon Scale-insects the trees were not cleared of Rust-mites. They usually reappeared in numbers, within five or six days, owing to the hatching of the eggs. As a remedy for Rust-mite, therefore, kerosene is not as effective as either whale-oil soap or sulphur.

In making applications for Scale-insect it is advisable to render the wash effective against Rust-mite also, and this can be in a measure accomplished by adding sulphur.

Experience has shown whale-oil soap to be superior to condensed milk in forming emulsions, and much cheaper. Emulsions made with soap do not thicken or ferment, as when milk is used.

The formula given in the preceding chapter (see ante, page 94) gives the best results.

The emulsion should be diluted with water ten times, or in the proportions 1 to 9, and applied in fine spray.

In cases where an application is needed for both Scale-insect and Rust-mite the above wash, with two or three ounces of sulphur added to each gallon of the mixture, forms the most effective combination that can at present be devised. It is best applied in early spring, but should never be used in midwinter or when there is danger from frost.

Carbolic Acid.—Several experiments with crude Carbolic acid, saponified with lard oil and lye, or dissolved in strongly alkaline solutions,

---

*A solution of sulphuretted hydrogen may be very simply prepared by boiling sulphur in lime-water. (See Sulphurated Lime, *ante*, p. 98.)

gave about the same results as 66 per cent. kerosene emulsions. The Mites were readily killed, but their eggs for the most part survived.

Carbolic acid is highly poisonous to plants, and must be used in small doses. Three or four fluid ounces of crude acid dissolved in one gallon of strong soap solution make as strong a wash as it is safe to apply. Although even cheaper than kerosene, it is not a more effective remedy, and, owing to the greater danger attending its use, it cannot be recommended in preference to the latter.

A strong carbolic or creosote soap can be purchased at a reasonable price, and will prove very useful to orange-growers, as it is not only a powerful insecticide, but also a remedy for "die-back," and possibly also for "foot-rot," or any disease of the plant of fungoid origin.

Potash.—Very strong lye is required to kill the Mites, and their eggs are not destroyed except by solutions sufficiently caustic to burn the leaves and bark.

The different commercial brands of concentrated lye and caustic potash vary greatly in purity and strength. The potash used in the following experiments was a superior article, put up in 1-pound balls, coated with rosin:

(1.) Solution: 4 pounds (48 ounces) potash to 1 gallon water. Leaves dipped in this solution were badly burned, and, together with them, the Mites and eggs were entirely destroyed.

(2.) Solution: 2 pounds (24 ounces) potash to 1 gallon water. Leaves charred. Mites and eggs destroyed.

(3.) Solution: 1 pound (12 ounces) potash to 1 gallon water. Mites nearly all killed. A single living adult seen. Molting Mites and eggs not all killed. Leaves devitalized, but not charred.

(4.) Solution: 8 ounces potash to 1 gallon. Adult Mites nearly all killed. One half-grown Mite seen crawling about among crystals of potash. Molting Mites and eggs not killed.

(5.) Solution: 6 ounces potash to 1 gallon. Adult Mites killed. Several recently molted Mites seen crawling on second day. Molting Mites not killed. Eggs uninjured.

(6.) Solution: 4 ounces potash to 1 gallon. Many adult Mites killed; some alive. Numerous young Mites alive on second day. Molting mites and eggs uninjured.

(7.) Solution: 3 ounces potash to 1 gallon. Same results as No. 6.

Solutions of 1 pound to the gallon have been used upon orange trees, and although all the leaves and portions of the bark were destroyed, they recovered rapidly from the effects of the application. Such heroic treatment for insect pests is, however, unnecessary and unadvisable.

Pyrethrum.—Applied in fine powder, this insecticide visibly affected the adult Mites and caused them to erect themselves frequently upon their anal prolegs. The free Mites left the leaves in a few hours, but it is doubtful if many of them were killed. The molting Mites and eggs remained uninjured. Continued exposure to contact with the strong powder disables and finally kills the Mites, but they are not as violently affected as many of the higher insects, and recover from slight applications.

Lime.—Not the slightest effect was obtained with applications of lime, as the following experiments will show:

(1.) Freshly air-slaked stone-lime dusted thickly over infested leaves. Mites continued feeding and propagating under the coating of lime-powder, and did not abandon the leaves during eight days in which they were kept under observation.

(2.) Slaked lime, 1 pint measure suspended in 1 quart water, and allowed to partly settle. Leaves dipped in the turbid liquid. No injurious effect upon the Mites or their eggs. Adult Mites were rendered restless by fine particles of lime adhering to them, and all left the leaves within two days, but were not killed.

(3.) Same solution as No. 2, clarified by standing several days. Leaves dipped in the clear lime-water. No effect whatever during eight days' observation.

Ashes.—Finely-sifted hard-wood ashes dusted upon the leaves produced no effect whatever upon the Mites, and did not seem to discommode them in the least.

The above experiments were made in December, during continued cold weather, which retarded the development of the Mites and interfered somewhat with observations as to hatching of the eggs under treatment.

CAUTION.

There is danger in applying penetrating liquids to orange trees during the winter. First, because any shock to a dormant tree is apt to start the buds and induce new growth at a time when there is danger of frost. Secondly, a succession of cold nights and cloudy days, such as frequently occurs in severe winters, following immediately after an application, will increase to an injurious extent its effect upon the plant, by preventing evaporation of the liquids used, and allowing them to remain too long in contact with the leaves and bark. Serious loss is liable to follow a disregard of this warning.

CHAPTER IX.

INSECTS AFFECTING THE ROOT, CROWN, TRUNK, AND BRANCHES.

INSECTS AFFECTING THE ROOT AND CROWN.

TAP-ROOT BORERS.

A grub or "Sawyer" is sometimes found boring into the tap-root of the Orange. No specimens have been examined, but from the descriptions given by competent observers, it can only be the larva of some longicorn beetle of moderately large size.

Mr. William H. Ashmead, in the Florida Agriculturist, February 16, 1881, mentions and gives a figure of a larva, which is possibly that of *Chion cinctus* (Drury), found boring in the tap-root of a Bitter-sweet orange tree. It was only discovered upon taking up the tree in order to transplant it, and may therefore be presumed to have done little damage.

A larva which appears to belong to this species has also been sent in Orange roots to the Department of Agriculture from Florida.

Other borers of this numerous and destructive family are likely to occur in the trunk and branches, as well as in the roots below the surface of the ground. It is difficult, without a previous knowledge of their habits, to suggest a remedy for these subterranean borers, but should they at any time become troublesome they may be removed by uncovering the roots and destroying the borer in its gallery with a pointed wire.

WHITE ANTS OR "WOOD-LICE."

Habits.—Termites or white ants are small, soft bodied insects resembling ants and living in numerous colonies. They shun the light and travel to great distances through galleries constructed beneath the surface of the ground. They feed for the most part upon dead wood and decaying vegetable matter, but sometimes attack living plants, especially those parts which lie below the surface of the ground. A certain amount of moisture is necessary to their existence, and very dry wood is usually free from their attacks.

TERMES FLAVIPES Kollar.

[Fig. 46.]

This species is common from Maine to Texas, and is especially abundant in the South, where it invariably attacks wood buried in or lying upon the ground.

Each colony consists of numerous workers, among which are several distinct forms, and a few males and females. The females never leave the home nest, but, like the queen of the honey bee, devote themselves to producing eggs, which are hatched and cared for by the workers.

The central nests, in which are hived the queens and eggs, are rarely discovered, but generally exist in deeply-buried roots or in the hearts of stumps and logs of the largest size.

The workers extend their operations to immense distances, and, in search of food, excavate slender subterranean galleries, hundreds and even thousands of feet in length. It is, therefore, practically impossi-

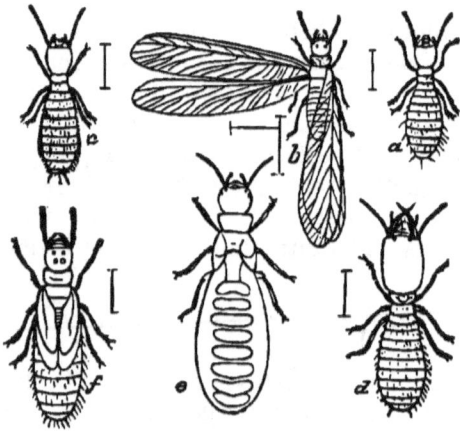

FIG. 46.—*Termes flavipes*: *a*, larva; *b*, winged male; *c*, worker; *d*, soldier; *e*, large female; *f*, nymphe. (From the Am. Ent., Vol. II.)

ble to trace these galleries to their source, and by finding and destroying the brood nest to break up a colony.

Twice each year, in spring and fall, multitudes of winged males and females are produced, which swarm forth during the cooler parts of the day or after rains, and fill the air with their fluttering forms. Most of these fall a prey to birds, reptiles, insects, and other predatory animals, but many escape, and, after coupling, lose their wings, and in pairs seek suitable places in which to found new colonies.

Injuries to Orange.—Owing to their subterranean habits and avoidance of light, Termites are very insidious foes. Their vast numbers enable them to very quickly accomplish the work of destruction, so that often the finding a tree in dying condition is the first intimation which the orange-grower receives of their presence. Upon removing the earth about the collar and root, the bark is found eaten away and the tree perhaps completely girdled.

The growing wood of plants is not the natural food of Termites, and is only attacked by them under exceptional circumstances. Thus in orange groves they may be impelled to escape from the heated soil by excavating galleries into the root bark of the trees, the moisture and coolness of which are grateful to them. It is to be remarked that they at first confine their galleries to the soft outer layers, and only subsequently penetrate and feed upon the heart wood as the tree dies in consequence of their injuries.

Recently transplanted trees whose roots have suffered mutilation, young groves set out on new land, and trees planted too deep or which have too much earth heaped about the crown, are exposed to danger from Termites, but old and well-established trees are little liable to their attacks, unless from disease or other injuries dead and unhealthy wood is present to invite their entrance.

Their Work easily distinguished from that of other Insects.—The galleries of Termites are seldom circular, but most frequently present a series of broad and shallow chambers, often overlying one another and connected by short passages. The walls of the galleries are always lined with a a layer of comminuted wood, which gives them a mottled appearance, very characteristic, and distinct from those of ants or other boring insects, and renders them easily recognizable in the absence of the Termites themselves. These latter are usually present, however, as they seldom leave a piece of wood in which they have effected a lodgment until every portion of its solid interior has been eaten away and reduced to powder, unless, indeed, the material becomes too dry for their further existence. Their entrance galleries are always beneath the surface of the ground or under cover of other material, for they never expose themselves to light.

In living orange trees, as has been said, their first attack is made at the base of the trunk, just beneath the surface of the ground. Not unfrequently this is betrayed, before extensive damage has been done, by a slight exudation of sap from the wounded bark, which moistens and cakes the ground at the surface.

SOURCES OF DANGER—PRECAUTIONS.—*Stumps and buried Roots of forest Trees.*—So abundant are Termites in the South that no buried fragments of wood long escape their visits. The hardest live oak, and the most resinous pine yield in time to these scavengers. The decaying stumps and roots of forest trees, therefore, form an element of danger to orange groves planted on newly cleared land, that cannot well be avoided; but the risk may be reduced to a minimum by removing the stumps, particularly those of oak and other hard woods, which stand nearer than five or six feet to any orange trees, and by care in removing chips and severed roots from contact with or too close proximity to the young trees.

On mulching and the use of decaying Wood as a Fertilizer in the Orange Grove.—A mulch of muck, leaves, grass, pine-straw, succulent vegetable matter, and even well-rotted and disintegrated wood from old brush piles, does not in itself attract Termites, and its use is not attended with any danger, provided it is not piled against the trunk of the tree, the crown of which should in all cases be left exposed to the air. It is well to maintain an open space immediately about the tree, and the mulching should not be allowed to approach nearer than six or eight inches to the trunk on any side.

The practice of bringing brush, logs, and chips of wood into the orange grove, and either burying or allowing them to rot upon the ground, is hazardous, and will surely attract and colonize Termites, which, under any circumstances, must be considered dangerous and undesirable neighbors for orange trees. If disintegrated wood is used at all as a fertilizer, all solid fragments should be carefully excluded.

Deep planting.—This is a most frequent cause of trouble, and should be obviated by raising the trees too deeply set. In cultivating, also, the tendency of the earth to heap about the trees should be corrected by turning the furrows toward the centers between the rows, or by drawing back the earth with the hoe.

REMEDIES.—*Exposure to Light and Air.*—As Termites require for their existence darkness and moisture, on discovering their attacks the first step should be to remove the earth about the affected parts, and uncover the crown and root to a depth of several inches, at the same time removing with the knife, as far as possible, all the dead wood and bark, and exposing their galleries to the drying action of the air. In cases of slight attack this will generally suffice to drive them away.

Hot Water.—If the galleries extend too deeply into the wood to be readily uncovered with the knife, or if a numerous colony is found to have established itself at a considerable depth beneath the surface, a liberal application of hot water will usually reach and destroy them without injury to the tree.

Pyrethrum.—Termites are exceedingly sensitive to the action of this insecticide, and are invariably killed by contact with the powder. It may be used to great advantage whenever it can be brought into contact with the insects. Pyrethrum loses its properties rapidly on exposure to the air, and although it retains its power for a longer time when covered with earth, it remains effective for a few days only, and cannot be relied upon to permanently protect the plant from the attack of this or other insects.

Penetrating Liquids.—Kerosene in emulsion is very effective, and may be safely used in moderate quantities; but all penetrating oils should be applied with great caution to the roots of plants.

Bisulphide of carbon is most useful for destroying colonies remote from the trees, but is far too dangerous a substance to use upon or near the roots. The central nest, when its position is known, may be broken up and the queens destroyed by pouring a few ounces of the liquid into the galleries, or into a hole made by a stake driven as close to the nest as possible. The hole should then be closed with earth to insure percolation of the vapor through the soil.

Ashes, Lime, and Sulphur are without effect in protecting orange trees from the attacks of Termites. In the cases where these substances have seemed effective in driving them away the result has been accomplished simply by the disturbance to their mines and exposure to the drying action of the air.

Ingrafting Scions.—Trees completely girded by Termites may be saved, if taken in time, by inarching scions between the root below and the stock above, thus reestablishing the connection between the two. The tree will in time restore the eroded bark, and the scions may be allowed to remain or may be afterwards cut out.

Supplementary stocks may also be planted close to the injured tree, and grafted in above the girdled portion, to sustain the life of the trunk and enable it to restore the severed connection. A poultice of mud and cow dung, applied to the injured part, will protect it and materially assist the formation of new wood and bark.

CALOTERMES CASTANEUS.

A second species of Termite, somewhat larger than *Termes flavipes*, but otherwise closely resembling it, has been found in decaying branches and stumps of orange; but as far as its habits have been observed it is a tree-inhabiting species, seldom forming very large colonies, and not likely to do injury to growing plants, as it prefers very dry wood, and is most frequently found in dead branches from the tops of forest trees. Should it prove injurious to the orange it will probably require the same treatment as the related species.

INSECTS AFFECTING THE TRUNK AND BRANCHES.

COLEOPTEROUS BORERS. "SAWYERS."

THE COMMON ORANGE SAWYER.

(*Elaphidion inerme* Newman.)

[Fig. 47.]

The larvæ of this beetle are cylindrical, whitish, fleshy grubs or sawyers, with rudimentary legs, which cannot be of much assistance to the animal in moving about, and a pair of strong short jaws. As with most borers of this family, the head is small and can be withdrawn entirely into the body. The first body-joint is somewhat enlarged, and covered above with minute horny asperities, which are pressed against the walls of the burrow, and serve to hold the body firmly in place while the jaws are forced into the wood. The full-grown larva is about one inch in length.

The pupa is formed in the gallery, in a rude cell made by pushing aside the chips with which the larva stops up all the approaches to its burrow.

The perfect insect has a long, cylindrical body with rather roughly pitted surface; the color is dark brown, dusted densely beneath, but

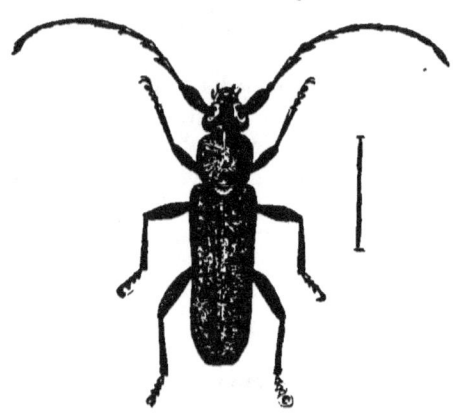

FIG. 47.—*Elaphidion inerme*. (Original.)

irregularly above, with fine ash-gray hairs; the antennæ are not longer than the body. The length varies from 11^{mm} to 15^{mm} ($\frac{44}{100}$ to $\frac{60}{100}$ inch); the males are smaller than the females.

Fig. 48 illustrates, in all its stages, *Elaphidion parallelum* Newm., a closely allied species, which lives in northern fruit-trees, and has habits similar to the Orange Sawyer. In the figure, *a* represents the larva; *b*, the pupa in its cell; *c*, the perfect insect; *d*, the head; *e, f*, and *g*, the mouth parts; and *h*, the antenna of the larva, enlarged; *i* and *j* show details of the antennæ and tip of the wing-cases, respectively, in the imago; *k*, the end of the twig which contains the borer.

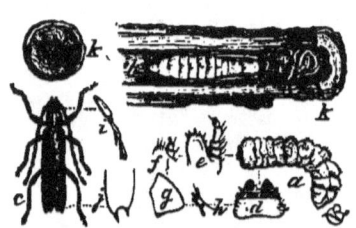

FIG. 48.—*Elaphidion parallelum* Newm.: *a*, larva; *b*, chrysalis in twig; *c*, adult beetle; *d, e, f, g, h*, head and mouth parts of the larva; *i*, part of antenna; and *j*, end of wing case of the adult; *k*, end of twig, cut off. (After Riley.)

The larvæ of this beetle are more properly scavengers or pruners, feeding by preference upon dead branches, not only of Orange, but also of Hickory and other hard-wood trees, and confining themselves to the dry and lifeless wood, unless compelled by hunger to enter the living portions of the plant.

The injuries caused by them result from careless pruning, and, especially in the case of budded nursery trees, from leaving untrimmed the dead end of the stock above the insertion of the bud. These dead stubs attract the mother beetle, and she deposits one or two eggs in each.

The grubs that hatch confine themselves to the dead ends until they are completely hollowed out and reduced to mere shells, filled with sawdust. But if the supply of dead wood fails, they are forced to descend into the living stock below, and thus weaken the bud if they do not kill it outright, undermining the tissues which support it.

Protection afforded the Tree by its Gum.—Very frequently the larva in penetrating the living tissues causes its own death by suffocation from the flow of gum, which rises in the gallery, filling it to the top. This is particularly apt to occur in the case of Lemon, Citron, and others of the citrus family, which produce an abundance of gum. When in vigorous condition the trunk of the Orange is perfectly protected by its gum from the attacks of boring Coleoptera, and it is only endangered when, from loss of vitality, such as follows transplanting or disturbance from disease, attacks of Scale-insects, &c., the circulation of sap and the flow of gum are decreased.

Necessary Precautions.—It follows from what has been said that dead limbs, especially the dead ends of budded stocks, should be carefully trimmed off, back to and even with the healthy wood. Trees transplanted during an unfavorable season, and which do not get a good or early start, are apt to die back and present dead ends, which attract borers. Such trees need to be closely watched and kept pruned until their vigor is restored.

When trees of large size are cut off and budded, the entrance of borers in the ends of the stump or large branches should be prevented by protecting them with a coating of shellac or grafting-wax. It is also well to allow a few suckers to grow for a time on the side opposite the bud, in order to preserve a healthy flow of sap on this side and encourage the more rapid formation of wood and bark over the exposed heart wood.

It is in consequence of the sluggish flow of sap and drier condition of the wood on the side opposite the growing shoot or bud that this side of a budded trunk is particularly exposed to the attacks of borers; and most of their damage is done by undermining and killing the bark, with long galleries running down one side of the tree.

Means of destroying the Borers.—Should the borer be found to have penetrated the wood beyond the reach of the knife, no simpler method of destroying it can be suggested than the old one of following it to the bottom of its retreat with a piece of annealed wire sharpened at the end. If the wire is also slightly hooked at the end, the sawyer may generally be pulled out and removed bodily.

THE TWIG GIRDLER.

(*Oncideres cingulatus*, Say).

[Figs. 49 and 50.]

This beetle is injurious to fruit and timber trees in all parts of the southern and eastern United States. The female has the singular habit of cutting off twigs and branches not exceeding three-fourths of an inch in diameter in which she had previously deposited a number of eggs. Fig. 49 shows the insect in the act of cutting a twig. In the South the Persimmon suffers most severely, but Oak, Hickory, Cherry, in fact, all hard-wood timber and fruit-trees, are attacked, and even climbers and ligneous shrubs like the Rose are not exempt.

FIG. 49.—*Oncideres cingulatus*. (After Riley.)

No extensive depredations upon the Orange have hitherto been reported, but in most groves an occasional branch is amputated. The loss is seldom noticed except in young trees, which it is sometimes provoking to find deprived of their leaders of the previous season's growth. The cutting is so cleverly done as to pass for a malicious use of the pruning shears, and few persons would suspect it to be the work of an insect.

The beetle is about 16^{mm} ($\frac{64}{100}$ inch) long, rather stout and cylindrical, dark chocolate-brown in color, speckled with lighter brown, and lightly covered with short, gray pubescence, resembling a coat of bluish dust or pruina, denser beneath and upon head and thorax, and forming a broad transverse band upon the wing-cases. The antennæ of the female about equal the body in length, and are somewhat longer in the male. There is but one brood each year. The eggs are laid in September and October, and are deposited singly beneath the bark, usually close to a bud. [Fig. 49, *b*; *e*, egg, natural size.] After placing an egg under each bud for a distance of two or three feet, the female cuts off the branch containing them by gnawing around it a deep, narrow groove, so nearly severing it from the tree that it falls by its own weight, or is broken off by the wind and falls to the ground, where it obtains the moisture necessary to the development of the young. The eggs hatch into white, fleshy larvæ of the form common to wood-boring beetles, and known in the South as "Sawyers." (Fig. 50, *a*.) The larvæ remain nearly a year feeding upon the wood of the fallen branch, which they riddle with their galleries, and in the latter part of summer form within the wood oval cells, in which they transform to pupa. (Fig. 50, *b*.)

FIG. 50.—*Oncideres cingulatus*. *a*, larva; *b*, pupa. (After Riley.)

The perfect beetles appear again in September. They are very shy, and remain perfectly motionless when disturbed. Their mixed coloration of neutral gray and brown is also admirably adapted for concealment upon all kinds of bark, and they are therefore not easily detected at their work.

Remedies.—The simplest means of destroying this pest is to gather up and burn during the winter the fallen branches which have been cut by them, and which contain their eggs or larvæ. Where persimmon bushes are abundant this will prove a work of some labor, but will be absolutely necessary if the Japan persimmon is cultivated for profit.

The Girdler is not likely to prove a very serious pest to the Orange, but should it ever become such some advantage may be gained by trapping the perfect beetles as soon as they begin to appear in the fall. This can be done by means of sirup daubed upon trees and fences. The sugared spots must be visited at night with a lantern, and the beetles, which will be found attracted to these spots, can be detected and destroyed. The sirup may be mixed with a little beer, wine, or alcohol to render it intoxicating, so that the beetles found feeding upon it will not be disturbed by the light of the lantern and try to escape.

INJURIES CAUSED BY ANTS.

SOLENOPSIS XYLONI McCook.

[Fig. 51.]

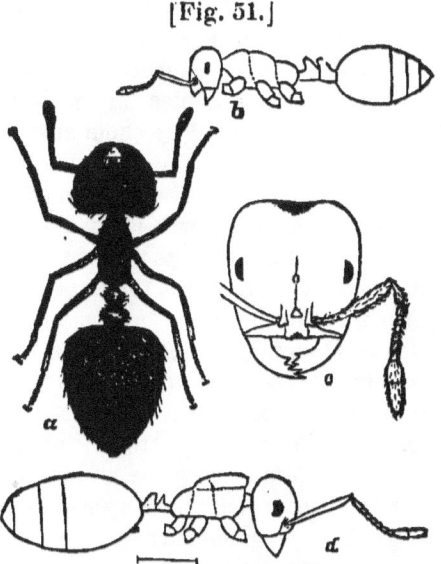

FIG. 51.—*Solenopsis xyloni:* a, ant from above; b, same, side view; c, same, view of head; d, queen, side view. (After McCook.)

The well-known carnivorous habits of this ant—it is one of the commonest and most effective destroyers of the Cotton Worm—would lead us to reject any but the most positive and direct evidence that it fed upon living plants. There is, unfortunately, no room to doubt that it does frequently and seriously injure the Orange by gnawing away the bark, and causing an exudation of gum which seems, at certain seasons of the year, to become one of its principal sources of food-supply.

In obtaining this the ant is led by its instinct to make incisions at the base of the largest and most vigorous leaders at a time when, having nearly or completely attained their full growth, the young shoots are in process of hardening and ripening their wood, and the flow of elaborated sap to these parts is greatest, giving in consequence the most copious exudation of gum from a wound.

The ants make their attacks in force, and either girdle and kill the shoots or cut so deeply into their bases that they bend over or break off by their own weight. Sometimes, but rarely, the ants attack the old bark of the trunk and larger branches and gnaw holes in it, eating away the cambium layer without waiting for gum to exude. When the flow is very copious the ants bring sand and mix with the gum. This enables them to tunnel into it, and while some individuals are continuing the excavation in the bark beneath, others are penetrating the gum thus hardened and removing it piecemeal to their nests.

Habits of the Ant.—*Solenopsis xyloni* is a mahogany-brown ant of medium size. It is very pugnacious and stings sharply. It lives in large colonies, making its nest in the earth, and after rains throwing up irregular heaps of finely-granular earth. These heaps swarm with ants, among which are seen occasional individuals (workers major) with enormously enlarged heads. It is exceedingly fond of the nectar of plants and the honey-dew secreted by insects, and is a constant attendant upon Plant-lice and Lecanium Scales on the Orange. During the greater part of the year it is attracted by them alone, and its visits to the trees are harmless, but in October and November, when these insects are scarce, the ant turns its attention to the gum of the tree itself. During these months the summer growth is hardening and the bark is full of elaborated sap, containing a large amount of saccharine matter. It is probably in this condition only that the ants find it palatable and accept it in lieu of their ordinary food.

Destroying Colonies.—When not too near the tree, bisulphide of carbon may be used in breaking up colonies of this ant in the same manner as recommended for those of Termites. Pyrethrum powder, to the action of which they are very susceptible, stirred into the soil about and within their nest kills great numbers of the ants and frequently causes the survivors to abandon the premises. Naphthaline, in the form of a crystalline powder, used in the same way is equally effective in breaking up colonies. After frosty nights in winter, when the sun shines warm on the following morning, the ants come out of the ground and gather in clusters under fallen leaves or other objects affording them protection from the wind with exposure to the warmth of the sun. At such times an excellent opportunity is afforded to destroy the entire colony by raking over the ground about the nests, at the same time spraying the disturbed ants with kerosene or dusting them with pyrethrum.

Means of preventing the Ants from ascending the Trees.—When they have begun to attack a tree it is with extreme difficulty that they can be permanently driven off. Pyrethrum dusted over those upon the tree, and scattered over the ground about its base, kills all the ants with which it comes in contact, and affords temporary relief, but its effect is not lasting, and it does not always prevent their return. Coating the raw spots with shellac and protecting the trunk with a band of tar and other viscid substances cannot be permanently relied upon to keep them off.

Sir John Lubbock, in his work on Ants, Bees, and Wasps, speaks of isolating nests of ants "by fur, with the hair pointing downwards," but we are not told what kind of fur was used. A broad band of fur tied around the trunk of the tree, and with the hair pointing downwards, is effectual in preventing their ascent. The skin of the rabbit has been used with success, but probably that of any fur-bearing animal would answer.

Fur does not form a barrier absolutely impassable to ants, and they will frequently clamber through a very narrow band, but they experience great difficulty in making their way against the hairs, and almost invariably become confused and turn back, if the distance exceeds 1 or 2 inches.

Still more simple and almost as effective is a barrier of chalk. This is applied by rubbing a lump of dry chalk over the bark to form a band at least 8 inches wide, and completely encircling the trunk. In attempting to cross such a band the ants nearly always slip and fall to the ground. The fine interstices of the bark are filled with loose grains of chalk, in which their claws find a very treacherous support. While fresh and dry the chalk band is well-nigh impassable to ants of the size and weight of the Solenopsis, but dews at night, or rains, and the moisture of the atmosphere in a short time change the character of the surface by causing the grains of chalk to cohere with sufficient firmness to support the weight of the insect and they then cross it in safety. The device cannot, therefore, be regarded as a permanent one and requires frequent renewal, but it may be resorted to temporarily when a piece of fur is not at hand.

Very soft, fine clay, fuller's-earth, or talc may be substituted for chalk, but in all cases must be applied by rubbing on from a dry lump. Good results cannot be obtained by using any of these substances in powder, dry, or as a whitewash applied with a brush.

CHAPTER X.

INSECTS AFFECTING THE TWIGS AND LEAVES.

INSECTS OF THE ORDER HYMENOPTERA.

LEAF-EATING ANT.

(*Monomorium carbonarium* Sm.)

A small black ant eats holes in the leaves of orange trees when they are very young and tender, but seldom does any damage beyond destroying a leaf or two, which in most cases the plant can very well spare. Should this ant, however, become destructive, it may be combatted in the same way as the Solenopsis mentioned in the preceding chapter. A band of fur around the trunk of the tree will prevent their ascending.

INSECTS OF THE ORDER COLEOPTERA.

BRACHYS OVATA (Web.).

This small beetle, belonging to the family Buprestidæ, is frequently met with upon the leaves, in which it occasionally eats small holes. The beetle is 5^{mm} ($\frac{2}{10}$ inch) long and nearly the same in width. The body is flattened, or very slightly convex, and shield-shaped. The color is a mixture, finely mottled, of dark and light bronze. When disturbed, the legs are drawn into grooves in the underside of the body and the beetle falls to the ground, where it bears a remarkably close resemblance to the seeds of some of the common wild vetches. The beetle has not hitherto been known to do appreciable damage to plants of the citrus family. Its natural food is the Oak, upon which its strangely-flattened larvæ live as leaf-miners, excavating galleries in the narrow space between the upper and lower surfaces of the leaves, and feeding upon the parenchyma.

THE ORANGE LEAF-NOTCHER.

ODONTOTA RUBRA (Web.)

A beetle of the leaf-eating family Chrysomelidæ is occasionally found eating the leaves of Orange, but never to an injurious extent. Like the preceding, its larva is a leaf-miner, and is found on various plants, but not upon the Orange.

NOTOLOMUS BASALIS Leconte.

[Fig. 52.]

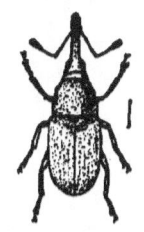

A weevil or snout-beetle (family *Curculionidæ*) of small size and light straw color, frequently found upon the trees, usually hiding in dead leaves or tangles of spider-web. It has been seen to eat the leaves and tender bark, but it nibbles rather than feeds upon the Orange, and cannot be convicted of doing serious harm. When the Orange is in bloom the beetle is quite common upon the flowers, and it feeds upon the pollen and nectar without injury to the plant. The early stages are not known, but it is suspected of a connection with the Saw-palmetto, upon the bloom of which the beetle is always found in abundance.

Fig. 52. — *Notolomus basalis*. (Original.)

THE ORANGE LEAF-NOTCHER.

(*Artipus floridanus* Horn.)

[Fig. 53.]

This is a snout-beetle of bluish-white color, stout, cylindrical form, 6^{mm} (¼ inch) in length. It is said to eat jagged notches in the edges of orange leaves (see Report of Commissioner of Agriculture for 1879, p. 207), and was also found by Ashmead on the Florida Keys feeding upon the Lime and other plants. (Orange Insects, p. 62.) The beetle is confined to the peninsula of Florida, and is rare except in the extreme southern portions of the State.

PACHNÆUS OPALUS, Olivier.

A weevil similar in form and color to the preceding, but one-half larger. Ashmead, in his Orange Insects, p. 61, says: "This weevil was caught by me in great quantities in South Florida on the Keys, feeding on the leaves of the lime-tree (*Citrus*). I also found it eating the leaves of *Baccharis halimifolia* and *Borrichia frutescens*, which I think are its natural food plants." It is certainly very rare on the mainland, and does not occur

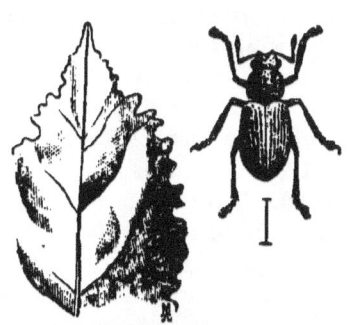

Fig. 53. — *Artipus floridanus*, and orange leaf with edges gnawed by the beetle. (After Comstock.)

in the northern part of the State. Both this and the preceding species may be removed, as suggested by Mr. Ashmead, by shaking them from the trees into cloths spread to receive them. They fold up their legs and simulate death, when disturbed. The early stages of both species remain unknown.

INSECTS OF THE ORDER ORTHOPTERA.

THE ANGULAR-WINGED KATYDID.

(*Microcentrum retinerve* Burm.)

(Plate IX.)

This large, green grasshopper, common in all parts of the United States, has been exhaustively studied by Professor Riley, and its full history detailed in his sixth Missouri report. It has been several times noticed in reports of the Department, and is quite fully treated in the report for 1880. The eggs—large oval objects, flattened like flax-seed and dark gray in color, are placed overlapping each other in a row along the edge of an orange leaf, or are deposited in two parallel rows along a twig. There are two broods each year. Eggs laid in December hatch in January or February. The young complete their growth in eight or nine weeks. The eggs of the second brood begin to appear in May, and are continually being deposited during the summer. Young of the second brood are first seen in July.

Throughout their lives, the Katydids feed upon the Orange. The young confine themselves to the tender foliage, but the adults often gnaw the bark of growing shoots and leaders, and thus inflict very serious injuries. Occasionally a tree is almost defoliated by Katydids, and this, of course, happens most frequently in the case of young trees; but, owing to the luxuriance of its foliage and the rapidity with which the orange-tree renews its lost leaves, the damage done by these insects is rarely sufficient to repay the cost of fighting them. Young groves should, however, be protected from their attacks, and early in the winter the trees should be examined and the leaves with eggs upon them removed. The young may very readily be killed by dusting the foliage with pyrethrum powder.

EGG-PARASITE OF THE KATYDID.—(*Eupelmus* [*Antigaster*] *mirabilis*, Walsh.)—(Plate IX, Fig. 2, female; Fig. 2a, male.)—The eggs of the Katydid are very frequently found with a small, round hole cut through the side. This is the exit-hole of the parasite which is hatched and bred within the egg of the Katydid, feeds upon its contents, and in due course issues forth, a four-winged fly. The larva, like that of most Hymenopterous parasites, is a transparent, white, footless grub; the pupa of the female is flattened, and is very curiously packed in its narrow quarters, so that it exactly fills the space within the egg-shell. To accomplish this, the abdomen and legs are folded back over the body, and it is remarkable that the perfect insect retains through life the power of thus rolling itself up into a ball. In the imago stage the two sexes are very dissimilar. The female has clouded wings, the body shows metallic reflections of purple, green, and copper-bronze, and the abdomen is black, with the first joint white. The male is smaller than the female, has clear wings, and is uniformly bright metallic green in color. It has not the power of rolling itself like the female.

THE LUBBER GRASSHOPPER.

(*Romalea microptera* Serv.)

(Fig. 54.)

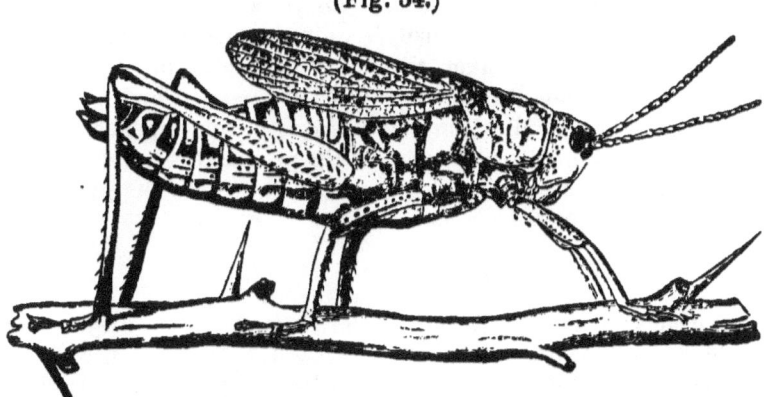

FIG. 54.—The Lubber Grasshopper. (After Glover.)

This huge locust has nomadic habits, and wanders about in search of food, attacking almost all succulent plants. It sometimes does damage to orange trees by feeding upon the leaders and tender shoots, and is at times sufficiently abundant to become a serious pest. The eggs are laid in the ground and hatch in March or April. The young are black, with bright yellow markings. For several weeks after leaving the ground they are gregarious, each brood in its wanderings keeping together and gathering at night in a cluster upon some low herbaceous plant. This habit, with their conspicuous coloration, renders it an easy matter to find and destroy them at first. Later in the summer they separate and become scattered, and the separate individuals must then be sought for and destroyed.

During its growth the insect several times changes its skin. After the final molt, which takes place in July or August, its appearance is entirely changed. The colors of the young are reversed in the adult; yellow becomes the predominant color, and the body is marked with spots and lines of black. The wings are tinged with pink; they are too short and rudimentary for flight. The adult insect is nearly 3 inches long, exclusive of its members; it is very heavy, clumsy, and slow in its movements.

There is but a single brood; after depositing its eggs, in September and October, the insect disappears and is not seen again until the young come out of the ground in the following spring.

Absence of enemies.—The Lubber Grasshopper has no known enemies. Predaceous animals cannot be induced to feed upon it, and doubtless its juices have an acrid and disagreeable flavor. Its sluggish habits, taken in connection with its conspicuous coloration, show that it has little need of concealment, and that it does not fear attacks of enemies. The eggs are probably preyed upon by some species of Bee-fly (*Bombyliidæ*), but if such an enemy exists it remains as yet undiscovered.

Remedy.—So large and conspicuous an insect is not likely ever to prove an alarming pest, and hardly requires elaborate directions for its management. If care is taken to destroy the young broods by trampling upon them when they appear in early summer, and before they have scattered, there will be an end to anxiety from this source for the season, and with a little pains taken at the proper time for two or three successive seasons a farm may be entirely rid of these 'hoppers, even if previously much infested by them.

OTHER LOCUSTS (*Acridiidæ*).

The various species of Acridiidæ, grasshoppers, as they are commonly called, nibble the leaves of orange trees, but do serious injury only where weeds are allowed to grow up around the trees. From their size and voracity the species of the genus Acridium, of which three are found in Florida, are most injurious. They are large insects, 2 or 2½ inches long, and are very active, jumping and flying to great distances.

In *Acridium obscurum* Burm. the general color is olive green, with fuscous dots and a yellow stripe from the head to the tip of the closed wings. The wing-covers are chocolate brown.

Acridium americanum Scud. (Fig. 55) is very similar, but the general

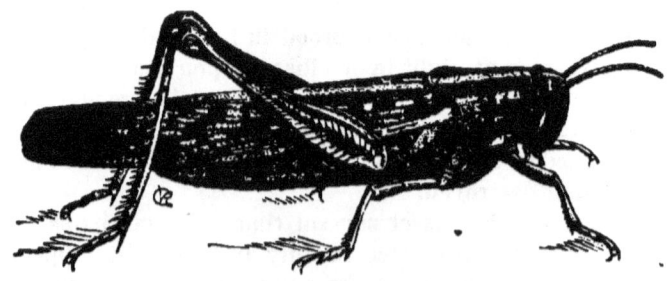

FIG. 55.—*Acridium americanum.* (After Riley.)

color is reddish-brown and the wing-covers are marked with large brownish spots.

Acridium alutaceum Harr. is dull brownish-yellow in color, and the wing-covers are marked with small spots. Like the Katydid, these larger grasshoppers occasion loss of growth, and stunt the plant by eating back the succulent ends of the shoots, as well as by consuming the leaves. With clean culture, and keeping the grove free from weeds and succulent plants, very little trouble will be experienced from the ravages of locusts, which are only attracted in numbers by dense masses of vegetation.

INSECTS OF THE ORDER LEPIDOPTERA.

THE ORANGE DOG.

(*Papilio cresphontes* Cramer.)

[Plate X and Plate XI, Figs. 1 and 2.]

The most important enemy to the Orange among this group of insects is a caterpillar 2½ inches long, of a dark brown color, with large blotches and markings of cream color. (Plate X, Fig. *b*.) The anterior part of the body is enlarged, and when at rest and not feeding the head is drawn in and turned under. The swollen extremity then presents a hideous, mask-like face, or dolphin head, of which the upper portion of the true head forms the snout, and two velvet-black spots in deep depressions on each side do duty as eyes. When irritated, the larva shoots forth from a fold just back of the head two long, fleshy, orange-colored tentacles, resembling a pair of horns. (Plate X, Figs. *c* and *d*.) These are scent-organs, emitting a penetrating odor, disagreeable alike to man and beast.

When full-grown, the larva retires to the vertical trunk or to some large branch of the tree, weaves a mat of strong thread to which it fastens itself by its terminal hooks, and with its head directed upwards slings itself at an angle to the trunk by means of a silken band passed around its body and fastened at the ends to the bark. Within this loop it changes to chrysalis by casting its larval skin. The chrysalis (Plate X, Fig. *e*) is a remarkable example of protective mimicry; the mixture of grey and brown colors, together with irregularities of form, such as projecting points upon the breast and at the upper end, give it a very close resemblance to a dead, lichen-covered twig.

From this somber-colored case issues in time a large and gaily-colored butterfly, with wings above velvet-black, crossed by a double series of large yellow spots, and beneath yellow with black veins (Plate X, Fig. *a*). The under wings end in tails, and are adorned above with a pair of eye-like spots of red edged with black and surmounted by a thin crescent of blue. Upon the under side these spots are repeated, with the addition of a second pair of red blotches and a complete row of pale blue crescent-shaped spots.

This showy butterfly is one of the commonest insects in the South, and is seen everywhere flitting about in the orange groves.

Life-history.—The eggs are spherical, smooth and pearly in luster, with a dull red or reddish-yellow tinge, and are deposited singly, invariably upon the youngest and most tender shoots, usually upon the tips of the budding leaves (Plate XI, Fig. 1). The butterflies appear with the opening of spring from chrysalids formed in November and December. The first eggs are deposited early in February, or as soon as the new growth appears upon the orange trees. The eggs hatch in ten or twelve days. The caterpillar completes its growth in about thirty days, and remains in pupa from ten to fifteen days. About two months is thus occupied by a single brood, and there are four full broods during the season beginning with February and ending with October. The breeding is, however, continuous during the summer, and eggs are laid whenever new growth appears upon the orange trees.

The ovaries contain over five hundred eggs, the laying of which occupies the female many days; she scatters them over a wide area, seldom depositing more than four or five upon a single plant. The young caterpillars feed at first only upon the tenderest leaves, but when well grown demolish both leaves and shoots which have not hardened into wood.

On account of its large size and voracity, the Orange Dog does great damage, particularly to young trees, which are sometimes completely defoliated. It has other food plants besides the Orange; among the number the species of Prickly Ash (*Zanthoxylum*) are mentioned by several authors. It is found commonly in the swamps of Florida, feeding upon the Tupelo (*Nyssa aquatica*, L.) and upon the Red Bay (*Persea carolinensis*, Nees). It seems, however, to prefer the Orange and its relatives to all other plants.

Defensive measures.—Hand-picking is not a very difficult task in the case of so large an insect, and must in most cases be relied upon to keep young trees free from Orange Dogs. As the eggs are quite large, and conspicuously placed at the tips of the growing stalks and budding leaves, it is a simple matter to find and pinch them between the fingers. A very little practice will enable the orange-grower to go rapidly through his young grove and destroy by hand nearly every egg. If this method is systematically pursued, the result will well repay the trouble. Two rules should be borne in mind, and will greatly facilitate the work. (1.) Only those trees which are pushing out tender sprouts need be examined for eggs and young larvæ.* (2.) In nearly all cases the eggs are laid upon sprouts at the top of the young tree and not upon those low down and near the ground.

---

* While this rule in regard to the disposition of the egg can be predicated with great confidence for the orange district of Florida, it is but just to observe that it may not hold good for Louisiana and other more northern localities. Mr. L. O. Howard has in fact found the eggs of *Papilio cresphontes* upon the older leaves, and on the twigs of orange trees, growing in public parks in the city of Savannah, Ga. The observation was made about the middle of August.

THE ORANGE DOG.

A great deal can be accomplished towards reducing the numbers of the Orange Dog, by destroying the butterflies; the most effective implement for this purpose is a light fowling-piece, loaded with dust shot or coarse salt. It may seem somewhat ridiculous to advocate the shooting of butterflies, but an insect which has a spread of wing of four or five inches affords a by no means despicable object for target practice. A more certain method for those not skilled at shooting on the wing is to attract the butterflies from a distance by planting in some convenient place a bed of flowering plants. It is a common sight to see a dozen or more individuals of this butterfly hovering over a garden bed of Phlox or Zænias, within easy range of the drowsy orange-grower, as he takes his midday siesta upon the veranda. What a loss of opportunity it is to allow these foes to escape and continue their havoc in the orange grove.

PARASITES.—A *Tachina* fly, with a hairy body, and somewhat larger than a common house-fly, which it superficially resembles, attacks the caterpillars when partly grown, and deposits upon each several elongate, oval, white eggs; these hatch maggots, which penetrate the skin of their host and feed upon its body-contents, eventually killing the worm. The tachinized caterpillar usually attempts to pupate, but strength fails, and it dies suspended in its silken loop. The parasitic maggots eat their way out and drop to the ground, in which they form oval puparia. They emerge as flies in twelve or fifteen days, or, if the season is far advanced, remain in the ground during the two or three months of winter, and issue with the return of warm weather in February. From four to eight flies are bred from a single Orange Dog.

Chalcis robusta Cresson. (Fig. 56.)—From the chrysalis of *Papilio cresphontes* there sometimes issues, instead of the butterfly, a four-

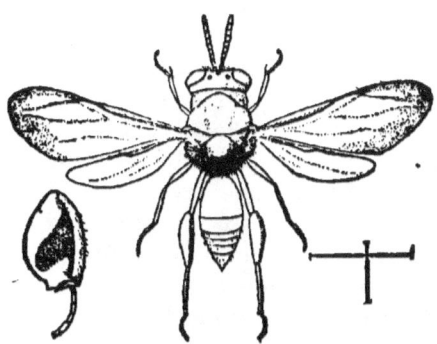

FIG. 56.—*Chalcis robusta*. (Original.)

winged fly. This parasite is a large and handsome member of a family, the Chalcididæ, composed for the most part of minute forms. It is 8.4^{mm} ($\frac{3}{10}$ inch) long; in color black, with golden-yellow legs. The posterior thighs are swollen, and adorned with an oblique band of black across the middle. The wings are smoky. The head and thorax are very coarsely punctured, and clothed with short, golden hairs. The fly in quitting its host makes a large, round hole in he side of the chrysalis. All the specimens obtained emerged in June or July from pupæ of the second brood. There can be no doubt that this parasite would in case of undue multiplication of the Orange Dog become an efficient check upon its increase. At present, however, it is somewhat rare.

SLUG CATERPILLARS—STINGING CATERPILLARS.

Several species of Bombycidæ, called "slug caterpillars," because of their apparent want of legs, and their gliding, snail-like movements, are occasionally found doing damage to orange trees by feeding upon the leaves. The hairy species are known as "stinging caterpillars," being provided with nettling hairs. They are all of rather large size, an inch or more in length, and have sluggish habits. They construct stout and very tough cocoons, attached to the bark of the tree, and they know how to conceal them with great art. The perfect insects are moths, with rather thick, heavy bodies, covered with long, downy hairs, and flying only at night. The four species which are known to feed upon the Orange are *Lagoa opercularis* Sm. & Abb., *Empretia stimulea* Clem., *Phobetron pithecium* Sm. & Abb., and *Limacodes scapha* Harr.

LAGOA OPERCULARIS Sm. & Abb.

[Figs. 57, 58, 59.]

The caterpillars of this moth are covered with long, silky hair, underneath which are concealed shorter, stiff hairs, exceedingly sharp at the points, and powerfully nettling when they penetrate the flesh. Upon some persons the invisible wounds made by these hairs produce swellings, and an amount of irritation equivalent to a sting; the larvæ are, in consequence, popularly supposed to be very poisonous. When young the caterpillars are white and resemble a flock of cotton wool. They undergo six molts, at one of the last of which they become darker, the color varying in individuals, from red-brown to light clay-color. When full-grown the larva presents the singular appearance of a lock of hair possessing sluggish life and a gliding, snail-like motion. It is 1½ inches long, bluntly rounded in front and diminishing rapidly to a point behind. The hair rises in a sharp ridge upon the back, and forms several tufts of rust-red color.

Fig. 57.—*Lagoa opercularis*, larva. (After Riley.)

The cocoon (Fig. 58) is placed in a crotch of the tree or upon a branch of considerable size; it is 20^{mm} ($\frac{8}{10}$ inch) long, oval, convex, flattened on the side next the tree, and fastened very firmly to the bark. The upper end is abruptly truncate, and fitted with a hinged trap-door, which is readily pushed open from within by the escaping moth, but does not yield to pressure from without, and is so accurately fitted that no tell-tale crack can be discerned. Upon the back of the cocoon is an elevation formed by the meeting of several folds and ridges, forming a marvelously exact imitation of a winter bud. The ends of a lock of hair from the body of the caterpillar counterfeit the down which in nature protects the dormant bud. The substance of which the cocoon is made is a tough parchment, composed of agglutinated silk, in which is felted the long, hairy covering of the larva. Its color is a neutral brown, closely approximating to that of the bark upon which it is placed. The entire arrangement is a most successful representation of the stump of a small branch broken off near its junction with the main stem, and upon which is plainly shown the swelling of a bud.

FIG. 58.—*Lagoa opercularis*, cocoon. (Original.)

The perfect insect (Fig. 59) is a moth with a very wooly body, pale yellow, tinged with brown. The fore wings are umber-brown at the base, fading to pale yellow outwardly; the surface is marked with fine wavy lines of silver gray, and the fore margins are nearly black. The legs are yellow, with dusky feet. The wings of the male moth spread about one inch; those of the female an inch and a half.

FIG. 59.—*Lagoa opercularis*, moth. (Original.)

Life-history.—The larva is a very general feeder, and although the Oak appears to be its principal food plant, it is occasionally injurious to the Orange. It never injures the bark or tender shoots, but subsists only upon the mature leaves.

There are two broods, one in early summer and the other in the fall. The larvæ of the second brood form their cocoons in November or December, and in them pass the winter, not changing to pupa until the following March or April, or about two weeks before the moths appear.

Parasites.—The same parasites have been bred from Lagoa as from the Orange Dog. Tachina flies issued in June from a cocoon found on Orange in March. The hymenopterous parasite *Chalcis robusta* issued September 15 from a cocoon collected August 27.

THE SADDLE-BACK CATERPILLAR.

(*Empretia stimulea* Clemens.)

[Figs. 60 and 61, and Plate XI, Fig. 3.]

The caterpillar of this species, also a general feeder, is short and thick, and very strangely marked with a large, quadrate patch of green, in the center of which is an oval spot of purple, so that the animal appears to have thrown across its back a green cloth surmounted by a purple saddle. The fringing hairs along the sides of the larva have irritating properties like the concealed nettling hairs of Lagoa.

The cocoons are short, oval, almost globular, flattened against the branch to which they are attached, and are of the same tough, parchment-like material and brown color as in Lagoa. They are usually placed in concealment, often against the main trunk of the tree, at or near the surface of the ground. The larva before pupating cuts a circular flap at the end, making an opening nearly equal to the entire diameter of the cocoon, through which the moth makes its escape by pushing open the door from within.

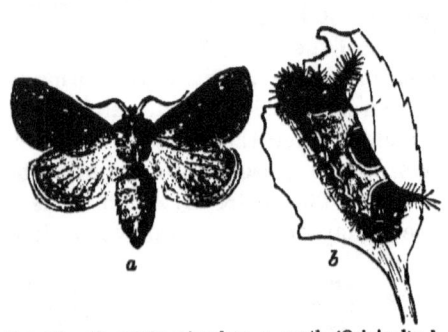

FIG. 60.—*Empretia stimulea*: *a*, moth (Original); *b*, larva (after Riley).

The moth has a wooly body and legs of rich maroon color, with the base of the abdomen and the under wings of lighter brown. The scales of the fore-wing lie flat and have a silken sheen upon the prominent veins and margin, while in the depressions between the veins they stand erect, as in velvet, giving an embossed appearance to the wing.

FIG. 61.—*Empretia stimulea*, cocoon. (Original.)

The upper surface of the fore-wing bears several dots of pale yellow, each consisting of a few opalescent scales. The dots are arranged in two pairs, one at the base and the other at the apex of the wing, with a single minute fleck placed half-way between the pairs.

Parasite.—The larva is destroyed by a Microgaster.

THE HAG-MOTH CATERPILLAR.

(*Phobetron pithecium*, Smith and Abbot.)

[Figs. 62 and 63.]

This insect receives its name from the curious hairy appendages which cover the back and project from the sides of the larva, and have a backward twist, like locks of dishevelled hair. These are, in fact, fleshy hooks, covered with feathery, brown hairs, among which are longer, black, stinging hairs. The larva is 15^{mm} ($\frac{6}{10}$ inch) long and has an oval body, over which, however, the flattened and closely applied appendages form a nearly square shield. The cocoon (Fig. 63) is almost spherical, like that of the Saddle-back caterpillar, and is defended by the hairy appendages which the larva in some way contrives to leave upon the out-

SLUG CATERPILLARS ON ORANGE.

side. These tufts give to the bullet-shaped cocoon a very nondescript appearance, and the stinging hairs afford a very perfect protection against birds and other insectivorous animals.

Unlike the preceding species, the Hag-moth larvæ do not seek to hide away their cocoons, but attach them to leaves and twigs fully exposed to view, with, however, such artful management as to surroundings and harmonizing colors that they are of all the group the most difficult to discover. A device to which this insect frequently resorts exhibits the extreme of instinctive sagacity. If the caterpillar cannot find at hand a suitable place in which to weave its cocoon it frequently makes for itself more satisfactory surroundings by killing the leaves, upon which, after they have become dry and brown in color, it places its cocoon.

FIG. 62.—*Phobetron pithecium*, larva. (After Riley.)

Several of these caterpillars unite together, and selecting a long and vigorous immature shoot or leader of the orange tree, they kill it by cutting into its base until it wilts and bends over.

The leaves of a young shoot, in drying, turn a light tan-color, which harmonizes most perfectly with the hairy locks of the caterpillar covering the cocoon. The latter is, consequently, not easily detected, even when placed upon the exposed and upturned surface of the leaf.

The moth has body and legs of purple-brown, with ochreous patches on the back and a light yellow tuft on the middle pair of legs. The abdomen is sable, ending in a tuft of ochreous scales. The fore-wings have the colors of the thorax finely mingled, as in graining. The hind-wings are sable, bordered with ochreous in the female. The fore wings of the male are long and narrow, the hind-wings short and very triangular. Both pairs are, in this sex, partly transparent.

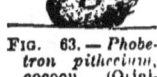

FIG. 63.— *Phobetron pithecium*, cocoon. (Original.)

The spread of wing varies in this moth from 20 to 24^{mm} ($\frac{8}{10}$ inch to $\frac{98}{100}$ inch).

THE SKIFF-CATERPILLAR.

(*Limacodes scapha* Harris.)

[Figs. 64 and 65.]

The generic name *Limacodes*, signifying slug-like, is very appropriately given to this naked and slow-moving caterpillar, which is thus described by Harris: "Body thick, and its outline nearly diamond-shaped; the back is a little hollowed and the middle of each side rises to an obtuse angle; it is of green color with the elevated edges brown. The boat-like form of this caterpillar induced me to name it *Limacodes scapha*, the skiff Limacodes." (Ins. Inj. to Vegetation, p. 419.)

The larva (Fig. 64) lives upon Hickory, Oak, &c., but has been reported as feeding also upon orange leaves. It forms a tough, rounded-oval cocoon. The moth (Fig. 65) is cinnamon-brown; upon each fore-

Fig. 64.—*Limacodes scapha*, larva.
(Re-drawn from Harris.)

Fig. 65.—*Limacodes scapha*, moth.
(After Packard.)

wing is a large tan-colored spot with a border of silver. It has a spread of wing, in the female, of 30^{mm} (1.2 inches).

The life-histories of the four species of slug-caterpillars are similar, and that given above for the first species may be assumed to apply to each of the others. The same parasites are probably common to them all.

BAG-WORMS.

[Plate XII.]

Worms living in cases made of sticks or leaves, and which they carry about with them from place to place, and enlarge with their growth. Pupæ formed within the the case of the larva. Males issuing as small moths, not differing greatly from others of the same family. Females remaining wingless, degraded forms, to the end of their existence, when they leave the protecting sack, in order to make room for their eggs, and die.

THE COMMON BAG-WORM OR BASKET-WORM.

(*Oiketicus abbotii* Grote.)

The baskets of this species are very large, those of the female over two inches long; the sack of the male is, however, only one-third as long as that of the female.

The caterpillar is dirty brown in color. The first three joints, which bear the legs, and are protruded from the case when the animal moves about, are protected by horny shields, and together with the head are mottled and streaked with light and dark brown. When young the case is carried erect upon the upturned end of the body, but as the worm grows larger and the basket becomes heavy with the weight of sticks and fragments of which it is composed, it is allowed to hang down.

The Bag-worm is an omnivorous and most voracious feeder; nothing vegetable appears to come amiss to it, and it sometimes is common enough upon orange trees to do serious damage, especially as it does not confine itself to the leaves, but also gnaws the tender bark of the shoots and cuts off bits of the twigs with which to form its basket. The basket is differently constructed to suit its surroundings; on oak it is usually formed of bits of rounded twigs, placed crosswise after the fashion of a log cabin; on trees with dense foliage like the Orange it is oftener fashioned with leaf material. In all cases it is thickly lined and firmly bound together with strong, grayish-white silk, and is too tough to be torn asunder with the fingers. Before the larva becomes a pupa the bag is suspended by a band of silk to a twig or branch.

The winged male escapes from the sack leaving the pupa shell protruding. It is a rather thick-bodied moth of dark brown color. The abdomen is very long, slender, and tapering to the point, which is armed with a pair of shell-like claspers, and these conceal the point of the intromittent male organ. These parts are very elastic and extensile, and enable the male to reach deeply into the sack of the female, in the act of coupling. The fore-wings of the male are rather long and narrow; they are slightly paler than the body, and are marked with a short oblique line, devoid of feathers, and situated just beyond the middle of the wing. The hind wings are short and angular.

The female is without wings or legs, and is, in fact, hardly more than a living egg-sack. When fully mature the pupa splits at the anterior end, and the body of the female protrudes. Without entirely leaving the pupa shell, but dragging it after her, she works her way to the mouth of the basket, where she awaits the visit of the male, having her head at the outlet.

In what precise manner the act of fertilization takes place is not well understood,* but as soon as it is accomplished, the female pushes herself backwards to the farther end of the basket, and, her hinder extremity being still within the pupa shell, she proceeds to fill it nearly full of pearly, cream-colored eggs, packed in silk. The vacant space at the end is then filled with a tangle of floss silk, mingled with feather scales, which the mother plucks from her own body. When finally her body is entirely withdrawn from the pupa shell the lips of the T-shaped slit at the end snap together, entirely closing the exit.

The female continues to work her way slowly outward, weaving as she goes a tangle of silk, mingled with scales stripped from her own body. Having filled the entire space within the basket, and lest she should imperil the safety of her young by remaining in the case to die, the mother completes the sacrifice by dropping from its mouth. Her exhausted body, shorn of its downy covering, falls to the ground, where, naked and defenceless, it becomes a ready prey to ants and other prowlers.

How wonderful an example is here shown of the power of the maternal instinct, which can thus overpower the instinct of self-preservation in an unreasoning insect, and compel her to yield to her offspring, unborn and unseen, a secure retreat, which otherwise in life she never leaves, and from which she could not be torn except piecemeal.

The eggs of the Bag-worm hatch in September. The young larvæ

---

* See Appendix III.

(Pl. XII, Fig. 2, *a*) push or eat their way out of the pupa shell of the mother, and emerge from the mouth of the basket. They almost immediately begin to form their cases, which they make of any material soft enough to be rasped by their jaws. A bit of cork, for example, is exactly suited to their wants. The process of forming the basket is curious, and, observed under a lens, is as follows: The larva cuts off with its jaws a fragment of cork, of a size and shape determined by the cavity of the mouth; each fragment is, in fact, a mouthful, which the larva ejects and places between its front legs, adding one to another to form a pile, which from time to time it fastens loosely with web. (Plate XII, Fig. 2, *b*.) Pieces are added at the sides until the pile becomes a transverse tangle about as long as the body and placed at right angles to it. Each end of the pile is fastened loosely to the surface on which it rests, and several strands of silk are laid along it from end to end. Then, standing with its body astride of the tangle, the larva bends down its head, and dives under the mass, turning a complete somersault, so that when its head and fore part of the body appear on the other side, the insect lies on its back, bound down by the fillet of silk and bits of cork, which still remain fastened to the surface at the ends. (Plate XII, Fig. 2, *c*.) With a quick movement the larva twists around and stands again upon its feet, having its neck, as it were, under a yoke. (Plate XII, Fig. 2, *d*.) It then makes of the yoke a complete collar by adding bits of cork to each end until the circle is complete. Row after row of fragments is added to this, until the collar becomes a hollow cylinder within which the body of the little workman gradually disappears. (Plate XII, Fig. 2, *e*.) Each fragment as it is ejected from the mouth is fastened by one end to the edge of the band, and secured with a few rapid passes of the silk-producing mouth-organs. From time to time the larva cuts the anchoring threads, shifts its work, and fastens it down again. Like a skillful artisan it works rapidly, not stopping to finish the work as it goes, but only occasionally strengthening it with a few strands of silk on the inside, until the cylinder is long enough to entirely cover its body. One end is then closed up and the inside well coated and finished with a tough lining of silk; the case meantime standing upright and fastened by one end. (Plate XII, Fig. 2, *f*.) When fully completed the larva cuts loose the anchoring cables, and marches off, with the case borne aloft like a cap, on the upturned end of its body. This case of the young larva is constantly enlarged, until it becomes the basket of the adult.

The Bag-worm appears to be single-brooded, and the winter is passed by the young larvæ in their cases. Pupæ are formed late in summer. The males emerge, the females deposit their eggs and perish, and the young hatch during the month of September. Hand-picking must be relied upon to rid the trees of Bag-worms whenever this becomes necessary.

Parasites.—The Bag-worm is attacked by an Ichneumonid, *Hemiteles thyridopterigis* Riley. (Plate XII, Fig. 3.) The females (*b*) are dull red, with banded wings, and are rather more than one-third of an inch (9^{mm}) long. The males (*a*) are slender, with black, shining bodies and clear wings; they are somewhat smaller than the females (8^{mm}). A number of the parasites inhabit a single case of the Bag-worm, which they partly fill with a consolidated mass of their own dark-brown, parchment-like pupa cases. (Fig. 3, *c*.). The parasites cut their way out through the thick sides of the Bag-worm follicle, each individual apparently making an exit-hole of its own.

Another Ichneumonid, *Pimpla conquisitor* (Say) (Plate XII, Fig. 4), will undoubtedly prove to be parasitic upon this Bag-worm, as it has been bred from other, closely related species, and is a very common enemy of many large caterpillars in the south. It has a rather slender body of black, banded with white, and clear wings. It is about 0.4 inch long. It is a solitary parasite, the female depositing but a single egg in each worm which she stings.

A third and much smaller parasite, *Microgaster* sp., issues late in September from the young larva cases of Oiketicus, in which it spins a snow-white silken cocoon of its own. The parasitic fly is red-brown in color, with dark antennæ and ovipositor. It measures 3^{mm} (0.12 inch) in length, exclusive of appendages.

NORTHERN BAG-WORM.

(*Thyridopteryx ephemeræformis*, Haworth.)

[Plate XII, Fig. 1.)]

This Bag-worm bears a very close resemblance to Oiketicus, and appears to replace it in the North, where it is particularly injurious to Cedars. It is not certainly known to occur in Florida, but may be found in the northern part of the orange belt. Its case is formed in the same way and its life-history is probably similar to that of Oiketicus. The pupa of Oiketicus is, however, chestnut-brown, while that of Thyridopteryx is dark mahogany in color. The baskets of both species vary in construction, and are not readily distinguished the one from the other. The male of Thyridopteryx is black, with transparent wings.

PARASITES.— Besides the Ichneumonid, *Hemiteles thyridopterigis* Riley, which was first known as a parasite of this Northern Bag-worm, and has been noticed above, several other related parasites are mentioned by authors as preying upon Thyridopteryx.

Pimpla inquisitor (Say) (Plate XII, Fig. 5) is mentioned by Mr. Glover as destructive to this Bag-worm. It has a black body, with parti-colored legs; the face is white in the male. Length about one-tenth inch.

The Yellow-banded Ichneumon (*Pimpla conquisitor*, Say) (Plate XII, Fig. 4).—This is also a common parasite of the Cotton Worm and other large moths. It closely resembles the preceding, but the joints of the abdomen are ringed with white. It is mentioned by Lintner as one of the parasites of the Northern Bag-worm.* The species varies in length from about one-quarter of an inch to over half an inch.

In Harris's Entomological Correspondence, p. 242, we find the following: "The parasite of the drop-worm is *Ichneumon concitator* Say, a very common and somewhat variable species, which attacks all sorts of larvæ. It is one of the most common parasites of *Clisiocampa americana*." No mention of this species can be found elsewhere than in Harris's writings, and the presumption is that a confusion has been made between names of similar sound, and that either *Pimpla conquisitor* or *Cryptus inquisitor* was intended.

THE CYLINDRICAL BAG-WORM.

(*Psyche* sp.)

The cases of a Bag-worm supposed to belong to the genus *Psyche* are sometimes seen upon orange trees; they are not spindle-shaped, as in the preceding species, but cylindrical, and the fragments composing the outside are laid on longitudinally. The fragments usually consist of bits of straw or dead pine-needles, some of which are very long and project beyond or out from the sides of the case. The basket of the female is about 38^{mm} (1½ inches); that of the male 25^{mm} (1 inch) in length, exclusive of projecting points. The female is wingless; its pupa-case is of a light chestnut-brown, and is 15^{mm} ($\frac{9}{16}$ inch) long.

Fig. 66 represents the basket of the male of *Psyche confederata*, with the pupa-shell protruding. (Reproduced from Trans. Amer. Ent. Soc., vol. II, Plate III, Fig. 67.)

FIG. 66.—*Psyche confederata* G. & R. (After Grote.)

The male remains unknown; it is a winged moth, which probably resembles *Psyche confederata* G. and R., but is larger and possibly lighter in color.†

The life-history of this Bag-worm is undoubtedly similar to, if not identical with that of Oiketicus and Thyridopteryx.

THE ORANGE BASKET-WORM.

(*Platœceiicus gloverii* Packard.)

[Fig. 67.]

A much smaller species than the preceding was first mentioned by Mr. Glover, who gave an account of its habits in the Patent Office

---

* First Annual Report of the Injurious and Other Insects of the State of New York, by J. A. Lintner, page 84.

† The male of *Psyche confederata* G. and R., is "entirely deep, smoky black. Antennæ plumose. Wings ample, closely scaled, rounded and full. * * * Expanse, 19^{mm}: Length of body, 7^{mm}." The specimens described by Grote and Robinson (Trans. Am. Ent. Soc., vol. II, p. 191) were sent from Texas. Plate III, fig. 67, gives a representation of the basket of this species. Similar cases, which may possibly belong to this species, have been seen upon the Orange in Florida.

Agricultural Report for 1858. Its basket is spindle-shaped, that of the female 18^{mm} ($\frac{7}{10}$ inch), and that of the male 13^{mm} ($\frac{1}{2}$ inch) long. It is covered with finely chopped bits of dry leaf, bark, moss and other scraps, supplemented not unfrequently with the scales of Bark-lice. As an additional protection, several small orange thorns are often fastened to the outside of the case, with their sharp tips projecting backwards and outwards. The pupa case is dark mahogany-brown, and the sutures between the joints are opaque, black, forming on the female pupa three, and on the male pupa four, very distinct rings. The male is a small, dark-brown moth, measuring 16^{mm} ($\frac{0.4}{100}$ inch) across the extended wings. The female, as in the preceding Bag-worms, is wingless, and undergoes a development similar to that of Oiketicus.

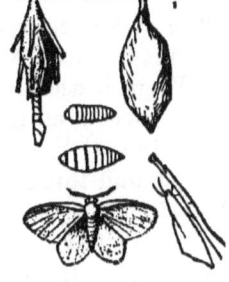

FIG. 67—*Platœceticus gloverii*. (After Glover.)

UNNAMED BAG-WORM.

[Fig. 68.]

A species of Bag-worm smaller than any of the preceding exists upon Orange, and is not uncommon. Its cases are long, slender, and cylindrical, and covered with fragments of bark, straw, &c.; many of these are linear, and have projecting ends. The female case (Fig. 68a) is

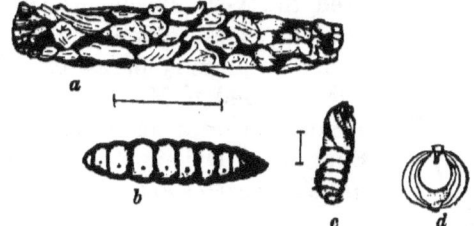

FIG. 68.—Unknown Bag-worm on Orange: *a*, case of female; *b*, pupa of female; *c*, pupa of male; *d* end of male pupa, enlarged. (Original.)

15^{mm} ($\frac{8}{10}$ inch), and that of the male 12^{mm} ($\frac{48}{100}$ inch) long. The pupa of the female (Fig. 68, *b*) measures 8^{mm} ($\frac{32}{100}$ inch) in length. The male pupa (Fig. 68, *c*; *d*, end of pupa enlarged) is very minute, being only half the size of the female. Both are slender, bluntly-rounded at the ends, and of a light chestnut color.

This small species is allied to *Psyche confederata*, by the slender form and light color of its pupa, as well as by the construction and cylindrical shape of its case. In Platœceticus, on the other hand, the fusiform shape and dark color of the case and pupa, indicate a closer relationship to Oiketicus.*

---

* The species of Bag-worms are more numerous than has been supposed, and several undescribed species are confused in collections with the few species hitherto described.

LEAF-EATERS WITHOUT CASES.

ARTACE PUNCTISTRIGA Walker.

The following account of this insect appears in the report of the Commissioner of Agriculture for 1880, p. 252:

"There is occasionally to be found upon the orange a fusiform white silken cocoon, an inch and a half in length. From this cocoon there issues in spring a thick-bodied woolly white moth, the female measuring an inch and three-quarters, and the male an inch and one-quarter across the wings. Each fore wing has five transverse rows of small black dots. We have not seen the caterpillar which spins this cocoon, but from an examination of the cast-off skin to be found at the end of the pupa, and from other facts, we may readily state it to be a rather thick larva, about an inch and a half in length, and covered with long mixed black and whitish hairs, giving it a grayish effect. These cocoons are not confined to orange, but are also found upon the grass at the foot of the tree, and one specimen received was evidently found upon cherry, as pieces of the bark still adhered. The species seems to be comparatively rare, but, as we have said before of other species, it is liable at any time to increase and become injurious; therefore the sooner it is treated of the better. As one of the causes of its rarity we may mention the existence of a large ichneumonid parasite, which we have not been able to breed, owing to the fact that it in its turn is parasitized by a chalcid, of which we have bred thirty-six specimens from a single cocoon, all having made their exit, as usual, from a single hole. It is possible that this chalcid may also be a primary parasite. The specimens were referred to Mr. Howard for study, and decided to be a new species of the genus Encyrtus of Dalman." It was described (*loc. cit.*) as *Encyrtus artaceæ* n. sp.

THE GRASS-WORM.

(*Laphygma frugiperda*, Sm. & Abb.)

[Figs. 69 and 70.]

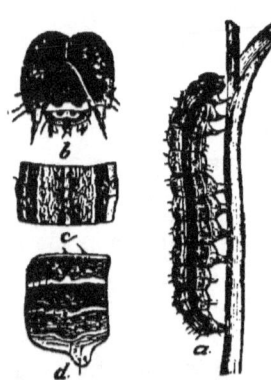

FIG. 69.—*Laphygma frugiperda:* a, larva, natural size; b, head; c, middle joint from above; d, do. from side, enlarged. (After Riley.)

Patches of the eggs of this common moth are very commonly found on orange leaves. But although the young caterpillars eat the leaves to some extent, they soon find their way to some other and more succulent food-plant. Full-grown caterpillars are scarcely ever seen upon the Orange, although they can be bred upon it in confinement.

The eggs are dull white, with a pearly luster. The clusters contain a variable number of eggs, and are covered with mouse-colored down from the body of the mother.

The caterpillars grow to the length of an inch and a half. They are very variable in color, the young being dark, sometimes nearly black, and the adults of lighter color, varying from brown to pale green, with fine mottlings of other colors. Several broad stripes of dark and light brown, running from head to tail, render this caterpillar conspicuous and easily recognized.

The moth belongs to the numerous group of Owlet Moths, called in the South "Candle Flies." It has narrow front wings of gray and brown, finely intermingled; and the semi-transparent hind wings of dull white, with smoky margins. Spread of wings about one and a quarter inches.

The pupa is polished, mahogany-brown, and is formed in a simple, unlined cell beneath the surface of the ground. The transformations of this insect are completed in one month. There are several broods, but the worms are most numerous in August, and the moths in September.

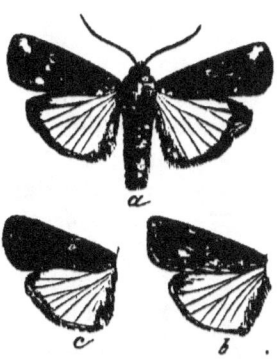

FIG. 70.—*Laphygma frugiperda;* a, moth, normal form; b, wings of variety *fusca;* c, do. of variety *obscura*—natural size. (After Riley.)

Orange groves which are kept clean will not be liable to injury from the Grass-worm, which feeds naturally upon grass and succulent herbs. Young groves are sometimes attacked when they are allowed to become foul and only cultivated at long intervals. The amount of damage done by this caterpillar is small, but it may, under special conditions, become a serious pest. Clean culture will in such cases prove an all-sufficient remedy.

LEAF-ROLLERS.

Slender, almost naked, worms, of small size, and usually yellowish-green in color, which roll up leaves, or bind together tender bud-leaves, to form a protecting tube, within which they lurk and feed, and in time transform to pupæ.

Before the moth issues, the pupa is pushed partly out of the tubular shield of leaves. Fig. 71 shows the pupa of *Platynota rostrana* protruding from the side of a folded orange leaf.

The adults are rather small moths, with pointed heads, and oblong, somewhat heavy fore wings, which, when folded, form a roof-like ridge over the body.

The eggs are laid upon the surfaces of leaves, in elongate, oval patches of transparent yellowish-green color. In these patches each egg forms an excessively thin overlapping scale, and the whole mass of fifty to eighty eggs is thus firmly knit together, and can be removed from the leaf without separating. The thinness and cellular structure of the egg-cluster give it a resemblance to certain low forms of vegetable life, and it might readily be mistaken for a mold or a lichen.

THE CORK-COLORED ORANGE TORTRICID.

(*Platynota rostrana*, Walker.)

[Fig. 71.]

The tubular webs of this species are very common and quite destructive to small seedling and nursery plants, as the worm is apt to select the tender budding leaves at the top of the plant, and by killing these check further growth. Both this and the other Tortricid leaf-rollers do occasional damage to the fruit by puncturing the rind beneath the shelter of a leaf, which they fasten with web to its surface.

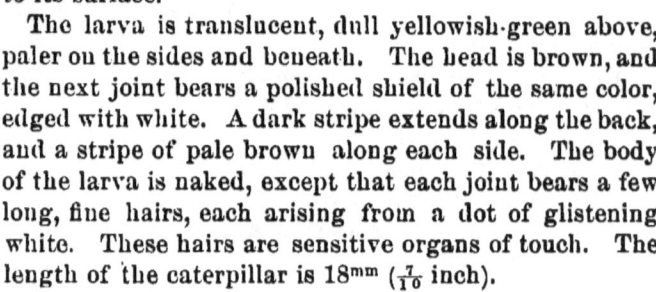

The larva is translucent, dull yellowish-green above, paler on the sides and beneath. The head is brown, and the next joint bears a polished shield of the same color, edged with white. A dark stripe extends along the back, and a stripe of pale brown along each side. The body of the larva is naked, except that each joint bears a few long, fine hairs, each arising from a dot of glistening white. These hairs are sensitive organs of touch. The length of the caterpillar is 18^{mm} ($\frac{7}{10}$ inch).

Fig. 71.—*Platynota rostrana*; pupa shell protruding from folded leaf. (Original.)

The pupa is of slender form and chestnut-brown color. It has six pairs of terminal hooks, with which it clings to its tubular web.

The male moths are much darker than the females, the upper wings cinnamon in color, with oblique bands of umber, and their surfaces much roughened with elevated tufts and ridges of coarse scales. The females are larger and the upper wings much lighter in color, the red being mingled with silver-gray. In this sex the tufts of scales are very minute, and the oblique bands are reduced to fine, elevated lines. Length of the male, with wings folded, 10^{mm} ($\frac{4}{10}$ inch); of the female, 12^{mm} ($\frac{48}{100}$ inch).

The eggs of each batch hatch simultaneously, the last caterpillar quitting its egg-shell a few minutes after the first. The young caterpillars immediately scatter over the plant, but hide in crevices at first, and do not begin rolling the leaves until they are three or four days old. They shed their skins five times during the eighteen or twenty days of their existence as larvæ. They remain eight or ten days in pupa. Allowing eight or ten days for the laying and hatching of the eggs, a period which is not certainly known, a single generation occupies less than six weeks. There are apparently four or five broods during the eight warm months, and an additional brood in mild winters, but the caterpillars may be found at all seasons of the year, and there is in fact very little evidence of a separation into distinct broods.

Hand-picking is the only remedy that can be relied upon, and by this method young trees can without difficulty be kept free from their attacks.

PARASITES.—*Trichogramma pretiosa* Riley.—This minute Chalcid fly, well known as the parasite which renders effective aid by destroying the eggs of the Cotton Worm, also infests the egg clusters of the Orange Leaf-roller. The mother parasite deposits a single egg in each cell like egg of the Tortrix, and within this narrow cell the young parasite finds food and domicile until it has completed all its changes. Then it eats its way out, making a ragged hole in the shell, and emerges as a perfect four-winged fly like its parent. The fly is 0.3^{mm} ($\frac{1}{100}$ inch) long, clear yellow in color, with ruby eyes and iridescent, hyaline wings, which are delicately fringed with hairs.

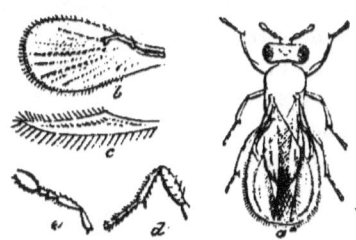

FIG. 72.—*Trichogramma minuta.* (After Riley.)

It has been bred from the Tortrix eggs in March and also in September. Fig. 72 represents *Trichogramma minuta*, a closely-allied species, which differs from *Trichogramma pretiosa* only in color and the form of the small joints of the antennæ.

Miotropis platynotæ Howard.[12]—A slender hymenopterous fly has been bred from the larva of the Orange Leaf-roller. It is honey-yellow; head lemon-yellow, with dark eyes and antennæ. The head is much wider than long, and bears above three dark-colored, simple eyelets (ocelli). The wings are hyaline. Three or four maggots of the parasite are found living within a single caterpillar of the Tortrix, which is at last almost completely devoured by them. The parasites form naked pupæ, loosely disposed within the tubular web of the destroyed Leaf-roller, and in about nine days change to adult flies by casting the thin, transparent skin of the pupa. The flies were obtained in September.

Polysphincta albipes Cresson.—Cocoons of slightly yellowish, coarse silk, loosely spun, were found by Professor Comstock on an orange leaf, at Rock Ledge, Fla. The flies issued in February. They have been described by Mr. Cresson in the Report of the Commissioner for 1879, p. 208. The body is dull red, smooth and polished; head black, with white mandibles; wings hyaline, and legs white. Length 7^{mm} ($\frac{28}{100}$ inch). This insect is somewhat doubtfully considered a parasite of *Tortrix rostrana*.

Goniozus n. sp.;[13] family *Proctotrupidæ*.—A minute parasite is bred from the caterpillar of the Leaf-roller. It has a shining, black body, with yellow legs and antennæ, and hyaline wings, with a dark-brown stigmal spot. Length 2.5^{mm} ($\frac{1}{10}$ inch). Four or five of the parasites are found in a single caterpillar. They spin oval cocoons of whitish silk within the tubular web of the Tortrix. The parasites issued October 1.

THE SULPHUR-COLORED TORTRICID.

(Dichelia [Tortrix] sulphureana, Clem.)

The caterpillars of this widely-distributed Leaf-roller are very general feeders. In the northern States they are frequently injurious to Clover; in the South the long list of their food-plants includes Cotton, Strawberry, Grape, and Orange; upon the latter they are somewhat rarely found, and it is probable that the thick leaves of the citrus family are not well adapted to the needs of this species. The caterpillar bears, a close general resemblance to that of *Platynota rostrana,* but is somewhat smaller, and the head and thorax are pale yellow. The pupa is dark mahogany brown, almost black. The moth is sulphur-yellow above; the upper wings are marked with red-brown, or purple-brown. The markings vary greatly in different individuals, forming a double letter Y or an X upon the folded wings, but are sometimes reduced to a series of dots, representing only the terminal and intersecting points of these letters. The under wings are varying shades between yellow and brown. Length from the tip of the beak to the extremity of the folded wings, 11^{mm} ($\frac{44}{100}$ inch). The life-history and habits of this species in Florida are probably the same as *Platynota rostrana.* In the Report of the Commissioner of Agriculture for 1880 will be found an account of both species. *T. sulphureana* is there said to have three generations in a year in the latitude of the District of Columbia, and probably only one in middle and northern Maine.

LARGER LEAF-ROLLER.

(Tortrix?)[14]

This is a somewhat larger insect than *Platynota rostrana,* from which, however, the larva differs only in minute details. The pupa also is similar to that of *P. rostrana.* The moth is rust-red, with three oblique bands of maroon-red upon the upper wings, and their anterior (outer) edge is sinuate.

The habits of this species are precisely the same as the foregoing, but the larva being larger is more destructive, and often half cuts off small twigs of tender growth, the leaves of which it folds and binds together longitudinally, and feeds without preference upon the wilted leaves within its retreat, or upon the fresh leaves of surrounding branches.

WEB-MAKERS.

THE ORANGE-LEAF NOTHRIS.

(Nothris citrifoliella Chambers.)

The caterpillars of a minute moth have been reported from the extreme southern portion of the orange district, as doing injury in the groves. The following account of it is found in the Annual Report of the Commissioner of Agriculture for 1879, p. 205:

" Specimens of this insect were last summer received from Brevard

County, Florida. We do not know enough of its habits at present to do more than describe it and its methods of work.

"According to Mr. H. S. Williams, of Rock Ledge, the larvæ have been very injurious to the orange trees in his vicinity. They infest the young leaves of the new growth. These they web together by a delicate white silken web, and feed upon the bud, entirely stopping the growth of the shoot. If disturbed, the worm drops by a thread. It is very active, and when removed from its web runs quite quickly.

"The full-grown larva measures about 12^{mm} ($\frac{1}{2}$ inch) in length. It is yellowish in color, with the head and first thoracic segment black and somewhat polished. The posterior margin of the black thorax is pale-yellow. The anal plate and legs are polished yellow, with the scattered hairs upon the former blackish; all other hairs are yellow. The first pair of legs is black and the rest yellow.

"When ready to pupate, the larva rolls a leaf around itself and spins a delicate silken cocoon, in which it transforms to a rather stout, dark-brown chrysalis. There is nothing so characteristic about the chrysalis as to merit description. The moths emerged from August 25 to September 5."*

THE ORANGE WEB-WORM.

(*Anæglis demissalis* Led.)

[Plate XIII, Fig. 1, 1*a*, 1*b*.]

The caterpillars of this interesting little moth are not uncommon upon orange trees, but so remarkably well protected are they by their form, color, and surroundings, that the skill of the collector will be taxed to the utmost in discovering them.

They surround themselves with a tangle of web, involving several twigs and small branches, together with their leaves. (Plate XIII, Fig. 1.) Caterpillars of different ages will be found in each web, which they occupy in joint proprietorship with a small spider. Between this spider and the Anæglis there exists the most perfect harmony. In fact, so close is the association of these allies, that the Web-worm is never seen except in company with the spider, and the webs of the latter are seldom without the presence of the caterpillars.

It must not be supposed, however, that the Web-worm is a mere pensioner upon the bounty of the spider. Both are web-makers; the spider toils by day, its companion is active at night. During the day time the caterpillars remain suspended here and there in the web, and feign death. Their slender bodies, slung in all sorts of positions, are rigidly extended, and the head is bent sharply upwards at the neck, as if in *rigor mortis*. No amount of disturbance can induce the insect to betray

---

* The original description of the moth will be found in Prof. Comstock's Report (Report of Commissioner of Agriculture for 1879, p. 205).

itself by a movement, and it will even suffer itself to be crushed without exhibiting any signs of life.

The color of the caterpillar—a cinnamon-brown—and its flattened, wrinkled form give it an extraordinary resemblance to a shriveled bit of twig or leaf. The deception is rendered perfect by the presence in the web, whether by accident or design, of dry fragments and petioles of orange leaves which have fallen from the surrounding branches.

In these web-tangles not only the spider lives sociably with others of its kind, hanging their egg-sacks in the net, and raising their young, sometimes in numerous colonies, but two other insects unite in the remarkable confederation, and form for mutual protection a sort of entomological happy family. These are a small tree Cockroach and a coral-red bug (Hemipteron), both of which breed and lurk in the tangles, passing with facility over and between the meshes of the net, and evidently feel perfectly at home there. The bug is, however, known to be a predatory species, and feeds upon the eggs and young of the Mealy-bug (see Chapter VI).

The caterpillar of Anæglis (Plate XIII, Fig. 1, *a*) is long, slender, and somewhat flattened, in color rusty or cinnamon-brown, with a faint tinge of green; beneath, dull green. The body is finely wrinkled and speckled with minute white dots and with a row of bristles on each side, having a large white dot at the base of each. The second joint and last joint of the body paler. Head mahogany-brown. Length, 19 to 20^{mm} ($\frac{8}{10}$ inch).

Pupa clear brown, finely and densely speckled with darker brown, the intermediate shades producing a dark mahogany color; the breathing pores on the sides are prominent and jet-black in color. Terminal point (cremaster) red-brown, furnished with six or eight rather long hooklets. It is usually suspended, like the larva, in a more or less horizontal position in the thicker parts of the web; sometimes naked, but generally with a light, loose tangle of web and bits of excrement gathered about it. The length is less than half that of the larva.

The imago is a dainty little moth, with silver-gray wings, marked with a broad band and several wavy lines of purple-black, and with parti-colored legs. It has the triangular form characteristic of the Pyralidæ sometimes called Deltoides, from the outline assumed by the wings when at rest, which is that of the Greek *Δ*. The eyes are large, prominent, and black. The rather heavy antennæ curving backwards, and the pointed maxillæ directed upwards like horns, instead of forward in line with the head, give an air of alertness to the insect.

The egg is laid singly upon a strand of the web, either of the larva or the spider with which it is associated. It is spheroidal, pearly, yellowish white, and adorned with a microscopic pattern, consisting of elevated points, from each of which five pairs of raised lines radiate to the five surrounding points.

Broods.—As in the case of the Leaf-rollers (*Tortricidæ*), there are many broods during the year. The moths have been bred in February, March, April, June, July, September, and October, and caterpillars of all ages are found at any time during the summer. In December and January, however, only the pupa is obtainable.

Remedies.—The extent of direct injury done to the Orange by these Web-worms is slight. It is, however, desirable to remove them from the trees, as the tangles of web harbor Scale-insects, and by protecting them from enemies foster their increase. In many cases Scale-insects will be found to have made their appearance; brought there, in all probability, by the spiders. It is therefore a wise plan to cut away the infested portion, usually comprising only a small inside branch. If this cannot be done without too much mutilation—as, for example, on young plants—after removing the web from the branches they should be sprayed with one of the washes recommended in the treatment of Scale-insects.

INSECTS OF THE ORDER HEMIPTERA.

THE ORANGE APHIS.

(*Siphonophora citrifolii* Ashmead.)

[Plate XIII, Fig. 3 *a*, *b*, *c*, and *d*.]

The history of the common Plant-louse of the greenhouse and garden has often been written and, briefly stated, is as follows: In the autumn eggs are deposited singly in sheltered places; from these hatch in the spring only wingless females, which do not lay eggs, but are viviparous and produce young without the appearance of males. During the summer one generation follows another with an astonishing rate of increase; each brood consisting solely of wingless agamic females. Finally, the last brood in the fall consists of winged males and females, by whom the winter eggs are produced and the perpetuation of the species secured in the ordinary manner.

The Aphis of the Orange (Plate XIII; *a*, wingless female; *b*, winged females) is a dark green Plant-louse, from 1.5 to 2^{mm} ($\frac{3}{100}$ to $\frac{8}{100}$ inch) in length, and hardly distinguishable in a popular description from some of the species common everywhere in greenhouses and gardens. It has parti-colored legs and garnet-red eyes. The hue of the body varies with age, from light yellowish-green or rusty green in the very young, to dark green in the adults. The winged individuals are of so dark a green as to have been described as black, and the young of this form are distinguishable at an early age from those destined to remain wingless, both by their darker color and more prominent tubercles upon the upper surface of the body. Two pairs of these prominences gradually develop into wing-pads, and after the final molt become well-formed and transparent wings.

The development of this southern Aphis differs from that of its northern congeners, in that the winged and the wingless individuals occur together at all seasons, and both forms produce their young living. The males remain undiscovered, and it is entirely possible that they rarely make their appearance, perhaps only at intervals of several years. In the warm climate of Florida the cold is never sufficiently severe to kill winged females, and the Orange not being deciduous a supply of food is nearly always at hand. A winter egg is not, therefore, a necessity, as in the North, and it may be that none are deposited in ordinary seasons. The late fall broods consist in great part of the winged females, while in spring, and especially in midsummer, the wingless form predominates.

In the act of birth, the hinder end of the young Aphis appears first. The young is slowly protruded from the body of the mother, until only the tip of the head remains unexpelled. During the process and for a few minutes after, all motion outwards ceases, the larva remains immovable and with its members rigidly applied to its body. Soon it disengages first one leg, and then another, until all are widely extended. The antennæ are then raised and brought forward. This movement severs the contact with the mother, and the new-born young drops upon its feet, in the full possession of its faculties (which it makes no delay in putting to the test). Within ten minutes from the time when its expulsion from the mother began, it is quietly feeding by her side, its sucking beak inserted in the tender tissues of the leaf, and its body rapidly becoming distended with the juices of the plant. In less than a week after its birth, the plant-louse has become adult, and begins in its turn to produce young.

Destructive powers.—The Orange Aphis attacks the tender new growth; it checks the growth of young shoots, and curls the tender leaves. With such a direct and rapid method of reproduction, and with a winged form of female ever present to spread the pest, it will be seen that this insect presents a truly formidable aspect as a destroyer. Were it not held in check by numerous enemies and parasites, it would soon ruin the trees by destroying the new growth, and render the culture of the orange for profit an impossibility.

The work of enemies.—Such, however, is the activity of its enemies that not a single individual Aphis escapes destruction, or is allowed to exert to the full its reproductive powers. Colonies rarely attain great size, and, in fact, are frequently exterminated in their very beginning, and before any appreciable injury has been done.

The parasite.—The principal agent in accomplishing this result is a parasite, whose larva, feeding internally upon the Plant-louse, finally kills it. In dying the body of the Aphis becomes distended to the utmost, assumes a globular shape, and turns to a dingy yellow color. In drying it adheres firmly to the plant. (Plate XIII, Fig. 3, c.)

Within the body-cavity of its victim, the space within which it nearly fills, the larva of the parasite, a little, white, footless grub, lies concealed, curled up, with its head touching its tail. In a few days it becomes a pupa, and six or seven days later it emerges through a large hole eaten in the dry shell of the Aphis, as a slender, black, wasp-like fly, with yellow legs. This fly is, of course, very minute, being $\frac{1}{100}$ inch in length. It is *Trioxys testaceipes* Cresson.* (Plate XIII, Fig. 4.)

Its work can always be seen where the Orange Aphis has been colonized for a week or more, in the numerous bloated remains of the Aphis, some of which may still contain the parasite, and others exhibit the round hole through which it has made its exit. (Plate XIII, Fig. 3, *c* and *d*.)

Although only a single fly is bred from each individual of the plant-louse, the numbers of the parasite increase more rapidly than those of its victim, and as every Aphis is in time parasitized, no colony long escapes extermination. Were it not for the facility with which new colonies can be started at a distance, through the flight of the winged females, this species of Aphis and some others which are similarly attacked would suffer complete extinction in a single season.†

Other enemies.—Numerous other enemies combine to thin the numbers of Plant-lice. Those which have fallen under observation as destroying the Orange Aphis are discussed in the chapter on Predatory Insects. Among the number are three species of two-winged flies (*Diptera*), whose larvæ subsist exclusively upon Plant-lice, and several species of Lady-birds (*Coccinellidæ*) which, both as larvæ and as perfect beetles, rely to a very great extent upon this source for their food supply.

Remedies for Aphis.—Moderately strong applications of whale-oil soap, or the kerosene washes recommended for Scale-insect, are perfectly effective in killing the Orange Aphis, and will not injure the young growth upon which they are found.

THE GREEN SOLDIER-BUG.

(*Raphigaster hilaris*, Fitch.)

[Fig. 74.]

A large green Plant-bug is sometimes observed to suck tender shoots of Orange, causing them to wither and die. The same insect is, to a certain extent, predaceous, and has been reported as sucking Cotton Worms and other insects, for which reason it has usually been classed among beneficial insects. The full-grown bug is bright green in color, with a very fine yellowish line around the entire margin of the insect, and a black dot at the outer angles of each abdominal joint. The form

---

* Described in Report of the Commissioner of Agriculture for 1879, p. 208.

† Mr. Ashmead has described another minute, black parasite, which he bred from the Orange Aphis, and to which he gives the name *Stenomesius* (?) *aphidicola*. (Orange Insects, p. 67.) Three of the flies issued from the body of a single Aphis, and it may be a secondary parasite, preying upon the Trioxys.

is broadly oval, the legs slender and of the same color as the body. Length, 17^{mm} ($\frac{88}{100}$ inch).

The following account of ravages committed by the Raphigaster is from a correspondent in Florida. It affords a good example of the sudden rise into importance as a pest of an insect which is ordinarily a quite insignificant enemy of the Orange.

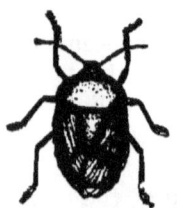

FIG. 73.—*Raphigaster hilaris*. (After Glover.)

* * * "You also request observations on the Green Soldier-bug. I forward by same mail twigs of the orange tree injured by the bug. The insects are coupling now. The females will soon lay the eggs in a cluster on a leaf, straddling over them while laying. The young appear in the latter part of February or the first part of March. As observed by the eye the young are black, with white spots, which color they retain until nearly full grown, when they acquire wings and change to a bright green. How this is done I do not know. They mature very quickly, and increase with surprising rapidity, continuing to breed until November. In the spring and early summer they confine their attacks principally to garden vegetables and succulent weeds. They are particularly abundant on tomato-vines, egg-plants, turnip-tops, and mustard, seldom doing much damage to orange trees at this season. When pea-vines are well grown, about or a little before the time of blossoming, they abandon nearly everything for the pea-vines. Last year they totally destroyed my garden. Not one tomato came to perfection. Where the insect had inserted its sucking-tube a reddish-yellow spot appeared. When cut the fruit was full of lumps and totally devoid of flavor. The tomato-vines grew so enormous a crop that the ground was almost covered by the fallen fruit. Last year I had 35 acres planted in cow-pea vines, which bore an enormous crop of peas; but not enough sound peas could be gathered to plant 5 acres additional land. Later it was impossible to find a sound pea. I attempted to turn under the vines, but so luxuriant was the growth that it could not be done. Towards the end of August the pea-vines were dead or dying, when the bugs swarmed to the orange trees, killing nearly all the new growth. Immense numbers were killed by keeping men constantly going over the grove, shaking the trees, and killing all that fell on the ground. The wingless individuals were readily killed, but the larger number of the mature insects saved themselves by flight. This method of destruction was kept up until the middle of December, by which time very few were found. On very cold days the winged insects were nearly dormant and could not fly. I have the trees frequently searched now, but rarely find the bug. The number of the insects is incredible. When thoroughly shaken, the ground under the trees would be alive with the fallen insects, and two days later just as many would be found. I despaired of getting rid of them until the cold weather commenced, when I found the number rapidly decrease until their nearly total extinction.

"As to the damage. The bug first attacks the latest growth, which wilts and droops while the bug is sucking; in a few days the shoot is dead; the same eye soon sends out another shoot which shares the fate of its predecessor, and so on until the eye has the appearance of a large bunch, as you will see on twigs sent. After all the tender growth has been destroyed the bug inserts his sharp sucking tube in the previous growth which has nearly hardened. Here I can only give you the facts and my theory; it is a fact that the insect sucks such wood, but the damage does not follow so quickly; but very soon after, on such wood known to be sucked, numerous bumps appear, which crack and exude a sticky sap, white at first, but soon a rusty red, and hard. Later on the insects suck the juice from fully-matured wood (an inch or more in diameter); on this wood the bumps do not appear, but the same kind of sticky sap exudes in tears, which soon harden and redden and are what I understand by "red rust." That the cause and effect are strictly true I can only surmise, but this much I and my men have seen: the insects sucking the sap as stated and the branches where sucked having the appearance described. In the winter months I have found clusters of the bugs on the stocks of the buds, two inches in diameter, and always an exudation of sap at these places, which I have never observed to redden as in the instances stated above. Why this is so, and why the insect leaves the more tender bud above to suck the sap from harder wood nearer the roots, I can offer no suggestion. At first I was strongly inclined to think that red rust was caused by soil-poisoning, but if so, why is it that trees have grown for so many years on the same soil and never had this disease until the introduction of the Green Bug? To illustrate: When I bought this place ten years ago there was a field of five acres which had been in partial cultivation several years, and on which grew spontaneously the tomato and mustard plant, the two plants on which the insects thrive the best. (At present I can only find the insect on the mustard.) Since my purchase I have kept this field constantly growing pea-vines, as well as the forty other acres which I have in orange trees, thus giving every encouragement to the increase of the pest. Adjoining this old field was a wild orange grove in a dense forest. Many of the sour stumps had large sweet buds, neither the buds nor sour trees giving any signs of the red rust until the winter following the clearing, and after a crop of pea-vines had been grown among the trees. Now the trees in this wild grove are just as much damaged as in the old field adjoining. Another case I will mention, and not trespass further on your patience. Five miles distant is the grove of L. Merritt, a wild grove budded. The buds are six years old and ought to be bearing heavy crops, but an occasional bloom is all. The trees have been in an unhealthful and "die back" condition for several years. When visiting his grove in the fall of 1881, I told him I had some trees in the same condition and was inclined to think the Green Bug was the cause. Since that time he has persistently hunted the bug, whipping it out of the large trees with poles, and killing wherever found; also he stopped planting peas. I have just visited his grove and found but two twigs damaged, and could not find a specimen of the bug. The trees have changed so remarkably in this grove that it was past recognition. Instead of a dense crop of dead twigs all over his grove, as at a previous visit, the trees had nearly doubled in size, and had a very large, healthy growth of branches in place of the dead twigs. I hear his trees are now in profuse bloom. I do not think that washes will do much damage to the bug. Very strong whale-oil soap rarely kills. Whale-oil soap, 1 pound; kerosene oil, 1 pint; water, 12 pints; sometimes kills when sprayed over them, nearly always when immersed. Pure kerosene kills, but not always instantly.

"The Green Bug has a parasite. I do not know what, but I frequently find their shells with the inside devoured. Last winter I buried a number to see if plowing under would kill them. In ten days none were dead; in three weeks 20 per cent. were dead, nothing remaining but the shells; in six weeks all but one were dead, empty shells remaining. The living insect I put in a bottle with a little earth over it, hoping to find the parasite, but unfortunately in about ten days the bottle was broken, the Green Bug was dead, the shell empty as in the other instances.

"At present the insect is very rare here; if found at all, generally on the mustard plant or weed locally known as nightshade. Yesterday, while showing a lemon tree to some visitors, I found some of the twigs drooping and remarked it looked like the work of the Green Bug. One was found under a leaf close to his work. I send you one of the shoots. If at any time you may consider the subject of suffiient importance to send a trained observer in the field, I will be happy to see him here and place every facility at his disposal."—[JAMES FRANKLIN, *West Apopka, Fla., January* 31, 1883.

THE THICK-THIGHED METAPODIUS.

(*Metapodius femoratus*, Fab.)

[Figs. 74 and 75.

A large dark-brown bug, emitting an unpleasant odor when handled, is addicted to sucking the juices of the Orange, attacking either the succulent shoots, the flowers, or the fruit. It has a heavy, clumsy body, with projecting angles to the thorax; the thighs of the hind pair of legs are swollen and spiny, and the shanks of the same pair are flattened with jagged edges. The adult bug is nearly one

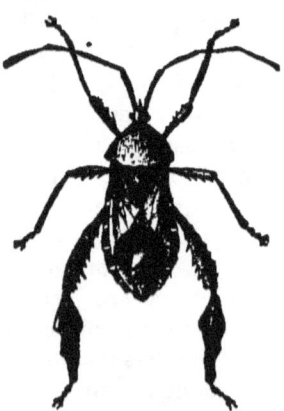

FIG. 74.—*Metapodius femoratus.* (After Glover.)

inch long. Although sluggish in habit, it takes wing when disturbed, and flies heavily with a loud, buzzing noise.

The eggs have the form of an oval casket, triangular in section, and are quite large; 3^{mm} ($\frac{12}{100}$ inch) in length. They are laid singly upon the leaves of plants, and are very beautiful objects, opalescent, and gleaming like a drop of molten gold. Figs. 76 a and b show the egg with the exit hole of the larva.

FIG. 75.—Egg of Metapodius femoratus. (Original.)

The young make their exit through a large hole eaten in the end. The young bugs are brightly variegated with red and black, and their bodies bristle all over with spines. They grow more somber in color with each casting of the skin, and gradually approach the adult in form and color.

OTHER SUCKING BUGS.

Metapodius terminalis Dallas.—This species can, with difficulty, be distinguished from the preceding, and the same account may be given of its life and habits. Both species of Metapodius vary greatly in size, but *M. terminalis* is usually the larger and heavier of the two. *M. femoratus* is the commoner species in the cotton-growing States, and *M. terminalis* is more abundant in the orange districts of Florida.

Like the Green Soldier-bug (*Raphigaster hilaris*), the species of Metapodius are known to prey upon other insects, particularly upon caterpillars, which are filled with the juices of plants, and there may be often a doubt as to whether they are injurious or beneficial.

Euthochtha galeator (Fab.). (Fig. 77).—This is another foul-smelling bug, having the general shape and appearance of Metapodius. It is however a smaller and lighter-colored insect; and the shanks of the hind legs are slender. The color is rusty-brown, and the length of the adult insect is 16^{mm} ($\frac{64}{100}$ inch).

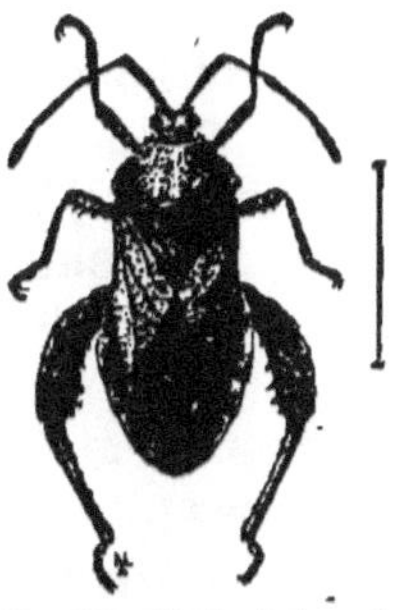

The eggs of *Euthochtha galeator* resembles those of Metapodius, but are only one-third as large, and are laid in irregular clusters on leaves or stems of plants. Their color is a ruddy gold.

The young bugs are purple-black, with orange heads and crimson abdomens. Their bodies are very spiny.

FIG. 76.—*Euthochtha galeator.* (Original.)

The habits of this bug do not differ from those of Metapodius. It is a very common and often a very destructive insect.

Other species of plant-sucking bugs will be found doing occasional damage to tender growth on Orange, but the above are the largest and best known of this class of offenders.

CHAPTER XI.

INSECTS AFFECTING THE BLOSSOM AND FRUIT, AND SCAVENGER INSECTS.

INSECTS AFFECTING THE BLOSSOMS.

During the season of blooming, insects of many species are seen flitting about the trees, attracted thither by the fragrance of the blossoms, and feeding upon the nectar, which they secrete in abundance. The greater number of these visitors are not only harmless to the plant, but are even of the greatest service, in securing the fertilization of the flowers, which could not otherwise be accomplished.

In fact, it is a fair inference that its fragrance and its sweets serve no other purpose in the economy of the flower than to call to its aid friendly insects which, in their restless movements from flower to flower, bear with them and distribute widely the fertilizing pollen dust.

A few injurious insects, however, frequent the blossoms. These are all sucking-bugs, and they cause the buds to blast and the flowers to fall prematurely, by tapping the juices from their stems and other parts. Among the most injurious are the Green Plant-bug, *Raphigaster hilaris* Fitch, mentioned in the preceding chapter, and the Leaf-footed Bug, *Leptoglossus phyllopus* (Linn.), an insect which will be considered among those especially injurious to the fruit.

THRIPS TRITICI (?) Fitch.

[Fig. 77.]

By far the most common insect found in orange blossoms is a little yellowish bug, whose slender body measures but 1^{mm} ($\frac{4}{100}$ inch) in length. The color of the eyes is dark red or brown; all the other parts are clear honey-yellow. The adults have narrow wings fringed with hairs. These hairs are characteristic of the family, and replace the membranous parts of the wing of most other insects.

Notwithstanding the rudimentary structure of their wings, these insects are capable of active flight, and they also have the power of leaping.

The Orange Thrips inhabits all sweet-scented flowers. In Lilies and Roses, as well as in orange blossoms, they sometimes swarm in countless numbers, and do great damage whenever they become unduly abundant.

From orange blossoms they are seldom wholly absent. They appear however to feed for the most part upon the stamens and petals, from which they suck the bland and fragrant oil. In the Orange, these parts of the flower are naturally deciduous, and the effect of the attacks of the Thrips is to hasten their fall; for the most part leaving uninjured the fruit-producing pistil, which moreover will not fail to have been fructified with the pollen which these active midgets distribute over every part. Figure 5 on Plate XI shows an orange blossom infested with these insects. The Orange, being a profuse bloomer, commonly sets more fruit than it can mature, and is constantly throwing off the surplus from the time when the buds begin to open until the branches are relieved of their burdens at the harvest. A large share of the energy of the tree is expended uselessly in the fruit which falls to the ground prematurely, and is lost.

The operations of the Thrips are confined to the flowers and therefore tend to anticipate and prevent this waste, by thinning out the superabundant bloom at the outset. For this reason the insect is more often a friend than a foe to the plant, and were it not for the fact that its numbers sometimes increase inordinately and to such an extent as to effect injuriously the forming crop, it could not be classed among the insect enemies of the Orange.

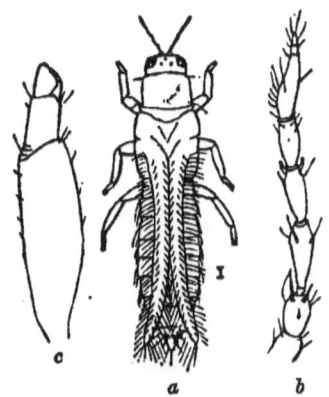

FIG. 77.—*Thrips tritici*: *a*, Thrips enlarged, drawn from living specimens; *b*, antenna; *c*, leg, much enlarged. (Original.)

The Orange Thrips is frequently an annoyance to persons occupied in flower gardens where Lilies and Roses are in bloom. It settles upon the hands and face, and bites sharply, although without poisonous irritation.

Remedies.—A moderately strong solution of whale-oil soap, one pound to four or five gallons of water, will suffice to destroy this insect if sprayed upon the flowers in fine spray. Applications of pyrethrum will also effectively reduce their numbers. It is best used in liquid, delivered in fine spray upon the flowers. One ounce of the powder in each gallon of water is sufficient to destroy the Thrips. The powder must be kept suspended by frequent agitation of the liquid.

INSECTS AFFECTING THE FRUIT.

THE COTTON STAINER OR RED BUG.

(*Dysdercus suturellus* Herrich-Sch.)

[Plate XI, Fig. 4.]

This Soldier-bug, well known to cotton-growers in Florida, as occasioning great loss by puncturing the cotton-bolls and injuring the fiber, has recently been found destructive to oranges by puncturing the rind and causing the fruit to drop from the trees and rot rapidly. Attention was first called to this new habit of the bug by letters to the Department of Agriculture from South Florida, in December, 1879. Since that time numerous reports have been received of excessive injuries done, especially in cases where cotton is raised among or in close proximity to the orange trees.

The Cotton Stainer may be distinguished from all other Soldier-bugs, some of which resemble it superficially, by its rather oval form, deep coral-red color, and white markings, which form a collar-ring behind the head, and a border upon each joint of the body. The wings of the young are mere pads of black color, but in the adult they cover the body, and are crossed with narrow lines of white, forming the shoulder-straps, from which these insects take the name "Soldier-bugs."

Broods, Habits, &c.—There are many broods during the warm months and even in mid-winter the young may often be found.

The principal food of the bug is the oil of cotton seed, to obtain which it punctures the hard seed-coats. It also feeds upon the seeds of other Malvaceous plants, although the precise species attacked have not been ascertained. In winter the Red Bug may be found gathered in vast numbers upon the heaps of waste cotton seed about the gin houses.

The eggs are oval in shape, amber-colored, with a pearly luster, and present, under a lens, a pattern of closely reticulated lines. They have been sent to the Department of Agriculture from the Indian River, Fla., in April, " laid in a group of twenty-one upon the under side of an orange leaf."* That this disposition of the eggs is normal may be somewhat doubtful. In winter at least, and around gin houses, the eggs are dropped loosely in the sand, and among the heaps of cotton seed upon which the bugs are feeding.

Attacks upon the Orange.—In January and February, if the weather is mild, the Red Bugs desert the fields where they have lingered upon the dead trash and waste of the cotton, and suddenly make their appearance in the orange groves. Usually this takes place only in groves adjoining fields that have been planted in cotton, but, as they are strong flyers, the bugs not unfrequently migrate in considerable numbers to a distance even of several miles.

At first, only adults are seen; these at once attack the fruit upon the trees. A week or ten days later, the wingless young appear; always upon the ground, clustering upon the fallen fruit. If the trees are not stripped and the fruit harvested before the young brood become adult and acquire wings, the entire crop will be lost. Even the packing-house is not safe from invasion, and fruit is apt to be destroyed after it has been gathered and stored in the bins.

In puncturing the orange, the bugs insert their slender sucking beak, often its entire length, and although the oil of the rind forms their principal food, they, nevertherless, frequently regale themselves with

---

* Report of the Commissioners of Agriculture for 1879, p. 204.

draughts of juice from the pulp within, and are sometimes seen to suck the juices from the surface of split or injured fruit, tapping it with the tips of their probosces, after the manner of flies.

The sucking-tube, having the fineness of a hair, leaves no visible wound upon the outside of the fruit, and within no indication of its passage. An orange which has been attacked therefore shows no outward sign of injury; nevertheless, a single puncture causes it to drop in a few hours from the tree, and to decay in one or two days

It is quite useless to pack for shipment to a distance the fruit from a grove which is attacked by Red Bugs, since the unsound fruit decays in the packages and soon ruins the whole.

Geographical distribution.—The Cotton Stainer is an inhabitant of warm climates. It is found in great abundance in the Bahamas, where, according to Mr. E. A. Schwarz,* it annually destroys a large part of the cotton crop. From the Bahamas or other West India islands it may have been introduced into the extreme southern portions of the cotton belt, in the United States. In Florida it has not been reported as occurring north of Gainesville, in Alachua County, and it is unknown to cotton-planters in the northern part of that county, although a familiar insect in cotton fields everywhere south of Gainesville.

The taste for oranges appears to have been recently acquired. Mr. Glover, in the Agricultural Report for 1875, gives an account of the insect and its depredations upon cotton, but does not mention it among the insects noted as injurious to the Orange. It should, however, be remarked that at the date of Mr. Glover's observations comparatively few bearing orange groves existed in the more southern portion of the State.

In 1879 the insect first attracted the attention of orange-growers, and the crop of that year was injured by it in several widely separate portions of the fruit belt. In various parts of the State it has since become a well known and much dreaded pest, and has occasioned very serious losses.

Freedom from Attacks of Enemies.—The Red Bug is one of those showy insects which are probably possessed of an acrid flavor, disagreeable to other animals, and are in consequence not much preyed upon by enemies. Certain it is that the Red Bug is not eaten by fowls or other birds, nor has any enemy of its own class been hitherto observed to attack it. The eggs will very probably be found to have parasites, as is the case with most other Hemiptera, but none have as yet been discovered.

Remedies and remedial Measures.—In default of aid from predatory animals it remains for man alone to combat this pest. Its extermination, in view of its gregarious habits, would not be a matter of great difficulty, if concerted action over wide areas could be secured. As was

---

* Report upon Cotton Insects, Department of Agriculture. 1879. Appendix I, p. 347.

long ago suggested by Mr. Glover, in his report above mentioned, the bugs may be attracted to small heaps of sugar-cane trash, with which Paris green or some other poison should be mixed; or the bugs, when collected upon piles of cotton seed in winter, may be destroyed by drenching them with boiling-hot water. The experience of several cotton-planters with this last method has shown it to be practicable, but to be effective it must be thoroughly carried out. As the eggs cannot all be reached and destroyed by the hot water, the operation needs to be repeated several times at such frequent intervals that the bugs are not allowed to reach maturity and deposit fresh eggs.

In the orange grove effective traps may be made with refuse oranges, orange peel, &c., and the bugs, when thus collected, may be destroyed with the kerosene washes used for Scale-insects. The kerosene solutions will also be more effective than hot water in reaching and killing the eggs.

The Red Bug can never become permanently attached as an enemy to the orange tree, since the fruit which alone supplies it with food lasts only a few weeks, and during the balance of the year the insect must seek its subsistence elsewhere. It is therefore an enemy to be dreaded only in the vicinity of cotton fields and gin houses, in districts where cotton is largely planted, or lastly, and with less probability, in case thickets containing numerous wild Malvaceous plants furnish the bugs with a supply of food during the months when the Orange is not in fruit.

In South Florida, at least, the planting of cotton in the vicinity of orange groves will necessarily be abandoned. Throughout the orange district the acreage planted in cotton has never been large, and it is for many reasons likely to diminish rather than to increase. With the abandonment of cotton planting, the Red Bug may be expected to disappear from this region.

THE LEAF-FOOTED BUG.

(*Leptoglossus phyllopus* Linn.)

[Fig. 78.]

This is a chocolate-brown bug, three quarters of an inch in length. It has the shanks of the hind legs very broadly flattened, and the edges jagged, resembling a tattered leaf fragment; hence its popular name. The markings, a white bar across the folded wings, and a small spot of the same color on each of the leaf-shaped shanks, are very characteristic, and render this species easily distinguishable among other bugs of the same family. The young bugs, with undeveloped wings, show the brighter red color of the body, and do not acquire the peculiar flattened hind shanks until nearly adult.

The eggs are golden brown in color, and are laid in a single row or chain, along a stem or the leaf rib of a plant. They are cylindrical, flattened on the under side and at the ends, and are closely applied end to end, forming a stiff, cylindrical rod in which each egg appears as a joint or cell. The young issue through a large hole eaten in the upper side of the egg.

The normal food of this bug in the South is a large Thistle, upon the heads of which young and old may be found clustering and sucking the juices of the plant. The young bugs are rarely found in Florida except upon the Thistle, or similar succulent plants, but the adult bugs, being strong on the wing, make excursions to very great distances, and enter the orange groves at the time of blooming, to suck the opening buds or tender shoots. Again they may be found attacking the ripening fruit, and causing it to drop in consequence of their punctures. The damage done in this way is often very considerable, and in some reported cases has amounted to an almost total loss of the crop.

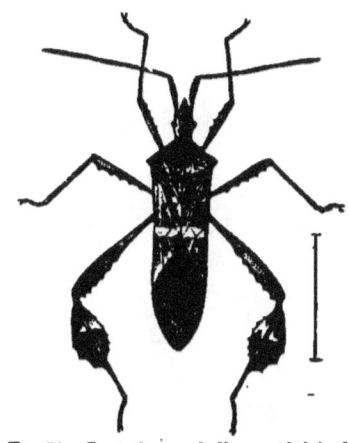

FIG. 78.—*Leptoglossus phyllopus.* (Original.)

Like many bugs of this family, they are particularly active in hot weather, and it is then very difficult to get within reach of the adult insects, as they take wing readily and fly away. But in cool or cloudy weather they are more sluggish and may easily be found and killed by hand-picking, or by knocking them into a bag or net with a stick.

Where Thistles are abundant this bug is sure to prove a serious pest, as the Thistles form a propagating ground from which they spread to a distance. A single large patch of Thistles has been known to infect a wide area, but when these were cut down and destroyed, the bugs in time disappeared from the groves in the neighborhood and gave no further trouble.

THE MEXICAN FRUIT WORM.

An unknown worm, of perhaps an inch in length, is said to be very destructive to oranges in Mexico. It penetrates the fruit to the core, and feeds upon the pulp, both fresh and after it has begun to rot in consequence of the attack.

A few years ago a very large percentage of the oranges sold in the markets at Vera Cruz contained these worms, and were entirely uneatable. It is said that no mark upon the outside of the fruit reveals the presence of the worm within.

In the absence of any definite knowledge in regard to this insect, it is only possible to point out the danger of its introduction first into the groves of Louisiana and then into Florida by means of oranges imported from Mexico at the port of New Orleans.*

SCAVENGER INSECTS.

INSECTS FEEDING UPON DEAD WOOD AND BARK.

TREE-INHABITING ANTS.

Several species of ants which live in trees make their nests in the dead wood of the Orange, more especially in twigs and smaller branches which have been killed by frost The wood of these winter-killed shoots being corky and easily excavated, they are frequently hollowed out by ants, and serve as places of deposit for their eggs and young.

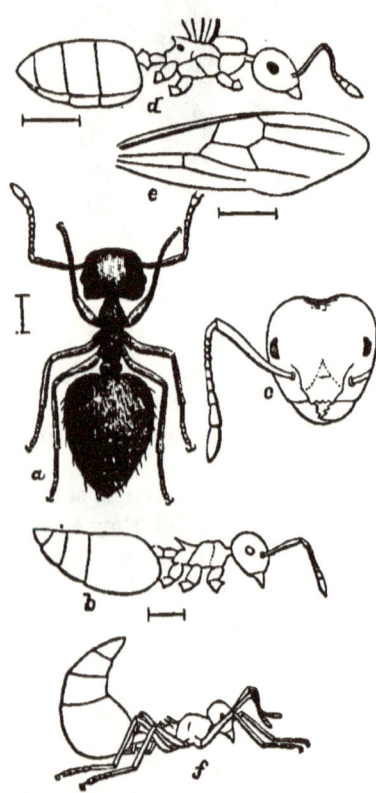

FIG. 79.—*Cremastogaster lineolata:* a, b, worker major; c, head of do.; d, female; e, wing; f, worker minor. (After McCook.)

Cremastogaster lineolata (Say). [Fig. 79.] This is one of the commonest of the species which have the above habit. It is jet-black, shining, and has a broadly triangular abdomen, which it elevates in a threatening manner when excited.

The species is very abundant upon Oak and other forest trees. It attends the various honey-producing insects found upon trees and feeds upon their honey-dew without doing any violence to the insects themselves. Its presence upon the orange tree, therefore, is of very slight importance either for good or evil.

Other species of ants which have been observed to make their nests in orange twigs probably have the same habits, and if not positively beneficial, certainly do little harm to the tree, and none of them gnaw or do injury to the growing parts.

---

*An Australian moth, *Ophideres fullonica* (L.), is said to pierce oranges with its proboscis and suck the juices of the pulp. In an article entitled "Les Lépidoptères à Trompe Perforante, Destructeurs des Oranges," M. J. Künckel describes and figures the proboscis of this insect, and shows its special adaptation to this end. (Comptes Rendus des Séances de l'Académie des Sciences, Paris, 30 Août 1875.)

THE ORANGE SAWYER.

(*Elaphidion inerme* Newman.)

This insect has been described in Chapter VIII, and is there shown to be injurious, under a careless system of pruning, in which the ends of branches are left untrimmed, with sufficient dead wood to attract the parent beetle, but not enough to support the larvæ; so that the latter are driven by hunger to enter and feed upon the living wood. It appears, therefore, that under natural conditions this beetle is merely a scavenger. Its grub feeds upon the wood of many trees, and, like most members of the Longicorn family, thrives only upon diseased and devitalized tissues, or upon wood which, though dead, has not entirely parted with its sap and become hard and dry.

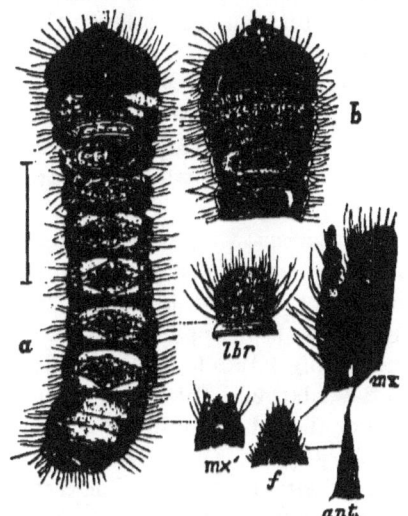

FIG. 80.—*Elaphidion parallelum*: *a*, larva from above; *b*, from beneath; *f*, ligula-like process, behind the labial palpi; *lbr*, labrum; *mx*, maxilla; *mx'*, mentum; *ant*, antenna. (After Packard.)

Fig. 80 represents the larva of *E. parallelum*, a closely allied species, having the same habits as the Orange Sawyer, but which lives in the Oak, &c.

THE ORANGE FLAT-HEADED BORER.

(*Chrysobothris chrysoela* Ill.)

[Plate XIV, Fig. 8.]

Dead twigs and branches of Orange are frequently found, upon which the bark is cracked and loosened, so that it comes off at a touch, bringing away with it considerable dust from the wood lying immediately beneath, a thin layer of which has been reduced to powder. When the loose bark and sawdust are removed, the surface of the branch presents an eroded appearance, indicating the path of an insect. The edges of the track form a succession of semicircular curves, as if made by the sweep of a miniature scythe. It is, in fact, the gallery of an extremely thin-bodied grub or sawyer, made partly in the bark and partly in the wood, and always filled with comminuted wood, which has passed through the digestive organs of the grub, and has been voided and deposited behind it as the insect made its way through the wood. The cell in which the pupa is formed is excavated in the solid wood. It lies parallel with but beneath the gallery, with which it is connected at one of its extremities. The short passage connecting the pupa-cell with the gallery is carefully filled with wood dust, firmly packed in place, so that even when the bark is removed and the gallery exposed to view, the mouth of the cell remains concealed, and is only disclosed upon the exit of the beetle. The cell is then found to be broad and shallow, oval in outline, and lined with a silken layer that is almost invisible by reason of its delicacy.

The Beetle.—In spring or early summer there issues a very handsome little beetle, broadly oval in form, and about 8^{mm} ($\frac{32}{100}$ inch) in length. The colors of the body are metallic bronze, greenish below and purple above. Upon the wing-cases are ten large spots of brilliant emerald green.

The Larva.—The form of the larva is characteristic of the family. It has the second joint greatly enlarged, forming a broad, flattened disk, into which the first joint and the small head are sunken, only the black tips of the jaws appearing beyond the cleft in the anterior border. The succeeding joints form a tail-like body, which is less than half as wide as the enlarged joint. In life the body is usually curved strongly to one side or the other, giving it still more the appearance of an appendage. The large joint is covered upon both of its flattened faces, with minute, horny denticulations, which serve to hold the body firmly against the smooth walls of the burrow while the jaws are forced into the wood.

The body of the lava is naked, or with scattered and nearly invisible hairs, soft, white, and without legs. It moves but slowly in its gallery, and only by means of the contraction and expansion of the enlarged flattened joint.

The pupa presents no especial peculiarities, and merely outlines the form and members of the perfect beetle.

Habits and Life-history.—The eggs are laid upon the bark of dead orange branches, and probably also on Hickory and other close-textured woods. The branches attacked are invariably dead and quite dry, but still retaining their bark. The larva never penetrates the living parts of the tree, and will perish of hunger if the supply of dead wood and bark is not sufficient for its support. The larvæ of different ages are found during the latter part of summer. Some of them change to pupæ in the fall, while others, after excavating their pupa cells, occupy them during the winter as larvæ, and undergo their transformations in the spring. Of those which pupate in the fall, some become perfect insects before cold weather, and beetles will be found in the cells as early as January; they do not, however, leave their retreats until summer weather has begun. The beetles continues to appear as late as May and June.

As a scavenger, assisting in the return to earth and air of the dead and useless material that has been assimilated by the plant, this can only be considered a useful insect, and certainly one that is incapable of doing any injury to the orange tree, either by causing disease or by direct loss of wood or bark.

THE CYLINDRICAL BARK-BORER.

(*Hypothenemus eruditus* Westwood.)

[Plate XIV, Fig. 1.]

This minute beetle is frequently an object of suspicion from its presence in great numbers in twigs killed by dieback. It is 1.6^{mm} ($\frac{8}{100}$ inch) in length, dark brown in color, cylindrical, and obtusely rounded at both ends. Under a lens it has a hoary appearance, owing to the short, stout hairs with which all parts of the body are clothed. On the wing-cases these stout hairs are arranged in numerous longitudinal rows, and the interspaces between the rows of hairs are deeply and coarsely pitted or punctate. The head is directed downwards and is not seen from above. The declivity of the thorax above the base of the head is covered with minute tooth-like asperities.

The larva as well as the beetle itself feeds upon dry corky wood and bark of various trees, and upon plants having soft or porous tissues, such as are found in the Grape and many other vines. They riddle the dead wood and bark with galleries, and quite rapidly reduce it to powder.

In the Orange their galleries are seldom found in solid wood, but invariably occur in the bark and in small twigs when from any cause they have been deprived of life and become dry. Succulent shoots killed by frost or disease attract the beetles in great numbers as soon as they become dry and brittle; but no part of the tree is attacked as long as it retains its sap or remains moist. The insect is therefore entirely harmless in its operations, and beneficial rather than injurious to vegetation.

Life-history.—The larva of Hypothenemus is a minute white grub, with a thick and stout cylindrical body, strongly curved, and without legs or other organs of locomotion, save that by the contractile movements of its body joints, it is enabled to crawl slowly through its burrows. The head is small, and all the parts surrounding the mouth, with the exception of the pair of stout jaws, are so minute that they can be discerned only after careful dissection upon the stage of a microscope.

The family *Scolytidæ*, to which this beetle belongs, number in the United States at least two hundred species,* divided among numerous genera. All of them have wood boring habits, and members of the same group resemble each other closely. The larvæ of the different species are for the most part indistinguishable; the points of difference, if any exist, are so minute that they have escaped observation.

The pupa is formed in a little cell, walled off from the galleries made by the larva. It shows the form of the beetle, and is white, turning brown as it approaches maturity.

The eggs are white, oval in shape, and are scattered by the mother either singly or in little groups at random in the galleries which she excavates.

---

*About one hundred and seventy species have been described.

Broods.—There does not appear to be any definite number of broods. The beetles are rather more abundant in spring and early summer, and the larvæ in midsummer and winter; but the insect propagates at all seasons, and its development is only interrupted by frosty weather.*

OTHER BEETLES BORING IN ORANGE WOOD.

In addition to the species hitherto mentioned, which are so frequently found in the wood of the Orange that may properly be considered a part of the regular fauna of the tree, there are numbers of other wood-eating Coleoptera, which are less obviously connected with the plant, but occasionally feed upon it, and have been bred from the dead limbs and twigs. A few species demand notice.

Two of these, *Leptostylus biustus* Lec., and *Hyperplatys maculatus* Hald., are closely allied Longicorn beetles, and belong to a group of that family, all the species of which are wood-scavengers, feeding only upon dead portions of plants.

Leptostylus biustus Lec. (Plate XIV, Fig. 2) is an ash-gray insect, with a rather broad and flattened body, the upper surface of which is broken by minute elevated points. The terminal third of the wing-cases is darker in color, and this darker portion is separated from the remainder by sharply defined lines meeting in a point upon the center line. Length, 7.6^{mm} ($\frac{3}{10}$ inch). The antennæ are one-third longer than the body.

The larvæ are cylindrical, slightly flattened sawyers, having the first joint of the body somewhat enlarged; the head is very small, and almost concealed within the enlarged first joint; color pallid, except the jaws, which are chitinous brown.

The larva tunnels dead branches the wood of which is not too hard, or excavates galleries under dead bark of the Orange, filling up the passage behind it with tightly packed sawdust. It transforms to the perfect beetle at the end of its gallery, in a cell-like cavity formed by the movements of the larva in the surrounding mass of loose woody fragments.

The beetles appear in April and May, and there is a supplementary brood in September, although the perfect insects frequently remain in their cells all winter.

Hyperplatys maculatus Hald. (Plate XIV, Fig. 3) is a somewhat smaller beetle than the preceding, and its form is more slender and flattened. The color of the body is ash-gray, spotted above with dots of velvet black, and with a large splash of the same on each wing-case near the tip; the legs are black, variegated with red; the antennæ are much longer than the body, and are also variegated red and black. Length, 6^{mm} ($\frac{24}{100}$ inch).

In its habits this beetle does not differ from *Leptostylus biustus*, and the larvæ of the two species resemble each other closely.

---

* Further notes concerning the habits of this beetle will be found in an article by Mr. E. A. Schwarz, in the Bulletin of the Brooklyn Ent. Soc., vol. VII, page 84.

Amaurorhinus nitens Horn.—This is a small, elongate beetle, shining black in color, and provided with a short beak or snout.

It is not uncommonly found boring in winter-killed twigs of Orange, or in portions of wood and bark which have been softened and rendered porous by the action of a wood-destroying fungus. The larva and other immature stages have never been observed.

The family of the *Cossonidæ*, to which this beetle belongs, comprises small insects, all of which, as far as their habits are known, feed upon dead bark, pith, or spongy wood, and fungus. The above species is as harmless as others of its family. It enters and feeds upon the wood after all life has left it, and is probably attracted by the presence of a fungus to the diseased portions which it infests.

INSECTS FOUND IN WOUNDS AND FOOT-ROT SORES.

Bleeding wounds, especially sores in which fermentation of the sap is taking place, are very attractive to insects of many kinds. It therefore frequently happens that some harmless sap-feeding insect is mistaken, by those who are ignorant of its habits, for the originator of the mischief.

A list of insects which through misapprehensions of this sort have been reported by orange-growers as causing foot-rot, includes (1) *Sap-feeders;* beetles of the families *Nitidulidæ* and *Monotomidæ*, which live in all stages upon the fermenting sap of plants. (2) *Euphoria sepulchralis* (Fab.), a Lamellicorn beetle, which is not unfrequently found sipping the sap; and the white, thread-like maggots of small flies, which almost invariably make their appearance in sour sap. (3) *Midas clavatus* Drury (Plate XIV, Fig. 4), a large black fly, with an orange-colored band on the abdomen, which hovers about the diseased spots in order to prey upon flies and other insects attracted to the flowing sap. (4) Scavengers, feeding upon the dead wood and bark; these include besides the Termites, of which mention has been made in a previous chapter, several sawyers or larvæ of beetles belonging to the Longicorn family, but of unknown species. (5) A number of minute beetles, *Læmophlœus, Lathridius, Sacium, Hesperobœnus*, and others, commonly found under the dead bark of trees, after it has been loosened by the gnawing of wood-eating insects. They are for the most part predatory upon the other insect inhabitants of these lurking places, and their larvæ may be found pursuing and devouring the young of the wood-scavengers, or even making war upon each other.

INSECTS FEEDING UPON DECAYING FRUIT.

SAP-BEETLES. (Family *Nitidulidæ*.)

Two species of this sap-loving family are so constantly found in rotting oranges, and also in injured fruit, before it has fallen from the tree, as sometimes to occasion the suspicion that they are responsible for the splitting of the rind at the time when the orange is maturing. It has, however, been ascertained that these beetles only attack the orange when the rind has been ruptured by accident or disease, or when it is softened by decay.

Carpophilus mutilatus (Fab.; Plate XIV, Fig. 5) is dull red-brown, with the disk of the wing-covers lighter; the latter do not reach the end of the body, and leave the last two joints exposed to view. The length of the adult is 2.8^{mm} ($\frac{11}{100}$ inch).

The larva has a rather long, cylindrical body divided into simple rings or joints; the color is dull white, with the head and first joint of the body brown; the last joint terminates in a pair of notched spines or conical projections toothed at the base.

Epuræa æstiva (Linn.; Plate XIV, Fig. 6) is shining, uniformly yellowish brown; the wing-covers nearly cover the body, leaving only the tip of the last joint exposed. The insect is smaller than the preceding; length, 2.2^{mm} ($\frac{8}{100}$ inch).

The habits of these two beetles are very similar and they are always found together, although the Epuræa is usually present in greater numbers than the Carpophilus.

In September they appear in great numbers in every grove where rotting fruit is allowed to remain upon the ground. The active larvæ, as well as the perfect insects, soon swarm in the rotting fruit, and being active in flight, the beetles seek out and penetrate the split or injured fruit even upon the trees.

They can, however, scarcely be considered injurious insects, as they are not capable of penetrating the fruit of their own accord, but merely take advantage of any chance opening to gain admittance to the pulp. The effect of their attack is simply to hasten by some hours the decay which inevitably follows any external injury to the rind.

The pupæ are formed in the earth; those of Epuræa just beneath the surface, and those of Carpophilus at a depth of several inches. They occupy small oval cavities made by the movements of the larva.

Development in these beetles is very rapid; the interval between broods does not exceed twenty-five days. Of this period, about ten days is passed as larva and eight or nine days as pupa; the remaining six or seven days are occupied by the beetles in coupling and ovipositing, and by the hatching of the eggs.

WINE OR POMACE FLY OF THE ORANGE.

Associated with the two beetles mentioned above is a little pale yellow fly of a kind that is familiar to most housekeepers under the name of "wine fly" or "vinegar fly." It has a rosy-red head and brick-red eyes; the joints of the abdomen are bordered above with black. Length of the fly, 2.6^{mm} ($\frac{1}{10}$ inch).

The maggots of this fly are found in great numbers in company with the larvæ of the sap-beetles in rotting oranges, through the pulp of which they burrow in every direction and greatly increase the rapidity of decay.

The maggot is transparent white, with a cylindrical body, thickest at the posterior end, and tapering to a sharp point at the head; the body joints are very prominently ringed. At the posterior end a pair of projections form the principal breathing organs. The head ends in a pair of hooked jaws, which have the raking movement common to most fly larvæ. The dark color of the jaws and frame-work which constitutes their base renders them visible through the transparent walls of the body.

In pupating, the larva enters the earth a short distance, or remains attached to the under side of the orange as it lies upon the ground. The larva contracts and its skin hardens, forming a casket-shaped puparium, about one-third as wide as long. The puparium is chestnut-brown in color; it retains the breathing-tubes of the larva, but is distended and slightly altered in form by the hardening of all the parts.

The wine-fly undergoes all its transformations within two weeks. This rapidity of development is evidently necessary, as the insect is dependent upon the juices of the orange, not only for its subsistence in the larva state, but also for the moisture necessary to sustain life in the pupa.

OTHER SPECIES.

The two beetles and the wine-fly above mentioned sometimes become annoying pests in the packing-house when piles of decaying fruit are allowed to remain about the premises, but are easily banished by clearing away the refuse, and maintaining cleanliness. In the grove, if the dropped oranges are picked up regularly, and the ground about the trees kept clean, these insects will rarely make their appearance. If, through carelessness in this regard, they are allowed to become numerous and infest the grove, thorned and split fruit, which might otherwise be used for wine-making, will, owing to their attacks, be rendered useless for this and other purposes, even before it has fallen from the trees.

Other closely allied beetles and other species of flies are found to infest injured or rotting fruit. Two only can be mentioned at present; they are—

(1.) *Smicrips hypocoproides* Reiter, a minute Nitidulid introduced from the West Indies, but which has become quite abundant in parts of the southern United States, and is found feeding upon sap and also in rotting cotton bolls.

(2.) *Europs pallipennis* Lec., a rare Monotomid beetle.

Fruit-eating Ant.—A small dark-brown ant, a probably undescribed species of Lasius, is sometimes found gnawing the pulp of split oranges upon the tree. A stream of the ants may be seen carrying bits of the fruit down the trunk of the tree.

INSECTS IN DRY FRUIT.

BLASTOBASIS CITRICOLELLA Chambers.

This small moth, belonging to the family Tineidæ, is described in the Report of the Commissioner of Agriculture for 1879, p. 207, where the following note concerning it occurs:

"From a dry orange which was found at Jacksonville, Fla., in the latter part of January, and preserved on account of its being infested by a small beetle (*Aræocerus fasciculatus*), there issued rather unexpectedly on March 17 a small gray Tineid moth, which was referred to Mr. Chambers for determination. * * *" The full description is given on the same page.

ORANGE-EATING TINEID.[15]

Another minute moth of the same family as the preceding (*Tineidæ*) was bred from the pupa found in a crevice of the rind of a split orange. The pupa was enveloped loosely with silk, in which were entangled the droppings of the larva, and was otherwise surrounded with evidences that the insect had fed upon the dry portions of the rind. The moth issued early in October and proved a very handsome insect of dark color, with scales of lustrous lead-color on the upper wings and body, the surface having a violet sheen. The head and thorax are iridescent dove-color. On the margin of the upper wing, at its base, is a membranous flap (costal fold), which can be folded beneath the wing or opened widely, disclosing a lining of delicate hairs, arranged in three tufts, the lower one forming, when erect, a rosette of lemon-yellow color; above this a tuft of orange yellow, and the upper tuft a pencil of purple hairs.

ARÆOCERUS FASCICULATUS (De G.).

This little brownish beetle is commonly found in dry or blasted bolls of cotton. It is also said to be injurious to coffee in Brazil. In the Report of the Commissioner of Agriculture for 1879, p. 206, mention is made of its occurrence in a dry orange. The larva and pupa, as well as the perfect insect, were obtained at the same time.

WHITE ANTS (TERMITES) IN FRUIT.

The fruit of the Citron, when growing upon recumbent branches and when touching the earth, is frequently entered by Termites and entirely destroyed by them. Oranges which have fallen from the trees and are allowed to remain upon the ground are also attacked, but less frequently than the citron. The Termites feed upon the thick inner rind of the citron, and upon the membranous divisions in the orange. They enter the fruit from beneath, through a small perforation made in the rind. The Termites never ascend the trees or attack fruit which is not resting upon moist earth. Their appetite for this sort of food is not very strong, and the loss they inflict cannot be considered serious. If citrons are attacked the fruit should be raised from the ground or allowed to rest upon a dry support, and the ground around and under the bushes should be frequently stirred with a rake.

CHAPTER XII.

PREDATORY INSECTS.

INSECTS PREYING UPON APHIS.

LADY-BIRDS.—COCCINELLIDÆ.

Several species of this family have already been noticed as predatory upon Scale-insects; nearly all the species, and they are very numerous, prey to a greater or less extent upon Aphis. Of the larger forms, which are familiar everywhere under the name of Lady-birds, four species are commonly found feeding upon the Orange Aphis in our groves. They are *Chilocorus bivulnerus* (Muls.);* *Exochomus contristatus* (Muls);† *Cycloneda sanguinea* (Linn.);‡ and *Hippodamia convergens* Guér.§ These have all been mentioned as preying upon scale-insects. Among the smaller members of this family are numerous species of the genus Scymnus, which prey upon Plant-lice, and most of them are found from time to time upon the orange trees. The form in Scymnus is rounded and very convex; the color in most of the species is a somber brown, sometimes relieved with blotches of dull red or yellow. The body is always hairy. In size the species range from one-tenth to one-twentieth of an inch in length. They are apt to resemble each other closely, and in some groups the species are distinguishable the one from the other only on the closest analysis.

The larva of Scymnus is rather thick and short, the body dark-brown, purple, or black, but entirely covered above with tufts of white wax, which are easily rubbed off in handling the insect.

The pupa is found within the split skin of the larva, as with the larger species of Lady-birds.

SCYMNUS CAUDALIS Lec.

In this species the body is black, with the head and parts of the thorax red; the end of the body and the legs yellowish-red. Length, 2^{mm} ($\frac{8}{100}$ inch).

---

* Black, with two red spots.
† Smaller in size. Red, with two black spots.
‡ Blood-red or brick-red, without spots.
§ Orange-red, with five or six spots on each wing-cover.

This is the commonest and one of the largest species found among Plant-lice on the Orange in Florida. Certain other species, almost equally common, are entirely black, and differ the one from the other only in size, and in characters too minute for popular description.

The larvæ of all the species bear white flocculent tufts, and have no marks by which the species can be readily distinguished. They are quite active when disturbed, but are usually seen quiescent in the midst of the unresisting herd of Aphis, feeding upon the young lice.

They undergo their transformations upon the leaves among the remains of the Aphis colonies destroyed by them and other enemies. The pupa is held in the split skin of the larva, and is dark-colored like the body of the latter.

SYRPHUS FLIES.—SYRPHIDÆ.

Whenever colonies of Aphis are found on the Orange there will almost invariably be found among them slug-like larvæ, which creep about among the Plant-lice with a leech-like movement, now contracting into an almost globular mass, and again elongating like the joints of a telescope. The minute terminal joint, which constitutes the head of the larva, is observed to possess a pair of retractile horny hooks, which work forwards and back, in and out of the mouth, like a rake. As the larva advances with a groping motion, for it is quite blind and eyeless, the outstretched neck and head sweep the surface, and the jaws continue their raking movement until they strike the body of an Aphis. Immediately the jaw-hooks grapple their unresisting victim, and soon through the transparent walls of the body the sucking stomach is seen pulsating and drawing through the œsophagus in a continuous stream the green juices of the plant-louse.

When actively engaged in feeding these larvæ continue with the greatest voracity to empty one louse after another, until they have destroyed dozens of them; and their bodies, distended with the contained juices, become translucent green in color. When filled to repletion, the larva falls into a lethargy, lasting two or three hours; during which the processes of digestion change the juices of the body to varying shades of brown, and dark masses of fecal matter gradually form in the intestines. The curious changes of color in the semi-transparent larvæ are therefore due entirely to the condition of the body-contents. Full fed individuals usually have a tinge of flesh color, owing to the formation of glandular, creamy masses of fat, which have a roseate hue. When fasting through scarcity of food, the fat is absorbed and the body becomes dark-brown and opaque. While feeding the larva is translucent green; while digesting the colors change to olive and brown, with distinct markings of reddish brown and black.

Transformations.—When full fed the larva attaches itself by means of a pair of terminal prop-legs, aided by a viscid secretion which it voids, and which in drying glues it to the surface of the plant. The body becomes distended and thickened, losing in length what it gains in girth. The skin of the larva is not split or shed, but hardens and forms the puparium, which protects the true pupa within. In the puparium the shape of the larva is profoundly altered, the body joints are obliterated, the anterior end becomes swollen and broadly rounded, and the form tapers suddenly behind.

The perfect fly issues by pushing off the convex end of the puparium, which splits at the suture between two of the old larval joints, and releases a circular cap, in the shape of a watch-glass.

The duration of the egg and larva periods in these Aphis-eating flies is short; the egg hatches in forty-eight hours after it is laid, and the larva becomes full grown and forms its pupa in five or six days. About ten days, the average time with insects having many broods, are passed in pupa. The reason of this extremely rapid development in the first two stages, the egg and larva, becomes obvious when we consider how brief is the existence of the Aphis itself, and how suddenly its colonies appear and disappear; for the life of a colony of Aphis is also very short. Upon the Orange the Aphis can feed only upon the very tender young leaves; in a short time these harden, and then the colony must scatter; but frequently, long before that time, their numbers are reduced almost to extermination by enemies and parasites. As the Syrphus larvæ cannot follow the winged insects, they must make the best of their limited opportunities and feed quickly or perish of starvation. It is curious to mark how nature in the case of these insects has responded to the necessities of the situation and given their larvæ restless activity, great rapacity, and destructive powers, notwithstanding their slow locomotion, and also a remarkably brief egg period, so that this wingless, blind, and almost legless maggot is enabled to compete with more perfectly organized rivals in the food struggle which takes place over every Aphis colony.

Broods, &c.—The larvæ of these Syrphus flies feed only upon Aphis and depend upon them for their existence. They therefore appear and disappear with the colonies of the latter, and the broods may be supposed to follow rapidly one upon another during the seasons of growth, when the appearance of new shoots upon the Orange gives support to numerous colonies of Aphis.

The seasons of growth in the Orange, after the renewal of the foliage in the early spring, depend in a great measure upon the prevalence of rains and vary from year to year, but are usually three or four in number during the year. The colonies of Aphis and likewise their Syrphus enemies are most abundant in June and September.

Three representatives of the family Syrphidæ are found among Aphis on the Orange. They belong to the genus Baccha.

THE FOUR-SPOTTED APHIS-FLY.[*]

(*Baccha babista* Walker.)

[Figs. 81, 82 and 83.]

This is a rather slender fly, with a large, well-rounded head, and a club-shaped hind-body, supported on a slender stalk or peduncle; the eyes, which cover the greater part of the head, are mahogany-brown; the thorax black, with a metallic luster, and with a golden-yellow shield; the wings are transparent; the club of the abdomen brown, marked with four pale triangular spots. (Fig. 81.) Length, 10^{mm} ($\frac{4}{10}$ inch).

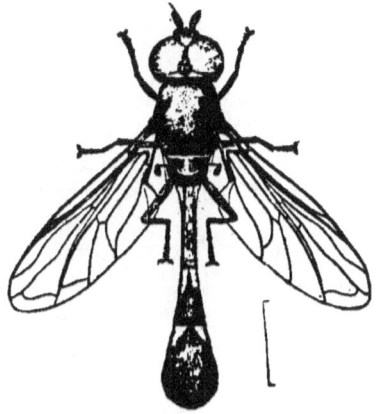

Fig. 81.—*Baccha babista*, adult. (Original.)

Fig. 82.—*Baccha babista*, larva. (Original.)

The larva (Fig. 82) has a cylindrical body, greenish, with a longitudinal band of dull red on the back; the joints about equal in size, except the first three, which are tapered, and form a retractile neck; the surface is covered with very short, stiff hairs, giving it a velvety appearance; each joint of the body is armed with a row of soft spines above and a pair of fleshy prop-legs below. Length, when at rest, 7.5^{mm} ($\frac{3}{10}$ inch).

The puparium, or chrysalis (Fig. 83), has the form of a cone, with one side flattened and fastened to the surface of the leaf; the large end is broadly rounded, convex; the color varies from dirty white to dull yellow, and there are more or less distinct cross-shaped markings upon the back; the spines of the larva shrink to minute prickles on the puparium.

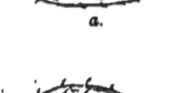

Fig. 83.—*Baccha babista*, puparium: *a*, dorsal view; *b*, lateral view. (Original.)

The eggs are elongate-oval, brilliant white, the surface marked with diamonds by obliquely intersecting engraved lines. They are deposited by the parent fly singly upon the leaves among Plant-lice.

Parasites.—Minute Chalcid parasites prey upon the Syrphus larva,

---

[*] This very common species has been described by Mr. Ashmead under the name *Conops? quadrimaculata.* (Orange Insects, page 69.)

and issue from the puparium, in numbers varying from six to eighteen, through a number of small holes which they gnaw in its top and sides. They are from 1^{mm} to 2^{mm} in length, and have the dark bronze and metallic colors with hyaline and iridescent wings so common in this family (*Chalcididæ*).

THE DUSKY-WINGED APHIS-FLY.

(*Baccha lugens* Loew.)

[Fig. 84.]

Another species of Baccha, scarcely less common than the preceding, has a more leech-like larva, in form flattened and dilated behind, but with the anterior joints lengthened into a very mobile and extensile neck. The surface of this larva is nearly smooth, without the spines or velvet hairs of the first species. In color the larva is dark, inclining to purple when not feeding, with cream-colored blotches, tinged with pink. The length in repose is about 8^{mm} ($\frac{32}{100}$ inch).

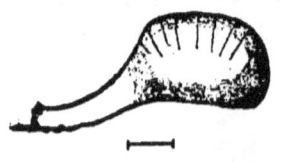

Fig. 84 — *Baccha lugens*, puparium. (Original.)

The puparium (Fig. 84) is dull brown, gourd-shaped; the anterior portion greatly inflated and behind suddenly flattened and contracted to form a sort of handle. The terminal spiracles of the larva are seen at the tip of the handle-like abdomen, where they form a pair of wart-like prominences.

The fly does not differ greatly in form from the preceding; it has eyes of brighter red, and the wings are distinctly clouded with spots of brown; the thorax less shining, dark bronze; the shield (metathorax) dark bronze, like the thorax; abdomen thicker, less broadly dilated at the end, uniform brown in color. The size of the imago varies greatly, from 8^{mm} ($\frac{32}{100}$ inch) (small males) to 12^{mm} ($\frac{48}{100}$ inch) (large females).

The egg is indistinguishable from that of *Baccha babista*.

THE RUDDY APHIS-FLY.

(*Baccha cognata* Loew).

A third species of this genus is found in company with the preceding species preying upon Aphis, sometimes upon Orange, but more frequently upon different kinds of Plant-lice found on herbaceous plants and weeds of the garden. In this species the form of the fly and its larva approach closely to that of *B. lugens*, but they are somewhat more slender and smaller than either of the preceding species. In the perfect fly the color of the eyes is mahogany-brown; the thorax black, not shining; the wings densely clouded with red-brown; the abdomen dull red, and very slightly dilated at the tip.

Larva.—The maggot has the form and smooth surface of *B. lugens*, but is more transparent and lighter in color, yellowish-green and white predominating.

THE PRUINOSE APHIS-FLY.*

[Figs. 85 and 86.]

A very common enemy of the Orange Aphis is a small two-winged fly. Its young is a greenish, slug-like maggot, 3^{mm} ($\frac{12}{100}$ inch) in length; the body is flattened beneath, convex above, with two deep longitudinal furrows on the back; the joints of the head and neck are small and tapering, as in the larva of Syrphus, and can be greatly extended or entirely withdrawn into the body; the body behind is rather broadly rounded; from the upper surface near the hind margin arises a pair of diverging appendages like the horns of a snail; the ends of these appendages are open pores, and the apparatus constitutes the principal spiracles, through which the animal breathes; the surface of the larva is roughened with minute knob-like excrescences.

FIG. 85.—The Pruinose Aphis-fly, larva. (Original.)

When ready to transform into pupa, the larva glues itself to the surface of the leaf by means of a black gum. The body of the larva shortens and thickens, becomes oval in shape, and assumes a golden-brown color, the breathing tubes are now very prominent, the lateral furrows of the larva are not obliterated, but divide the puparium into longitudinal lobes, and appear as broad bands of darker color upon the surface of the casket.

When vacated by the fly the puparium splits in a ring near the anterior end, releasing the tip in the form of a conical cap the cap also splits across the middle, dividing into two valve-like halves, only one of which is usually thrown off by the fly in its exit.

The fly (Fig. 86) is a small, thick bodied insect, about 2^{mm} ($\frac{8}{100}$ inch) in length, with deep purple eyes, transparent wings, and particolored legs; the body is bluish-white (pruinose), with sparsely placed black hairs; the upper surface of the thorax is marked with four longitudinal stripes of umber-brown. The egg is white, elongate oval, with fine longitudinal lines; it is fastened to the surface of the leaf among the living Aphis.

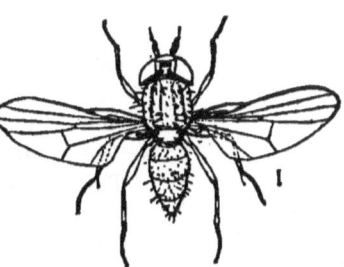

FIG. 86.—The Pruinose Aphis-fly. (Original.)

Transformations.—What has been said of the habits and transforma-

---

* Dr. S. W. Williston writes concerning this species: "They are evidently Anthomyids, but I cannot place them in any of the European genera. I am acquainted with a number of the Authomyid genera, but this species differs from any I know in the few bristles on the head and face."

tions of the Aphis-eating Syrphus-flies will apply equally to this insect, and it is found in company with them not alone upon the Orange, but among various species of Aphis on other plants as well.

Parasite.—A minute Hymenopterous fly (a Pteromalid)[16] attacks the larva and issues from the puparium through round holes eaten in its side. Two specimens of the parasites were bred from a single puparium of the fly. They issue in September.

OTHER PREDATORY INSECTS FREQUENTING THE ORANGE.

PREDATORY WASPS.

POLISTES AMERICANUS (Fabr.).

[Figs. 87 and 88.]

This large red wasp is fond of making its home under the dense foliage of the orange tree, and suspends its comb of paper to the branches.

FIG. 87.—*Polistes americanus.* (After Comstock.)

It is a large species, and its sting is equal in severity to that of the white-faced hornet. Fortunately, it is not an irritable wasp, and is little inclined to use its weapon, except when its nest is attacked.

Like most insects of its kind this wasp is carnivorous, and to a great extent preys upon caterpillars and soft-bodied insects. With these it feeds its young, first masticating the food into a pulpy ball, in order that it may readily be swallowed by its young, which are not provided with horny jaws, and then presenting it to the latter in their cells in much the same fashion that a bird feeds its nestlings. Not only the grubs are fed in this way, but also the young wasps which have recently issued from the pupa, and which do not for some time leave the nest or take part in the labors of the colony.

FIG. 88.—*Polistes* nest in spring. (After Riley.)

The nest consists of a single comb or layer of cells, which is increased in size by the addition of new cells around the edges until it sometimes attains the diameter of 10 or 12 inches. The comb is not protected by a covering of paper, as in the nest of a hornet, but the cells are built with the mouth downwards, and the back of the comb is made very thick and strong, so that it sheds water.

The wasps make their comb of wood masticated to a pulp. They may be seen gathering for this purpose from fence rails and unpainted wood surfaces the fibers beaten out by the action of the weather. The leaf-rolling caterpillars which injure the buds and tender shoots of the Orange form a very considerable portion of the food of all colonies of Polistes which have established themselves in the vicinity of orange groves. Numerous other insects are also destroyed by them. The orange-grower should not, therefore, be concerned to find them building their nests in his orange trees, and it is greatly to his interest to allow them to remain. The ordinary operations of cultivating and pruning rarely disturb these insects, who pay no attention to the methodical movements of the horticulturist, and only resent a direct attack. Before the time for gathering the oranges the nests are usually deserted by the wasps and the colonies dispersed, for they do not continue to breed during the winter months even in Florida.

THE VASE-MAKER WASP.

(*Eumenes fraterna* Say)

[Fig. 89.]

This is also a useful predatory wasp, and is never known to use its sting unless caught and held in the hand. It is $\frac{8}{10}$ inch in length; the color is black with white markings. The abdomen is borne on a slender stalk or peduncle, and forms a rounded knob, prolonged at the extremity in a rather blunt point. Each side of the swollen portion of the abdomen is marked with a white spot.

The female of this wasp is solitary and makes single cells of mud and sand, which she attaches to various plants, and not infrequently to the twigs of orange trees. These mud cells are almost spherical, about three-fourths inch in diameter; the walls are thin and fragile; they have an opening

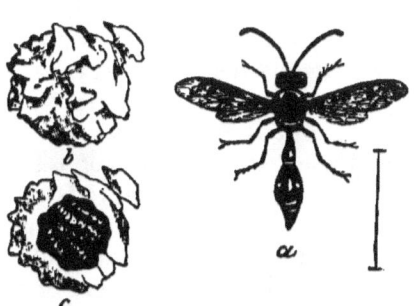

FIG. 89.—*a*, the Vase-Maker Wasp; *b*, nest; *c*, nest showing interior stored with caterpillars. (After Riley.)

which is provided with a projecting lip or ring and the structure resembles a globe-shaped flask, with a very short neck. Within the cell the female deposits a single white egg. She then packs it with small caterpillars, each of which is paralyzed and rendered helpless by a stab from her sting, and seals the opening with soft mud.

Each female constructs a number of cells, but scatters them about, seldom placing more than one or two in the same place. When filled and sealed up they are abandoned. The grub of the wasp feeds upon the caterpillars stored for its use; when all are consumed it forms its pupa within the cell, and in due course of time issues as a perfect insect, removing with its jaws the earthen stopper of its doorway.

Broods.—There are broods in spring and fall. The summer months are passed as pupæ, and the winter as perfect insects.

Parasites.—This wasp, in common with many other cell-making Hymenoptera, has an enemy which destroys the grub and occupies its place within the cell, issuing in its stead through a round hole made in its side. This parasite is a brassy-green Cuckoo-bee belonging to the genus Chrysis. It is remarkable for its bright metallic green or blue color, hard texture, and coarsely pitted surface, and the peculiar form of the abdomen, which is abruptly truncate behind and hollowed from the under side and is capable of folding over upon the head and breast, protecting the members in its hollow under surface, and making of the insect almost a compact ball. This position the insect is apt to assume when captured or disturbed. The perfect insect is 11^{mm} in length ($\frac{44}{100}$ inch) when fully extended.[17]

Other parasitic Hymenoptera have been bred from the cells of this wasp, but some of them (*Braconidæ*) are parasitic upon the caterpillars stored as food by the wasp, and not upon the young of the wasp itself. The eggs of these parasites existed in the bodies of the caterpillars before they were captured and placed in the cells by the mother wasp, and it is noteworthy that such parasitized caterpillars are not eaten by the wasp-grub; probably because they are soon destroyed by their internal enemy, and their bodies rapidly become too hard and tough for the weak jaws of the wasp-grub. It is also to be remarked that the poisoned sting of the wasp while paralyzing the caterpillar, does no injury to its internal parasite, but the latter completes its transformations as well shut up within the tightly sealed cell of the wasp as under normal conditions in the open air. The parasite fly, having cut its way out of the hardened skin of the caterpillar, finds itself still inclosed within the wasp cell, the walls of which it is unable to penetrate, and it therefore remains imprisoned until released by the exit of the wasp, for the presence of the caterpillar parasite in its cell in no way interferes with the transformations of the latter.

THE CAMEL-CRICKETS OR SOOTHSAYERS.

These are large insects, with attenuated bodies and long, slender legs, the first pair of which are elbowed and provided with sharp spines and hooks for capturing and holding their prey. The latter consists of insects of any sort, not protected by too hard a shell or other covering, but chiefly of flies and soft-bodied active larvæ. The camel-crickets do not molest Bark-lice, or other sedentary insects, and do not prowl about or spy into hidden places in search of food, but lie in wait for their prey, taking only that which comes within their reach; or they creep cautiously and slowly upon any small moving object which their keen and watchful eyes discover in their vicinity. When within reach of their prey, they seize it with the rapidity of lightning, and hold the struggling victim firmly clasped between the spines and grappling hooks of their fore legs.

PREDATORY INSECTS FREQUENTING THE ORANGE. 189

Their manner of feeding is very unlike that of other insects, and reminds one of a monkey eating fruit; they appear to masticate their food very deliberately before swallowing, biting off a piece from time to time, while they hold it in their claws.

The head swings upon a very mobile neck, and can be turned so far to the side as to look almost directly backwards over the shoulders. Their quick movements betray an alertness, in striking contrast with the feigned sluggishness of habit. This evidence of watchfulness, while the insect, with fore-arms folded, and claws clasped in the attitude of prayer, remains motionless and apparently absorbed in meditation, gives an irresistably comic air of hypocrisy to its actions. These peculiar habits were well known to the ancients, for the group is represented by numerous species in many parts of the world, and they early received the name Mantis (prophet, or soothsayer).

MANTIS CAROLINA.

[Figs. 90 and 91.]

This, the largest of our species, is not very abundant in Florida, but is sometimes seen upon orange trees, catching every moving insect that comes within the reach of its claws. It is yellowish-green in color, and

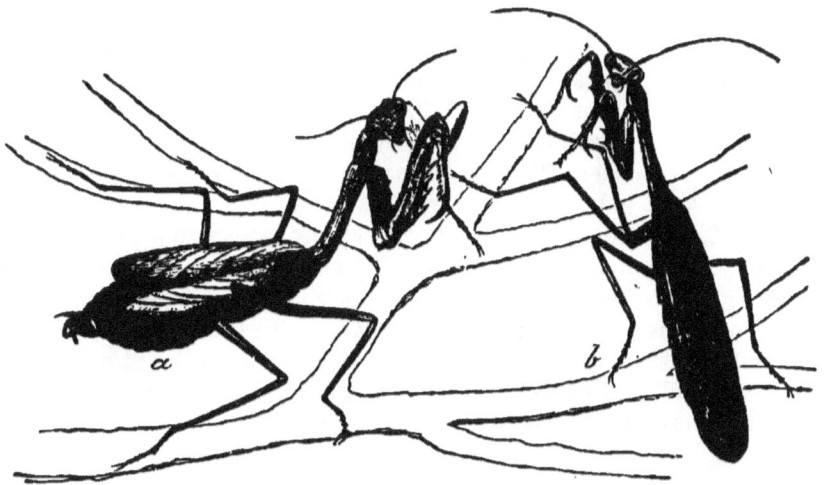

FIG. 90.—*Mantis carolina:* a, female; b, male. (After Riley.)

about two inches in length. It has wings in the adult state, which somewhat resemble folded leaves; each fore-wing bears a brown spot; in some exotic species the center of this spot is transparent, and resembles a hole eaten in the leaf by some insect. There is but one brood each year. The young hatch in early summer and complete their growth in the latter part of the season. The large egg-masses are glued to the twigs of trees; they are elongate, irregularly oval, about an inch in length, and contain forty or fifty eggs. The eggs (Fig. 91) occupy flattened cells placed in two ranks, alternating with each other; the cluster of cells has a braided or woven appearance, but consists simply of a continuous ribbon of mucus folded in close flutings, and having an egg deposited in the bight or angle of each fold. The eggs are deposited simultaneously with the deposition of this ribbon by the mother insect, and the whole mass is at first soft and flexible, but rapidly hardens by exposure to the air.

MANTIS MISSOURIENSIS?

In this species the body, though over two inches long, is but little thicker than a darning needle; the legs are very long and so slender that they seem hardly competent to sustain the weight of even so meager a body. The extreme attenuation of all its parts, and the light brown color of the insect, afford it protection from enemies, and enable it to advance unnoticed upon its prey. Its ghost-like form is difficult to detect upon plants, and it has the appearance of a straw caught in spiders' webs, an illusion which the insect with apparent design strengthens by frequently giving to its body a swaying motion as if vibrated by air currents.

This species is very common, and is frequently seen upon the Orange as well as upon other plants. It has a spring and fall brood. The egg-masses are brick-red in color, about half an inch long, and flattened upon the sides. They are usually deposited between the folds of a dry leaf or in crevices of the bark. The structure is the same as in the preceding species, but the cells are more distinct and regularly placed. The food of this Mantis consists chiefly of small flies, and neither this nor the preceding species are of much importance to the cultivator of plants, since they do not at all discriminate between his friends and foes, and do not seek out or destroy the more insidious enemies which lurk in hiding places, or those which protect themselves with a covering or scale.

Fig. 91. — Eggs of *Mantis carolina*. (After Riley.)

SOLDIER-BUGS.

Among the true bugs (*Hemiptera*) are numerous predatory species, of which not a few frequent the orange trees. It is not easy to distinguish the predatory from the plant-sucking kinds, and, indeed, in some instances, the same bug has both habits. The most noteworthy instance of this is in the case of *Raphigaster hilaris*, already noticed in Chapter IX. This species, on occasion a very destructive pest of the plant, is at other times a useful insect, killing and sucking the juices of plant enemies, particularly the leaf-eating caterpillars. Others of the Soldier-bugs feed upon the juices of the plant for a short time after hatching, and afterwards live exclusively upon insects.

The most rapacious of the bugs belong to the family Reduviidæ, and have the head well separated from the body by a more or less slender neck; they possess a stout, curved beak and long legs, well fitted for rapid movements. Many of these species bristle with spines, especially in the younger stages, and the usual colors are dark brown variegated with red.

THE SPIDER-LEGGED SOLDIER-BUG.

(*Leptocorisa tipuloides* Latr.)

[Plate VI, Fig. 4.]

This species has already been discussed among the enemies of Bark-lice (see Chapter VI). It is very commonly seen upon the Orange, and frequents, often in great numbers, trees infested with Lecanium Scales, and not only sucks the juices of the Bark-lice, but also captures ants and other insects which are attracted by the lice.

This predaceous bug should not be confounded with the plant-sucking Red bug (*Dysdercus suturellus*), which does injury to the fruit. In Leptocoris the form is slender; the body seven-tenths of an inch long and the legs longer than the body; the colors are orange and black.

The stouter form and deep-red color of the Red-bug render the two species distinguishable at a glance.

Leptocorisa must be classed among beneficial insects, since it feeds to some extent upon Plant-lice and Bark-lice; but, like many predatory bugs, it captures and destroys indiscriminately the friends as well as the foes of the plant. Possibly at times it subsists almost entirely upon the honey-dew ejected by Plant-lice. Acids as well as sweets appear to be suited to its taste, and it is one of the few insects known to prey upon ants, the juices of whose bodies are strongly flavored with formic acid.

The following soldier-bugs form part of a great army of predaceous insects which frequent the orange tree, but have no very close connection with the plant or its especial fauna.

THE RAPACIOUS SOLDIER-BUG.

(*Sinea multispinosa*, De Geer.)

[Fig. 92.]

Colors brownish, with a red stripe along the upper surface of the abdomen. The body is slender, but less so than Leptocorisa. The young bugs are said to feed upon Plant-lice; the adults, however, attack insects of large size.

FIG. 92.—*Sinea multispinosa*. (After Glover.)

THE WHEEL-BUG.

(Prionotus cristatus, Linn.)

[Fig. 93.]

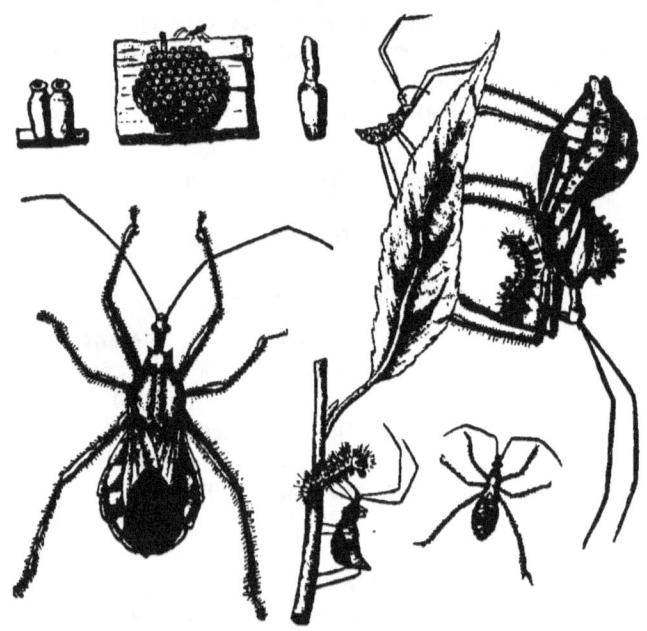

Fig. 93.—*Prionotus cristatus.* (After Glover.)

This large bug is not uncommon in orange groves. Its body and legs are covered with a coat of very fine, close down, giving it an ash-gray color; the thorax rises in a semi-circular ridge, which is provided with short, projecting spines, regularly placed, like the teeth of a cog-wheel; the head is small, but is armed with a powerful beak, which is capable of giving a poisonous stab, more painful to man than the sting of a hornet.

Mr. Glover, in the Report of the Commissioner of Agriculture for 1875, gives an extended account of this insect, and shows that it is very voracious in all its stages; the young prey upon Aphis and other small or soft-bodied insects, and after paralyzing them with their deadly sting suck and empty them of their juices.

The eggs are urn-shaped, as shown in the figure, and are deposited in large clusters, firmly cemented to each other, and placed in all sorts of situations, but usually upon some firm support, such as the trunk of a tree or the side of a building, or fence rail.

The young wheel-bugs are bright red with black markings.

The Green Soldier-bug (*Raphigaster hilaris* Fitch), the two species of Metapodius (*M. femoratus*, and *M. terminalis*), with the closely allied species, *Euthochtha galeator* Fabr., have already been noticed as partly plant-feeding, but with rapacious habits also.

INNOXIOUS INSECTS.

CASE-BEARERS ON ORANGE.

The trunks of orange trees are favorite feeding-grounds for the larvæ of several small moths of the family Tineidæ, which protect their bodies with cases formed of fragments of their food material. In the case of those species which are met with upon orange-tree trunks the food consists of lichens or other minute cryptogams found growing upon the bark.

A very common species belongs apparently to the genus Coleophora. Its case is dull white, about the size and somewhat the shape of a grain of oats; it is rather smooth outside, and seems to be formed of finely comminuted bark.

THE ORANGE CASE-BEARING TINEID.

(*Coleotechnites citriella* Chambers.)

This species was first made known in the Report of the Commissioner of Agriculture for 1879, which contains the following account of its habits. Mr. Chambers' descriptions of the genus and species will be found in the same report, page 206:

"At Manatee, Fla., in the latter part of April, I found upon the trunk of an orange tree the case of a Tineid larva. This case was rather slender, 11^{mm} (.43 inch) long, and rather pointed at the hinder extremity. It was dark gray in color, resembling the bark upon which it was found, and was apparently composed of small bits of lichens and excremental pellets, with much gray silk. The moth issued March 6, and upon being referred to Mr. Chambers proved to be a new species representing a new genus."

BARK CLEANERS.

Among the host of harmless insects that from time to time make their appearance upon the orange tree, there is a group of scavengers that frequent the trunks and assist in cleansing the bark, by devouring the fungi, molds, or excreta of other insects that befoul its surface. Of these the most conspicuous examples are certain nerve-veined insects (Neuroptera) belonging to the genus Psocus.

PSOCUS VENOSUS Burm.

The adult of this species is smoky-brown; head dark bronze; antennæ dusky, lighter at the base, densely hairy in the male; thorax margined with yellow; fore-wings almost black, the three basal veins yellow, with a triangular spot of yellow color (pterostigma) near the margin toward the tip; hind-wings smoky, hyaline; feet yellowish, with dusky tips; length 5^{mm} to 8^{mm} ($\frac{2}{10}$ to $\frac{3}{10}$ inch).

These little animals are seen upon the trunks of orange trees in flocks numbering from a dozen to forty or fifty individuals. They feed in companies and browse upon the lichens which they cleanly remove from the bark, leaving a clear space behind them. The colonies consist of one or more families and include individuals of all ages, the wingless young herding with the adult insects.

The adults, although winged, do not readily take flight. When alarmed the troop huddles together for mutual protection like sheep, but if directly attacked, or when seized with a sudden panic, they scatter in every direction and run nimbly over the bark, with which their drab colors harmonize so closely that they are not easily distinguished upon its surface. If left undisturbed, the herd in a short time reassembles and quietly resumes its methodical attack upon the lichens.

The eggs are oval, glistening white; they are laid upon the bark in batches of 15 to 30, deposited on end in several rows obliquely overlapping each other, and the batch is protected by an oval, convex shield of comminuted wood which surrounds and adheres closely to the eggs.

The females watch their eggs, and as soon as they are hatched lead their young ones forth to pasture.

This delicately organized insect is fond of shade and moisture and is most commonly seen in densely-shaded groves and old gardens. It is not restricted to the orange, nor is it compelled to live upon plants alone; it may thrive on walls or fences, wherever lichens grow. The smooth bark of the orange, when conditions favor the growth of fungi, affords excellent pasturage to this Psocus and it frequently becomes very abundant.

It is hardly necessary to point out that to the extent of its feeble powers this is a useful insect, and its presence should excite no alarm. *Psocus venosus* is more distinctively a northern than a southern insect and does not inhabit the extreme southern portion of the orange district in Florida. The adult insects hibernate and begin breeding early in the spring.

THE ORANGE PSOCUS.

(*Psocus citricola* Ashmead.)

This is a smaller species than the preceding. Length 2.5^{mm} to 3^{mm} ($\frac{10}{100}$ to $\frac{12}{100}$ inch). The color is white or pale yellow; the adults have very transparent, hyaline wings. At all ages the semi-transparent body shows the color of the intestinal contents, which varies considerably with the condition and nature of the food. This consists of the wax and other soft excretions of Bark-lice, of honey-dew, and probably also of minute fungi or their spores, which germinate on leaves and bark infested with insects.

The eggs are pearly-white and are laid in hollows upon orange leaves, in clusters of ten or twelve, tightly covered with a shield of black excrementitious matter. Over this is stretched a light canopy of web, in which are entangled a few minute black grains of excrement. The extreme transparency of the egg envelopes as well as of the animal itself affords an unusually favorable opportunity for the study of the changes that precede its birth.

Just before hatching the embryos lie with their backs to the surface of the leaf and are not curled in the egg, but the head only is bent over upon the breast. As the egg-shell is absolutely transparent and the embryo very nearly equally so, all internal changes of form can be plainly seen.

In hatching, the first movement seen is the formation of air bubbles, which pass in rapid succession between the mouth organs and collect in a larger bubble within the head of the embryo. From time to time this larger bubble passes through the constriction of the neck and disappears in the body cavity. The head of the embryo gradually swells, elongates, and distends the elastic egg-shell at the end, until this finally bursts and the young insect protrudes its body, curving upwards and forwards.

Air continues to pass through the neck into the abdomen, which becomes greatly distended and elongated, showing the segments. A muscular movement not connected with the passage of the air bubbles is seen in the frontal part of the head and the occiput is frequently drawn inwards, forming a deep depression.

The bursting of the first larval skin was not witnessed, but it evidently takes place soon after the abdomen is fully distended. The larva remains for many hours in an erect position, with the tip of the body clasped by the egg-shell and the cast larval skin. The head, at first elongate, becomes transverse and there is a general contraction and change of form in all the parts.

After the larva has freed itself from the egg-shell and envelopes, the abdomen is gradually contracted by the exertion of considerable and long-continued muscular effort and changes from a cylindrical to a cordate form.

The process of hatching occupies several days, and the young, as we have seen, make their entrance into the world, like a marsupial, in a somewhat rudimentary condition.

The Orange Psocus lives chiefly upon the leaves of plants, associated in small flocks or families. It passes the greater part of its life hiding under the canopies of web erected over the egg-clusters. Here the mother awaits the appearance of her brood, and here the young insects cluster, sallying forth from time to time with the adult in search of food.

The species breeds continuously in summer and some eggs are hatched even in winter. The adult insects hibernate in protected places, but are more delicate than their northern relative and probably do not extend beyond the region in which the Orange is grown.

The operations of this Psocus are apparently of trifling importance; it is, however, one of the commonest of orange insects and as such attracts considerable attention.

APPENDICES.

APPENDIX I.

THE MEALY BUG AT ORANGE LAKE, FLORIDA.

[Extracted from a letter by Jos. Voyle, Gainesville, Fla., June 12, 1884. Reprinted from Bulletin 4, Division of Entomology, U. S. Department of Agriculture, p. 85.]

Having business near Orange Lake during the past week, I visited several orange groves. I found all of the Florida varieties of Scale-insects in abundance. Oranges are already rusty, and the Rust-mite in many places, on both leaves and fruit, in such large numbers as to give a distinct coloration, distinguishable at a distance of ten feet.

But the most destructive insect, at present absorbing all the attention of the orange-growers there, is the Mealy-bug, *Dactylopius destructor*. This insect causes the fruit to rot under the colonies. A favorite place of lodgment is at the stem, under the calyx; the result is, the fruit drops.

I staid there three days to examine methods used and experiment in their destruction.

The cottony armor repels all watery solutions.

The methods used are: spraying each separate colony with pure kerosene by means of bellows atomizers; and mechanical action—rubbing or pinching each separate colony (by colony I mean the little clusters consisting of from ten to several hundred individuals); this is done by the fingers.

I examined the trees that had been treated with the kerosene spray and found both the leaves and fruit spotted yellow. I was also informed that fruit saved in this way two years ago was useless, having absorbed the odor of kerosene. The effective progress made by the means used is trifling, in consideration of the work to be done. I tried experiments with solutions of murvite sprayed on, but with no good result; then tried kerosene butter, using thick, milky solution of murvite, which combines in exactly the same way as with cow's milk, and found that an effective emulsion could thus be made.

After using and watching the action of this for some time, I saw that the interior insects of a dense mass were protected by the exterior ones; further experiments were made to meet this difficulty. By watching the men at work I saw that nearly every infested orange was handled to turn all of its sides to the eye; that wherever a large colony found lodgment in a fork of twigs or in a depression of the bark they were handled, also that the bunches of Spanish moss (*Tillandsia*) formed formidable breeding places. All of these require force for their dislodgment.

A strong stream of water was tried and proved effective, but laborious, and the insects falling to the ground were not killed.

Experiments with solution of murvite, made under a microscope, showed that in all cases where the solution came into actual contact with the skin of the insect the bug was instantly killed. Acting upon this and the knowledge gained by previous observation and experiment, I tried the effect of a fine, solid stream issuing under pressure, using a solution of murvite, one part, to water two hundred and fifty parts.

The results were excellent; the solution being forced into the colonies broke them up, and coming into contact with the insects killed them, the method of working being one man at the pump, another to guide the stream. The apparatus improvised being badly adapted to the purpose is very awkward. The work, although about four times as fast as with the bellows atomizer, is not adequate to the economical requirements. This method has the merit of no loss by damage to fruit or leaves by the material used; the waste, falling on the leaves and branches, will exterminate both scale-insects and rust-mites, these being plentiful, but neglected in the presence of the more pressing necessity of saving the growing crop from destruction by the Mealy-bug.

APPENDIX II.

EXPERIMENTS WITH INSECTICIDES.

[In part a reprint of matter published in the Report of the Entomologist, Annual Report of the Commissioner of Agriculture for 1881-'82. pp. 120-126.]

TABLE I.—KEROSENE EMULSIONS.

In Table I are given the results of seventeen experiments with kerosene in milk emulsions of varying strength. When the percentage of Coccids killed is given, this was obtained by cutting twigs, leaves, and portions of infested bark from all parts of the tree, and examining microscopically in the laboratory large numbers of the scales upon them. Under the head of young Coccids are included all those which have well-formed scales but have not begun to lay eggs. The youngest Bark-lice, or those which have not yet molted, were almost invariably killed, and are not included in the enumeration.

The percentage of young Coccids killed is given separately, including under this head all ages between the formation of the permanent scale and the appearance of eggs, but no larvæ before the first molt; the latter were in nearly every case all killed. Of scales which contained eggs three classes were examined and the percentage of each obtained: (1) Scales in which a portion only of the eggs were destroyed; (2) Scales in which all the eggs were killed; (3) Scales in which no eggs were killed.

Purple Scales (*Mytilaspis citricola*) were not abundant, but appear to be somewhat less readily destroyed than Long Scale. All the experiments were made upon young orange trees from three to six years old. An Aquapult pump of medium size was used, and in each case the trees were sprayed from the ground and on four sides. Where the trees were more than eight or ten feet in height the upper branches did not receive the spray with sufficient force, and show in some cases a smaller percentage of Bark-lice destroyed than the lower portions of the same tree. For full-grown trees a larger pump is needed, and the apparatus should be placed in a cart or otherwise raised above the ground when used.

The emulsions used were made as follows:

No. 2. Kerosene, 1 pint; sour cow's milk, 2 fluid ounces, dashed with a ladle; 2 drachms of powdered chalk were first added to the milk, and 2 ounces water during the stirring.

An imperfect emulsion, not readily suspended in water.

No. 3. Kerosene, 1 quart; solution of condensed milk, 3 parts; water, 5 parts, 12 fluid ounces.

Emulsion made by spraying through the Aquapult pump and back into the pail. Stable, and readily suspended in water.

No. 9. Kerosene, 1 quart; condensed milk, 12 fluid ounces, diluted with water, 36 ounces; emulsified with the Aquapult.

No. 10. Kerosene, 25.6 fluid ounces; condensed milk, 4.8 fluid ounces; water, 14.4 ounces; emulsified with pump.

No. 11. Kerosene, 2 quarts; condensed milk, 12 fluid ounces (1 can); water, 20 ounces; with pump.

No. 13. Kerosene, 2 quarts, 4 fluid ounces; condensed milk, 12 fluid ounces; water, 24 ounces; with pump.

200 INSECTS AFFECTING THE ORANGE.

TABLE 1.—*Kerosene emulsions.*

No. of experiment	No. of emulsion	Kerosene in the emulsion.	Emulsion diluted with water.	Amount of diluted wash applied.	Date of application.	Date of examination.	Long Scale (*M. gloverii*).				Chaff Scale (*P. pergandii*).				Remarks.
							Young coccids killed.	Scales containing eggs.			Young coccids killed.	Scales containing eggs.			
								Eggs, in part killed.	Eggs, all killed.	Eggs, none killed.		Eggs, in part killed.	Eggs, all killed.	Eggs, none killed.	
		pr. ct.	Parts.	Qts.			pr. ct.	pr. ct.	pr. ct.	pr. ct.	pr. ct.	pr. ct.	pr. ct.	pr. ct.	
10	2	80	1 to 16	10	Oct. —	Oct. 22	98	30	61	0					Bark, leaves, and twigs of lower branches. Thorns from upper branches. November 10, a few gravid females still living, also a few young scales forming from eggs recently hatched. Second application effectively cleared the tree of scales; only an occasional gravid scale found alive on upper branches.
						Oct. 25	93	58	29	13					
10	11	67	1 to 16	6	Nov. 14	Nov. 17									No appreciable effect upon eggs or mature coccids.
11	3	73	1 to 64	6	Oct. 22	Oct. 25	25-30		0	99+					Thickly infested bark of lower limbs. Upper branches give variable results.
29	11	67	1 to 9¼	8	Nov. 14	Nov. 19	71	43	18	39					
						Dec. 26	100		100		63	05	0	35	Bark, twig, and leaves from all parts. Prolonged examination; not a living coccid or egg can be found. Mites swarm under the dead scales and have probably completed the work of the wash.
24	11	67	1 to 16	6	Nov. 11	Nov. 18	91	37	19	44					Result about the same as in No. 24, or slightly less effective and variable.
28	11	67	1 to 16	6	Nov. 14	Nov. 19									
25	11	67	1 to 16	4	Nov. 11	Nov. 19	78	29	8	63					Variable; some branches give poor results. Evidently not enough liquid used for thorough application.
31	11	67	1 to 16	3	Nov. 14	Nov. 18					22		5	95	Small tree, but not sufficient wash used. Effect on Long Scale about equal to No. 25. Lecanium Scales killed only where the spray struck with force.
26	11	67	1 to 16	2	Nov. 11	Nov. 19									Small tree, but amount of wash applied entirely insufficient. Many branches show no effect. Very few Long Scale killed.
38	13	65	1 to 16	5	Dec. 8	Dec. 12									Result about the same as in No 24. Second application four days later.
38	13	65	1 to 16	9	Dec. 12	Feb. 4									Almost complete extermination of Long Scale. A few living coccids found upon a twig from upper branches. On the same twig a few living Chaff Scale were also found.

APPENDIX II.

										Remarks
17	10	57	1 to 16	6	Nov. 4	Nov. 9	25 to 50			Action very unequal upon different parts of the tree. Examination made too soon after application to show full effect of the wash.
18	10	57	1 to 16	6	Nov. 4	Nov. 10 / Jan. 30			Few	Effect upon Chaff Scale very slight. On some leaves nearly all killed. Tree less infested than formerly and condition much improved, but not cleared of scales. Chaff Scale beginning to increase again. Some Long Scale still living.
20	9	40	1 to 8	6	Nov. 4	Nov. 10 / Jan. 30				Chaff Scale not appreciably affected. Long Scale killed to some extent. *Lecanium hesperidum* not killed. Application not effective in clearing the tree. Chaff Scale will soon begin to increase.
16	9	40	1 to 11	6	Nov. 3	Nov. 9 / Nov. 9 / Nov. 10	45 / 36 / 72	37 / 20 / 40	14 / 19 / 0	Leaves and twigs............ } Chaff Scale much less affected. Exposed bark of upper branches. } Leaves, twigs, and bark of main branches. Chaff Scale less affected; not counted.
						Nov. 11 / Jan. 25	100			A single large leaf. Long Scale and Chaff Scale beginning to increase and entering upon a new brood.
19	9	40	1 to 24	6	Nov. 4	Nov. 10				Tree infested with Chaff Scale only. Effect on scales scarcely appreciable. Application has had little or no effect. Number of living scales has neither increased nor diminished. New brood beginning to hatch.
						Jan. 30				
23	9			6	Nov. 4	Nov. 11				Imperfect emulsion made by churning together one-half pint of kerosene, 12 fluid oz. (?) condensed milk, and 6 quarts water. Application very unequal owing to imperfect mingling of the oil and water. Young of Long Scale killed on some branches and not killed on others. Eggs for the most part uninjured. Some infested leaves show all coccids killed on one side; all living on the other side.

Cost of kerosene wash.—The following is the estimated cost for a standard wash of whale-oil soap and kerosene emulsion containing 67 per cent. of oil, and diluted 1 to 9:

Kerosene, 2 gallons, retail at 20 cents	$0.40
Soap, ¼ pound, retail at 10 cents	5
Water, 1 gallon	0
Emulsion, 3 gallons	45

At wholesale rates, 18 cents for kerosene and 8 cents for soap, three gallons of emulsion cost 40 cents = 13⅓ cents per gallon. One gallon of emulsion = 10 gallons of diluted wash; cost, 15 cents. Cost of wash per gallon, 1½ cents.

With the "Aquapult" pump and "Cyclone" nozzle, four gallons of wash is sufficient for thirty nursery trees of one and two years from the bud. Cost per tree, two-tenth cent.

Trees which have been transplanted and have made two years' average growth in the grove (3 or 4 years from the bud) require about two-thirds of a gallon of wash. Cost, 1 cent per tree. Bearing trees of full size will require from 5 to 10 gallons of wash. Cost, 7 to 15 cents; average about 10 cents per tree.

TABLE 2.—WHALE-OIL SOAP.

In Table 2 are given the results of experiments with solutions of whale-oil soap applied in fine spray to all parts of the trees by means of the aquapult pump. The solutions were all applied hot, being either solid when cool or too thick for spraying through the pump.

TABLE 2.—*Whale-oil soap*.

No. of experiment	Soap (Lbs.)	Water (Qts.)	Whale-oil soap solutions	Date of application	Date of observation	Long Scale (*M. gloverii*) — Young coccids killed (pr. ct.)	Eggs, in part killed (pr. ct.)	Eggs, all killed (pr. ct.)	Eggs, none killed (pr. ct.)	Chaff Scale (*P. pergandii*) — Young coccids killed (pr. ct.)	Eggs, in part killed (pr. ct.)	Eggs, all killed (pr. ct.)	Eggs, none killed (pr. ct.)	Remarks.
34	1	4	4½ quarts applied hot.	Dec. 6	Dec. 17 / Jan. 28	100	0	0	100	85(?)	0	0	100	Tree infested with Long Scale and a few scattered Chaff Scale; nearly every coccid, old and young, killed; a very few Chaff Scale still alive; eggs of both scales absolutely uninjured; tree rather large; not enough liquid used.
33	1	6	6 quarts applied hot.	Dec. 6	Dec. 16 / Jan. 28	100	24	15	61					Long Scale completely exterminated; eggs and young probably destroyed by mites; living Chaff Scale, nearly all young or nearly adult, numerous on some parts.
35	1	8	8 quarts applied hot.	Dec. 8	Dec. 17	65	0	0	100					Small tree; very thorough application; at noon in the sun. Both Long and Chaff Scale completely exterminated upon nearly all parts of the tree; several twigs, however, have escaped thorough wetting, and are still moderately infested with one or both kinds of scale.
36	1	10	5 quarts applied hot.	Dec. 8	Dec. 26	90	0	0	100					Tall tree; difficult to cover with liquid; adult female coccids not all killed. A few individual Long Scale found alive on some branches; 1 or 2 per cent. living.
37	1	12	6 quarts applied hot.	Dec. 8	Dec. 26	70	0	0	100	0(?)	0	0	100	Small tree; Long Scale which have not completed the first molt are all killed; the proportions given include coccids from passed first molt to adult; a few Chaff Scale seen, all living; no gravid female coccids killed. Small tree; thorough application; a few Chaff Scale intermingled seem not to have been affected.

TABLE 3.—LYE SOLUTIONS.

The following is a synopsis of experiments with potash and soda in caustic solutions:

Experiments with potash.—*Experiment No. 90.*—Solution, 1¼ pounds potash to 1 gallon water. Applied in fine spray to two thrifty young trees, about four years old. Leaves and tender shoots wilted visibly and changed color during the application, showing, a few minutes later, spots of brown. Two days after the application all the leaves were dead and dried up as if by fire, and remained adhering to the branches. Young growth entirely killed and pitted with holes. Three weeks later all branches under one inch in diameter were found to be entirely killed, the bark of larger branches partly destroyed, the bark of trunk blackened and hardened, but not destroyed. Upon the latter buds had begun to appear. Upon those portions of the tree where the bark was entirely destroyed the insects themselves were destroyed, but one-tenth of the scales upon the dead bark contained living eggs. Where the bark was not entirely destroyed half of the Coccids and more than half of their eggs escaped. The tops of both trees were killed and their shape and symmetry ruined. A 40 per cent. kerosene emulsion would have been as effective in destroying the Scale-insect, and would have had no appreciable effect on the tree. A 67 per cent. emulsion, which would have exterminated the insects, would have partially defoliated the most thickly infested branches, without affecting the vigorous portions of the tree.

Experiment No. 91.—Solution, 1 pound potash to 1 gallon water. Applied to two small trees very badly infested with Scale-insects. Owing to the enfeebled condition of the trees, the effect of the lye was as severe as in the preceding experiment. Five weeks later one of the trees was recovering, the other dying, and Scale-insects in both cases increasing.

Experiment No. 94.—Solution, two-thirds pound potash to 1 gallon water. Applied to several young trees. Nearly all the leaves dropped and many branches killed.

Experiment No. 92.—Solution, one-half pound potash to 1 gallon water. Applied to two small trees badly infested with Long Scale. Both trees badly, one completely, defoliated. Tender bark and smaller branches killed. Four or five weeks later the trees were recovering, but young brood of Scale-insect had thickly coated all the living branches.

Experiment No. 95.—Solution, four-tenths pound potash to 1 gallon water. Applied to a tree of medium size and in good condition. Great injury to foliage and tender bark. One month later the trees were recovering, but Scale-insect increasing.

Experiment No. 93.—Solution, three-tenths pound potash to one gallon water. Devitalized branches completely defoliated; other portions less severely affected. Bark blackened and hardened. One month later trees recovering; Scale-insect not dimin-diminished in numbers.

Experiment No. 96.—Solution, one-fourth pound potash to 1 gallon water. Applied to a vigorous tree. Tree not severely defoliated. Four weeks later Scale-insect increasing.

Experiment No. 86.—Solution, one-sixth pound potash to 1 gallon water. Applied to a tree rather badly infested, but still vigorous. Tree slightly defoliated. Scale-insect not checked and no eggs killed.

Experiments with soda lye.—The strongest application of soda lye, two-thirds pound to 1 gallon water, was not more severe in its effects upon the tree than one-half this amount of potash applied in Experiment No. 93. The bark was blackened, but not destroyed, and the tree was severely defoliated. The application had no permanent effect in removing the Scale-insects, but these were afterwards destroyed by an application of kerosene emulsion, and the tree in consequence fully recovered its vigor. The remaining experiments with soda lye—1 pound to 2, 1 pound to 2½, and 1 pound to 3 gallons of water, respectively (Nos. 43, 44, and 45)—failed to check the increase of the Scale-insect. One year later these trees had lost instead of adding to their growth, and appeared to be in dying condition, the continued presence of the insects having prevented a recovery from the effects of the lye. The Scale-insects were subsequently removed by applications of kerosene, and the trees began to improve rapidly.

APPENDIX II.

TABLE 3.—*Lye solutions.*

Number of experiment	Concentrated lye diluted with water.	Amount of solid lye used in single application. (lbs.)	Amount of diluted wash applied. (qts.)	Date of application.	Date of examination.	Long Scale (*M. gloverii*). Young coccids killed.	Scales containing eggs. Eggs in part killed.	Eggs, all killed.	Eggs, none killed.	Chaff Scale (*P. pergandii*). Young coccids killed.	Scales containing eggs. Eggs in part killed.	Eggs, all killed.	Eggs, none killed.	Remarks.
	Strength of the solution.					*pr. ct.*	*pr. ct.*	*pr. ct.*	*pr. ct.*	*pr. ct.*	*pr. ct.*	*pr. ct.*	*pr. ct.*	
42	Soda lye, 1 lb. to 6 qts.	1	6	Dec. 31	Jan. 20	37	0	0	100	0	0	0	100	Only a few Chaff Scales examined; all of them alive.
43	Soda lye, 1 lb. to 8 qts.	1	8	Jan. 2	Jan. 9	0	0	0	100					Long Scale only. No appreciable result.
44	Soda lye, 1 lb. to 10 qts.	½	5	Jan. 2	Jan. 9	0	0	0	100	0	0	0	100	Long and Chaff Scale together. No result whatever.
45	Soda lye, 1 lb. to 12 qts.	½	6	Jan. 2	Jan. 9									Do.
90	Potash lye, 1 lb. to 2¾ qts.	1½	4	May 18	June 7 June 7	94 55	4 31	89 11	7 58					All small branches killed, bark of trunk burned and hardened, but not destroyed, pushing out adventitious buds. Upon portions where bark is interly destroyed 8 per cent. of the scales have eggs all alive.
91	Potash lye, 1 lb. to 4 qts.	1	4	May 31	June 6 June 5 July 4	88	38	12	50	60	50	0	50	Tree badly injured, completely defoliated and killed back to larger branches.
94	Potash lye, 1 lb. to 6 qts.	3	18	June 22	July 2 July 3	78	43	10	47	18 25	6 5	0 0	94 95	Tree reduced to trunk and one living branch, the latter covered with new brood of scale.
92	Potash lye, 1 lb. to 8 qts.	1	4	May 31	June 6	96	32	0	68					Several trees. Results unequal.
95	Potash lye, 1 lb. to 10 qts.	1/15	5	July 22	July 3 June 6	78 70	20 40	0 0	80 60	46	12	0	88	July 4. Two trees, branches more or less killed back; trees, however, recovering. Living branches thickly coated with forming brood of Long Scale. Application not effective.
93	Potash lye, 1 lb. to 13¾ qts.	1/15	4	May 31										
96	Potash lye, 1 lb. to 16 qts.	¼	4	June 22	July 3 July 19					40	4	0	96	Chaff Scale very slightly affected. Eggs all alive. Adult females of Long Scale part killed. Females of Chaff Scale not killed. July 4 trees recovering. Scales as bad as before.
86	Potash lye, 1 lb. to 24 qts.	¼	6	May 3	May 7 July 5					15	0	0	100	Few Long Scales examined, few or no eggs killed. Scales increasing. No appreciable effect. A few young killed. Eggs hatching. Tree covered with new brood of Long Scale. No effect.

Table 4.—Crude Carbolic Acid (Oil of Creosote).

In Table 4 are given results of experiments with carbolic acid in solution and combined with other substances.

In experiment No. 27, 9 fluid ounces of carbolic acid was applied to a single tree about five years old. The tree, which was badly infested with Long Scale, and had many branches dead and dying, was severely defoliated, and lost some moribund branches, but recovered in six weeks and pushed out new growth in midwinter.

In experiment No. 30 a pint measure of crumbled carbolic soap was applied. The actual amount of acid contained in this soap did not exceed 2 fluid ounces. The extermination of Long Scale was complete. The tree, which was very badly infested and in poor condition, was almost completely defoliated and lost half its branches, but recovered very rapidly and pushed out new leaves within thirty days. (January 25.)

In experiment No. 21 the other substances added to the carbolic solution increased the injury to the foliage of the tree and it was very severely checked, but entirely recovered and was stimulated to vigorous growth at a time when all surrounding trees were dormant.

In the remaining experiments, 13, 14, 15, and 12, the quantity of carbolic acid used was not sufficient to kill the Scale-insects. The effect upon the trees was also very slight.

APPENDIX II. 207

TABLE 4.—*Crude carbolic acid or oil of creosote.*

Number.	Carbolic acid; amount used in single application.	Diluted with water.	Amount of diluted wash applied.	Date of application.	Date of examination.	Long Scale (*M. gloverii*). Young coccids killed.	Scales containing eggs. Eggs, in part killed.	Scales containing eggs. Eggs, all killed.	Scales containing eggs. Eggs, none killed.	Chaff Scale (*P. pergandii*). Young coccids killed.	Scales containing eggs. Eggs, in part killed.	Scales containing eggs. Eggs, all killed.	Scales containing eggs. Eggs, none killed.	Remarks.
		qts.	*qts.*			*pr. ct.*	*pr. ct.*	*pr. ct.*	*pr. ct.*	*pr. ct.*	*pr. ct.*	*pr. ct.*	*pr. ct.*	
27	9 fluid oz.	Dissolved in soap, 2 ounces; hot water, 1 pint.	4¾	6	Nov. 12	Nov. 14	94	41	17	42					Long Scale only. Very few young and no eggs killed
						Nov. 21	77	21	12	67					Bark of vigorous shoot infested with scales of last brood, and nearly all young. All scales before first moult are killed and not enumerated. Older scales still dying.
						Nov. 21 Jan. 25									Leaves from less infested portions of the tree. Scales completely exterminated upon most parts. In a few pieces young are forming.
30	2 fluid oz.	Creosote soap*—10.8 fluid oz.	6	6	Dec. 5	Dec. 16 Jan. 25	100	26	29	45					On exposed branches very few or no scales alive. Other portions give 3 per cent. living. Gravid females all killed. Long Scale only.
47	1⅓ fluid oz.	Id .... 9 fluid oz.	6	6	Jan. 10	Jan. 21	100	43	48	9	00	11	4	85	On minute and careful examination, not a single living coccid or egg can be found. Chaff Scale on outside have been killed; scales protected by others overlapping them are alive. Eggs but little affected. Chaff Scale
						Feb. 2									Long Scale nearly exterminated. Chaff Scale but slightly checked, and now increasing.
32	1 fluid oz.	Id .... 8.4 fluid oz.	6	6	Dec. 5	Dec. 16	99+	20	0	80					A single living coccid seen. Eggs slightly affected.
46	⅔ fluid oz.	Id .... 4.5 fluid oz.	6	6	Jan. 10	Jan. 21	96	13	2	85	42	0	0	100	Two small trees washed; (1) infested with Long Scale; (2) infested with Chaff Scale. On some twigs of the latter, only of pupae appear to be killed. Lecanium Scales nearly all killed.

*Creosote, 12 per cent. by volume; lard oil, 60 per cent. by volume; concentrated lye, 20 per cent. by volume; water, 8 per cent. by volume. (Solidified by long continued boiling, loss by evaporation estimated, and above proportions given as approximate only.)

TABLE 4.—Carbolic acid.

Number	Carbolic acid; amount used in single application		Diluted with water. Qt.	Amount of diluted wash applied. Qt.	Date of application	Date of examination	Long Scale (M. gloverii)				Chaff Scale (P. pergandii)				Remarks
							Young coccids killed. pr. ct.	Eggs in part killed. pr. ct.	Eggs all killed. pr. ct.	Eggs none killed. pr. ct.	Young coccids killed. pr. ct.	Eggs in part killed. pr. ct.	Eggs all killed. pr. ct.	Eggs none killed. pr. ct.	
46	....	[Continued]	....	....	....	Feb. 2	....	....	....	....	....	....	....	....	Living eggs and young scales found on both trees. Long Scale slightly checked; Chaff Scale not at all.
21	4¾ fl. oz.	Dissolved in soap, 2 ounces; hot water, 12 ounces; together with silicate of soda, 13 fl. ounces; water, 12 ounces; urine, 7 fl. oz.	4	5+	Nov. 7	Nov. 10 Nov. 19	91 99	56	0	44	....	....	....	....	Many scales full of dead larvæ which have hatched since application, but unable to issue. In many scales the eggs are partly or all killed; mother coccids in many cases still alive. Scales severely checked; no new scales forming.
13	2 fluid oz.	Emulsified with condensed milk, 4 fl. oz.; water, 1 oz.	5	5+	Oct. 26	Oct. 31	....	....	....	....	....	....	....	....	Tree infested with Long Scale. No appreciable effect upon the scales.
14	1.13 fl. oz.	Emulsified with sour condensed milk, 78 pr. ct.; to creosote, 22 pr. ct.	6	6	Oct. 31	Nov. 5	....	....	....	....	....	....	....	....	Long Scale. No appreciable effect.
15	1⅗ fl. oz.	Emulsified together with 2.7 fluid oz. of kerosene and 2.64 fluid oz. of sour milk curds. Oil creosote......14 pr. ct. Oil kerosene......42 pr. ct. Curds of milk......44 pr. ct.	6	6	Oct. 31	Nov. 5	....	....	....	....	....	....	....	....	Long Scale very slightly affected. Not over 20 per cent. of the young scales killed. No mature females and no eggs killed.
12	¼ fluid oz.	Solution in water, made by triturating 1 fl. oz. creosote with 2 oz. carb. magnesia and filtering in 1 quart water.	2	2	Oct. 25	Nov. 2	....	....	....	....	....	....	....	....	Long and Chaff Scale. No effect whatever.

TABLE 5.—BISULPHIDE OF CARBON.

In table 5 are given the results of several experiments with this insecticide. The emulsion, of which the ingredients are given in the table, was formed by beating together with a spatula the carbon and lard oil and then adding the milk and water, and emulsifying in the same manner.

The trees in experiments 40 and 41 were very severly checked, although not seriously injured, and all subsequently recovered. In experiment 39 the mixture was applied during a rain, and was entirely without effect upon the tree or scale.

TABLE 5.—*Bisulphide of carbon emulsion.*

[Bisulph. carb., 56 per cent.; lard oil, 19 per cent.; condensed milk, 6 per cent.; water, 16 per cent.]

Number of experiment.	Amount of bisulphide used in single application.		Diluted with water.	Amount of diluted wash applied.	Date of application.	Date of examination.	Long Scale (*M. gloverii*).				Chaff Scale. (*P. pergandii*).				Remarks.
							Young coccids killed.	Scales containing eggs.			Young coccids killed.	Scales containing eggs.			
								Eggs, none killed.	Eggs, all killed.	Eggs, in part killed.		Eggs, none killed.	Eggs, all killed.	Eggs, in part killed.	
			Qts.	Qts.			pr. ct.	pr. ct.	pr. ct.	pr. ct.	pr. ct.	pr. ct.	pr. ct.	pr. ct.	
41	9 fluid oz.	In emulsion, 10 fluid oz.	5¼	6	Dec. 31	Jan. 20	52	0	0	100					Very tall tree. Application made on a windy day and upper branches not thoroughly sprayed; gives varying results, some young and nearly all eggs alive. Other parts of tree have been entirely cleared of living young, but a large proportion of eggs escape. (*a*) Thorn from upper branches. Long Scale. Leaves, thorns, and twigs from lower branches. Gravid females of Long Scale all killed. A few Chaff Scale examined; coccids killed, but eggs alive.
40	5.6 fluid oz.	In emulsion, 10 fluid oz.	6	4 / 2	Dec. 31 / Dec. 31	Jan. 21 / Jan. 21	100 / 100	35	43	22					Two trees sprayed, one very small; both infested with Long Scale and Chaff Scale together. Trees nearly cleared of scale in part by the aid of parasites. Application more thorough than No. 41.
39	3+ fluid oz.	In emulsion, 6 fluid oz.	6	6	Dec. 15	Dec. 28		3	96	1	97	2	98	0	Applied in rain on windy day; not a satisfactory application. No eggs, and apparently no young coccids killed. Examination January 25 gave same results; scales increasing.

TABLE 6.—SILICATE OF SODA.

Table 6 gives the results of a single experiment in which silicate of soda, in the form of a thick liquid, was diluted ten times and applied in fine spray.

In other trials, with stronger solutions, the best result obtained was 80 per cent. of the young Coccids killed, and trees were cleared of scale by repeated applications at intervals of several weeks; but in these cases the bark was hardened and the growth of the trees somewhat checked.

TABLE 6.—*Silicate of soda.*

Number of experiment.	Amount used in single application.	Silicate of soda, diluted 1 o 9.	Diluted with water.	Amount of diluted wash applied.	Date of application.	Date of examination.	Long Scale (*M. gloverii*).				Chaff Scale (*P. pergandii*).				Remarks.
							Young coccids killed.	Scales containing eggs.			Young coccids killed.	Scales containing eggs.			
								Eggs, in part killed.	Eggs, all killed.	Eggs, none killed.		Eggs, in part killed.	Eggs, all killed.	Eggs, none killed.	
							pr. ct.	pr. ct.	pr. ct.	pr. ct.	pr. ct.	pr. ct.	pr. ct.	pr. ct.	
22	16 fluid oz.	Silicate of soda, diluted 1 o 9.	Qts. 4½	Qts. 5	Nov. 7	Nov. 10	43	0	0	100	......	......	......	......	Gravid females and eggs not injured. Chaff Scale; young slightly affected, eggs not at all.

APPENDIX III.

THE COITION OF BAG WORMS.

The following is an extract from an account of certain Australian Bag-worms, by William W. Saunders, as read before the Entomological Society of London, February 1, 1847.*

"*August* 30.—On this day I first observed a yellowish-white substance protruding at the lower end of the largest cases, which upon close examination proved to be a portion of the females in the imago state, one-third of their bodies being exposed. About an hour afterward, examining the cases again, I found the females had receded, and in opening a case the female moth became evident within, and thus they emerge and recede as occasion may require. The female is a large apterous moth, with a very little of the ordinary appearance of an insect of the moth kind. The length is about 1¾ inches, diameter full half an inch, color yellowish white, fawn, or buff; head and three first segments of the body naked and glossy on the upper part; feet very short. Antennæ none, or at least not visible to the unassisted eye; anal segment of the body clothed all round with a dense covering of silky down [42] of a deeper color than the rest of the body; ovipositor well developed.

"*September* 5.—Examined some of the females, no males having yet appeared. Two or three were dead; one nearly so, having deposited a great number of ova in the pupa case, which were enveloped in a short silky material. When the female has deposited all her ova, she is literally nothing but thin skin, which soon desiccates, leaving room for the young larvæ to pass. I have examined other species of *Oiketicus*, and find all the females are apterous.

"*September* 20.—A male imago appeared this morning. It had been in active operation a good while, as evinced by its wings, being much broken at the tips and otherwise much abraded. It is an insect of very peculiar construction, and seems to have some affinity with *Zeuzera*. It has the extraordinary power of extending the abdomen to 2 inches in length, and of turning and twisting it in all directions. When in this state it has alternate rings of black and yellow, with a curious appendage at the extremity. The male appears very eager to accomplish the grand object of nature, namely, the continuation of its species, as its existence appears to be of short duration. The large fat or rather distended females have not room to turn their bodies so as to present the generative organs conviently to the male, consequently the immense development of the abdomen in the males is of the greatest importance; but it appears very extraordinary that the head of the female should be inverted, when it is known that she never emerges from the case unless by accidentally falling therefrom, which position obliges the male when in the act of coition to stretch his abdomen all along the side of the female full 1¾ inches. This peculiarity appears to me to be the design of the all-wise Creator, in order to afford a secure place for the defenseless larvæ, viz, that of the pupa-case of their parent, from which they emerge after the disappearance of their mother's body, and immediately form themselves silken cases covered with small pieces of anything they can procure, arranged in every respect like the larger ones."

---

* Remarks on the habits and economy of a species of *Oiketicus* found on shrubs in the vicinity of Sydney, N. S. W., by W. W. Saunders, esq., F. L. S., &c. Drawn up from notes furnished by W. Stephenson, esq. Transactions of the Entomological Society of London, Vol. V. 1847-1849. pp. 40-33.

Recently Professor Riley has given a more detailed and exact account of the manner by which the act of coition takes place. A portion of his article which was published in the Scientific American Supplement of April 3, 1878, and republished in the Proceedings of the Biological Society of Washington, Vol. ii, 1882–'4, p. 81, is here reproduced:

"We have seen that, by means of the partial elongation of her puparium and her partial extraction therefrom, the female is able to reach with her head to the extreme lower end of her follicle, causing, in doing so, the narrow elastic portion of the follicle to bulge, and the orifice to open more or less, as it repeatedly did while the larva was yet feeding, whenever the excrement had to be expelled. Fig. 94, *a*, shows a follicle cut open so as to exhibit the elongated puparium, and the female extended from it as she awaits the male; *b* represents this degraded female more in detail. A cursory examination of the male shows the genital armature, which is always exposed, to consist of (1) a brown, horny, bilobed piece, broadening about the middle, narrowing to and notched at tip, concave, and furnished with a tuft of dark hairs at tip inside; (2) a rigid brown sheath, upon which play (3) the genital hooks or clasps, which are also concave inside, strongly bifid at tip, the inner finger furnished with hairs, the outer produced to an obtuse angle near tip, and generally unarmed (Fig. 95, *e*). In repose, this armature appears as in Fig. 95, *c*, from beneath, and as at *d*, from above, and is well adapted to prying into the opening of the follicle. The male abdomen is telescopically extensile, while the tip easily bends or curves in any direction, but most naturally beneath, as at *b*, where it is represented enlarged about six times, and with all the genital parts expanded ; *k*, the fixed outer sheath ; *f*, the clasps ; *g*, a pale membranous sheath upon which the præputium (*h*) plays, as on the finger of a glove ; *i*, the fleshy elastic penis, armed with retorse hairs, and capable of extending to nearly one-fourth of an inch ; *j*, showing the end still more fully enlarged. With this exposition of details, not easily observed or generally understood, the act of fecundation is no longer a mystery."

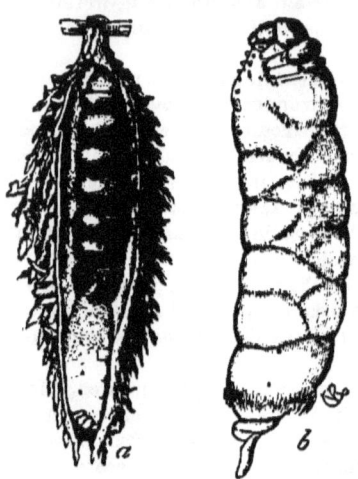

FIG. 94.—THYRIDOPTERYX EPHEMERÆFORMIS: *a*, Follicle cut open to show the manner in which the female works from her puparium and reaches the end of the bag, natural size; *b*, female extracted from her case, enlarged. (After Riley.)

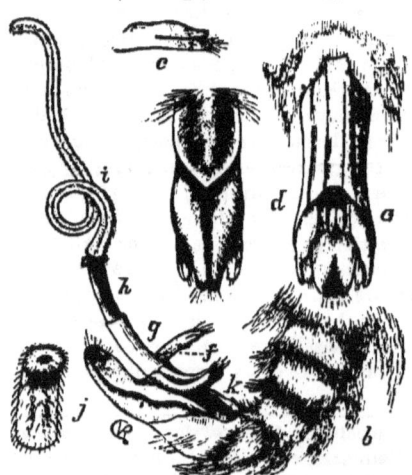

FIG. 95.—THYRIDOPTERYX EPHEMERÆFORMIS: *b*, The end of male abdomen from the side, showing genitalia extended; *c*, genitalia in repose, ventral view; *d*, do., dorsal view; *e*, tip of bifid clasp; *j*, tip of penis; all enlarged. (After Riley.)

NOTES.

NOTE 1 (p. 59).—Mr. Howard states that this Tetrastichus has never since been bred, and that the material is too poor for determination. April 18, 1885, I bred two additional species of parasites from the Florida Ceroplastes at Crescent City, which were determined by Mr. Howard as (1) *Coccophagus vividus* Howard (see Bulletin 5, Division of Entomology, U. S. Dept. Agr., page 24, species 37) which I had previously bred from *Lecanium hesperidum*, on Orange, at Crescent City. (2) A species of *Encyrtus* represented by one ♂ which was mounted in balsam and so badly crushed as to admit only of a generic determination.

NOTE 2 (pp. 69 and 77).—In looking up the saved material in order that this species might be determined, but a single crippled and inferior specimen was found, and Professor Riley prefers not to describe it for the present from this unsatisfactory specimen.

NOTE 3 (p. 79).—This parasite was handed to Mr. Howard, who has given me the following concerning it:

"While at first glance I determined the *Leptocorisa* egg-parasite for you as a species of *Telenomus*, a more careful subsequent study, and a comparison with a number of Mayr's types of this genus, show that it belongs rather to the allied genus *Hadronotus* of Foerster. The great majority of the species of the subfamily Scelioninæ, to which these two genera belong, are egg-parasites. This species may be described as follows:

"HADRONOTUS LEPTOCORISÆ n. sp.

"*Female.*—Length, 1.4^{mm}; expanse, 2.5^{mm}. Head and face evenly covered with small round punctures, except in the facial impression, which is transversely striate; antennæ subclavate; lateral ocelli nearly touching the margins of the eyes. Mesonotum a trifle smoother than the head and furnished with a very fine white pubescence. First segment of the abdomen dorsally longitudinally striate; remaining segments closely covered with fine round punctures; ventral surface sparsely punctate. Color, black; scape, brown; all coxæ, black; all trochanters, femora, tibiæ, and tarsi, light brown; mandibles and wing-veins, light brown.

"*Male.*—Length, 1.3^{mm}; expanse 2.5^{mm}. Antennæ filiform. In other characters resembling the ♀."

"Described from many ♂ and ♀ specimens, bred from the eggs of *Leptocorisa tipuloides*, at Crescent City, Fla., by H. G. Hubbard."

NOTE 4 (p. 80).—These bugs belong to the genus *Rhinacloa*, but the species is undetermined.

NOTE 5 (p 81).—This species is so far undetermined. It is a beautiful and well-marked species, the prevailing color being brown. The mesoscutum has two yellow stripes converging posteriorly, the mesoscutellum is entirely yellow, the metascutellum is marked with yellowish, and the abdomen has yellow rings.

Just as these notes are going to press, I am able to add the following concerning this species, received from Mr. Cresson:

"The specimen arrived minus its abdomen, but judging from what is left it seems to belong to the genus *Hemiteles*. I have looked over the material belonging to that genus in the society's collection, and do not find anything there agreeing with your specimen. I do not think it has been described, but as I have never worked up the genus, I cannot say definitely that it is new."

Notes 6, 7, 8, 9, and 10 (pp. 83 and 84).—These mites were mounted in balsam for subsequent study by Professor Riley, with a view of possible determination. He has kindly examined them and furnished the following notes and descriptions:

"The so-called 'Hairy Orange Mite' (Note 6) is one of the 'Harvest-mites' belonging to the section *Eupodidæ* and comes nearer to *Penthalodes* Murray than to any other defined genus, having 6-jointed legs of about equal length. It may be described as follows:

"Penthalodes mytilaspidis n. sp. Average length, 0.3^{mm}. Broadly oval; abdomen tapering to a point. Color dark red, with pale hairs. Head distinctly separated, narrow, elongate, conical. Mandibles scissor-like, projecting. Palpi inserted at apex of cephalothorax, close to the head, stout, 4-jointed, the first joint stoutest, first and second of about equal length, third shortest, the fourth ending in a stout, curved claw at the base of which an elongate oval thumb is inserted. Eyes barely discernible near the side of the cephalothorax between the first and second pairs of legs. Cephalothorax rounded in front, merging posteriorly into the abdomen, so as to leave no distinct division except in shrunken specimens. Surrounded by rather long and stout bristles, about 8 on each side, and with two rows of similar bristles dorsally. Legs about equal in length, the first pair very slightly longest; third joint longest. Claws 3, much curved at tip, the middle one curved upwards.

"Of the 'Spear-head Mite' (note 7) the mounted specimens are unfit for study and no determination can be made of them.

"The so-called 'Spotted Mite' (note 8) is also represented by such poor specimens from the Orange Coccidæ that they could not be used for determination, but I have obtained a closely-related species from twigs containing the eggs of *Cicada septendecim*, and have thus been able to make out its characters. It belongs to the Beetle-mites or Oribatidæ, and the one-clawed section; but it cannot strictly be placed in any defined genus. As I would not care to erect a new genus in these fragmentary notes, the species may be described under the genus *Hermannia*, to which it approaches nearest structurally, though bearing no great resemblance to the commoner species of that genus.

"Hermannia (?) trinebulosa n. sp.—Length, 0.38^{mm}. Color whitish, pellucid. Pyriform, surface apparently smooth and polished; three dusky abdominal patches, one large and central, and one at each lower side with a central, elongate-ovoid corneous plate; two dorsal rows of rather long hairs, with a few others at sides, a rather stouter one on each shoulder, and three anal pairs, the intermediate or second pair longest—all very minutely barbed. Cephalothorax broadly conical, bluntly rounded in front, separated from the body by a distinct transverse suture; on each side towards the base is a conspicuous, strongly clavate bristle. Palpi 6-jointed, the 2nd joint as long as the others together. All legs of about equal length, 6-jointed; terminal joint longest, tapering quite suddenly from about the middle to the end, especially in the posterior pair of legs. Claw simple, large, and strongly curved. All legs sparsely beset with rather long, simple bristles, which are most numerous on the terminal joint.

"Of figs. 39 and 40 (notes 9 and 10) the slides are not to be found, but, judging from the figures, the former is a *Tyroglyphus*, the species of which are very commonly found preying on animal matter, and the latter a *Sejus*, one of the Gamasid genera. I should not care to describe them by name without study of the specimens."

Note 11 (p. 98).—Prof. H. W. Wiley, chemist, U. S. Department of Agriculture, gives the following reactions of sulphur upon lime, treated with boiling water.

"Depending on the proportion of sulphur used, the products may be considered as follows:

$$3\ CaO + S_6 = 2\ CaS_2 + CaS_2O_3$$
Calcium disulphide + Calcium thiosulphate

"Or, with a greater amount of sulphur,

$$3\ CaO + S_{12} = 2\ CaS_5 + CaS_2O_3$$
Calcium pentasulphide + Calcium thiosulphate.

"In fact, probably both reactions go on at once, and even more complicated ones.

"The reaction of lime in the act of slaking on sulphur would probably be small, owing to the short time during which the heat would continue."

NOTE 12 (p. 153.)—The specimens of this parasite were turned over to Mr. Howard, who has given me the following description:

"MIOTROPIS PLATYNOTÆ n. sp.

"*Female.*—Length, 1.65^{mm}; expanse, 3.0^{mm}. Head broader than thorax; vertex broad; ocelli very close together; scape reaching almost to vertex. Pro and meso scutum somewhat rugose; mesoscutellum nearly smooth; metathoracic carina well marked. Hind coxæ with an external longitudinal groove. Abdomen moderately long oval, flattened. Color uniform honey-yellow (in dry specimens; Mr. Hubbard, in his general description, says: "Honey yellow; head, lemon-yellow"); eyes and ocelli, dark red; tip of scape, dorsal surface of pedicel, and all of flagellum, dusky; two large occipital dark spots, sometimes confluent; abdomen brownish at lateral border and with a brownish central spot varying in size; legs, light honey-yellow.

"*Male.*—Slightly smaller than female; abdomen widening from base to near extremity. Face with two converging black streaks from insertion of antennæ to middle ocellus; hind tibiæ with a distinct dusky tinge near extremity; abdomen more distinctly edged with brown and with a central translucent spot.

"Described from 5 ♂, 1 ♀; bred from larva of *Platynota rostrana*, at Crescent City, Fla., in September, by H. G. Hubbard.

"This species will probably ultimately form a new genus, as in the structure of the thorax at least it differs from the descriptions of *Miotropis*. It is, however, more nearly related to this genus than to any other Elachistid genus, and I therefore place it here temporarily."

NOTE 13 (p. 153).—This species was also referred to Mr. Howard, who describes it as follows:

"GONIOZUS HUBBARDI n. sp.

"*Female.*—Length, 2.4^{mm}; expanse, 4.4^{mm}. Face and notum very sparsely punctured and furnished with fine white pile; also delicately shagreened in addition to the round punctures. Abdomen very smooth and shining and ovate-acuminate in form; somewhat pilose, especially towards tip. Wings clear; stigma brown, with a hyaline spot at its center; stigmal cell nearly complete. Color black; all legs, including coxæ, honey-yellow; mouth-parts and antennæ honey-yellow.

"Described from 1 ♀ specimen, bred in October, from the larva of *Platynota rostrana*, at Crescent City, Fla., by H. G. Hubbard, for whom I have named the species."

NOTE 14 (p. 154).—This is evidently a dark form of *Cacœcia obsoletana* Walk. which Professor Riley has bred from oak, but it doubtless has several food-plants, as it is allied to the wide-spread and polyphagic *Cacœcia rosaceana* Harr., which feeds on rose, apple, peach, cherry, yellow birch, plum, cotton, clover, honeysuckle, bean, strawberry, *Negundo aceroides*, *Cornus stolonifera* and *Cratægus* spp.

NOTE 15 (p. 178).—The single specimen of this species preserved is badly damaged and minus all the head parts. It appears to be a *Blastobasis*, like the species which immediately precedes it.

NOTE 16 (p. 186).—This parasite was referred to Mr. Howard, who has given me the following:

"PACHYNEURON ANTHOMYIÆ n. sp.

"*Female.*—Length, 1.4^{mm}; expanse, 2.6^{mm}; greatest width of fore wing 0.56^{mm}. Head, face, and thorax delicately shagreened; antennæ inserted at the middle of the face; scape reaching to the first ocellus; club flattened, oval. Petiole of the abdomen slightly punctured. Abdomen flattened, oval. Subcostal vein of fore wing with seven strong forward-directed bristles. Mesoscutellum not especially prominent. Rear coxæ with four or five bristles above at tip. Color, very dark metallic green; scape of antennæ honey-yellow; pedicel dark above, yellow below; flagellum light brown; all legs honey-yellow; front and middle coxæ brownish above, verging upon metallic green at base; hind coxæ metallic green; all femora brownish in the middle, honey-yellow at either extremity; wing veins dark brown.

Male.—Length, 1.1^{mm}; expanse, 2.5^{mm}. Antennæ slenderer than in the ♀ and markedly pilose. Abdomen flattened, spatulate in form. Color, metallic green, lighter and more brilliant than in the female; legs of a brighter, nearly lemon, yellow; femora without the brownish central band.

"Described from 1 ♂, 1 ♀ specimen bred by Mr. Hubbard at Crescent City, Fla., September 6, from the puparium of an undescribed Anthomyid fly, called by Hubbard 'the Pruinose Aphis-fly.'

"This species may be at once distinguished from *P. altiscuta* Cook, the only other described American species of the genus, by its smaller size, its less prominent scutellum, more oval abdomen, and by the coloration of its legs and antennæ.

"*Pachyneuron altiscuta* is said by Professor Cook* to have been bred in large numbers from a scale insect on basswood, probably *Lecanium tiliæ* Fitch, and, as he there quotes me as saying, the only other recorded instance which I can find of the breeding of *Pachyneuron* is the case of *P. aphidis*, bred from an Aphis by Reinhard. It is not at all likely, however, that species of this genus infest both Hemiptera and Diptera, and as Professor Cook found a Syrphus larva feeding upon the eggs of his Lecanium, it seems probable that *P. altiscuta* comes from this dipterous larva. The same may be the case with *P. aphidis*. The circumstantiality of Mr. Hubbard's notes leaves no doubt as to the breeding of *P. anthomyiæ* from the puparium of the Anthomyid."

NOTE 17 (p. 188).—This species has since been determined as *Chrysis fasciata* Fabr.

---

* Notes on injurious insects. Entomological Laboratory, Michigan Agricultural College [1884].

EXPLANATION TO PLATES.

PLATE I.

YOUNG ORANGE TREE, HEALTHY AND DISEASED.

(From photographs.)

FIG. 1. Young Orange tree in healthy condition.　|　FIG. 2. Young Orange tree in diseased condition.

PLATE II.

DIE-BACK OF THE ORANGE.

(Original.)

FIG. 1. Die-back of the Orange, natural size and slightly enlarged.　|　FIG. 2. Bark fungus on twigs of Orange infested with Long Scale, natural size and slightly enlarged.

PLATE III.

COMMON ARMORED SCALES OF THE ORANGE.

(From Comstock's Report for 1880.)

FIG. 1. *Mytilaspis citricola* (Pack.): 1, scales on Orange, natural size; 1*a*, scale of female, dorsal view; 1*b*, scale of female with ventral scale and eggs; 1*c*, scale of male, enlarged.

FIG. 2. *Mytilaspis gloverii* (Pack.): 2, scales on Orange, natural size; 2*a*, scale of female, dorsal view; 2*b*, scale of male; 2*c*, scale of female with ventral scale and eggs, enlarged.

FIG. 3. *Parlatoria pergandii* Comst.: 3*a*, scale of female; 3*b*, scale of male, enlarged.

PLATE IV.

TWIGS OF ORANGE INFESTED WITH LONG SCALE.

(Original.)

FIG. 1. Larger branch sparsely covered.　|　FIG. 2. Twig thickly covered.

PLATE V.

CHAFF SCALE OF THE ORANGE.

(Original.)

PLATE VI.

ENEMIES OF BARK-LICE.

FIG. 1. *Aphelinus mytilaspidis*: *a*, the parasite; *b*, antenna; *c*, larva, enlarged. (After Riley.)

FIG. 2. *Hyperaspidius coccidivorus*: *a*, larva, enlarged; *b*, head of larva, much enlarged; *c*, side of head, showing eyes and antenna, still more enlarged; *d*, beetle. (Original.)

FIG. 3. *Dakruma coccidivora*: *a*, egg; *b*, larva; *c*, pupa; *d*, moth, enlarged; *e*, moth at rest upon a bark-louse, natural size. (After Comstock.)

FIG. 4. *Leptocorisa tipuloides*, slightly enlarged. (Original.)

FIG. 5. Roseate Orange Mite, greatly enlarged. (Original.)

PLATE VII.

APPARATUS FOR SPRAYING ORANGE TREES.

(From a photograph.)

EXPLANATION TO PLATES.

PLATE VIII.
ORANGE RUST.
(After Hubbard.)

PLATE IX.
KATYDIDS ON ORANGE.
(After Comstock.)

FIG. 1. *Microcentrum retinerve*: 1, adult; 1a, eggs; 1b, young, natural size.

FIG. 2. *Eupelmus mirabilis*: 2, female; 2a, male, enlarged; 2b, eggs of katydid from which *E. mirabilis* has emerged, natural size.

PLATE X.
ORANGE DOG.
(Original.)

FIG. 1. *Papilio cresphontes*, adult.
FIG. 2. *Papilio cresphontes*, full-grown larva, natural size.
FIG. 3. *Papilio cresphontes*, head of full-grown larva with horns extended, from the side, natural size.
FIG. 4. *Papilio cresphontes*, head of full-grown larva with horns extended, from the front, natural size.
FIG. 5. *Papilio cresphontes*, chrysalis suspended on twig, natural size.

PLATE XI.
MISCELLANEOUS ORANGE INSECTS.
(Original.)

FIG. 1. *Papilio cresphontes*, twig of orange, showing eggs and young larva, natural size.
FIG. 2. *Papilio cresphontes*, larva, one-third grown, natural size.
FIG. 3. *Empretia stimulea*, full-grown larva, natural size.
FIG. 4. *Dysdercus suturellus*, enlarged one-third.
FIG. 5. *Thrips tritici* on Orange blossoms, natural size.

PLATE XII.
BAG-WORMS AND PARASITES.

FIG. 1. *Thyridopteryx ephemeræformis*: a, larva; b, pupa of male; c, adult female; d, adult male; e, sack of female cut open, showing pupa-case and eggs; f, larva carrying case; g, sacks of young, natural size. (After Riley.)
FIG. 2. Young Bag-worms (*Oiketicus*), forming their sacks, a to e; f, sack of young completed, enlarged. (Original.)
FIG. 3. *Hemiteles thyridopterigis*: a, male; b, female; c, sack of bag-worm cut open, showing cocoons of parasite, natural size. (After Riley.)
FIG. 4. *Pimpla conquisitor*, slightly enlarged. (After Comstock.)
FIG. 5. *Cryptus inquisitor*. (After Riley.)

PLATE XIII.
MISCELLANEOUS ORANGE INSECTS.
(Original.)

FIG. 1. *Anæglis demissalis*, web-tangle of the caterpillars and spider, natural size: a, larva; b, moth, slightly enlarged.
FIG. 2. Aphis of the Orange: a, wingless female; b, winged female; c, parasitized female, greatly enlarged; d, colony on leaf, all parasitized, slightly enlarged.
FIG. 3. *Trioxys testaceipes*, greatly enlarged.

PLATE XIV.
MISCELLANEOUS ORANGE INSECTS.
(Original.)

FIG. 1. *Hypothenemus eruditus*, enlarged.
FIG. 2. *Leptostylus biustus*: a, beetle, enlarged; b, work and cocoon cell, natural size.
FIG. 3. *Hyperplatys maculatus*, enlarged.
FIG. 4. *Midas clavatus*, natural size. (Re-drawn from Harris.)
FIG. 5. *Carpophilus mutilatus*, enlarged.
FIG. 6. *Epuræa æstiva*, enlarged.
FIG. 7. Pomace-fly of the Orange: a, adult fly; b, larva; c, puparium, all enlarged.
FIG. 8. *Chrysobothris chrysoela*, enlarged.

YOUNG ORANGE TREE HEALTHY AND DISEASED

REPORT ON INSECTS AFFECTING THE ORANGE — Plate II

Report on Insects affecting the Orange. PLATE III.

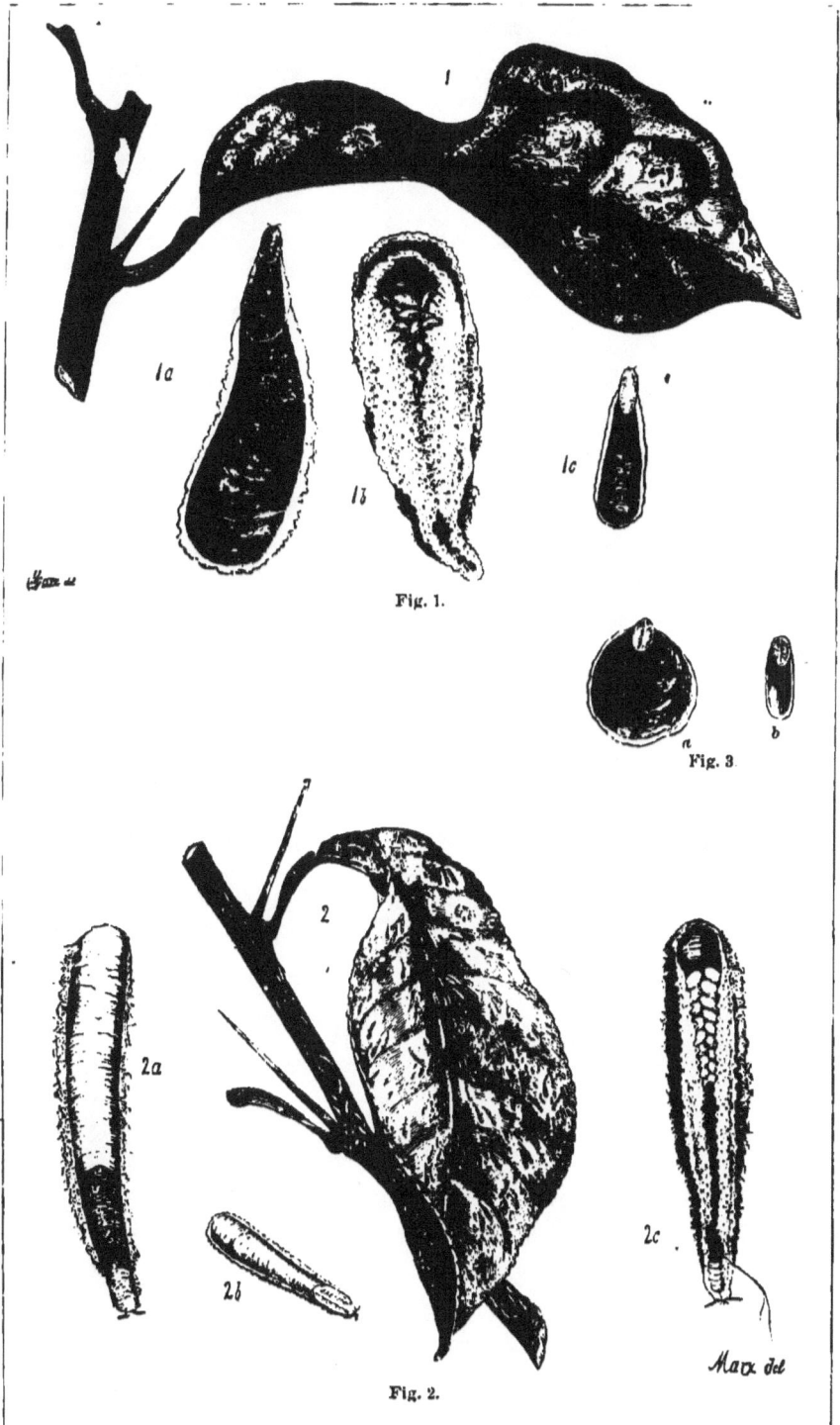

Fig. 1.

Fig. 3.

Fig. 2.

THE COMMON ARMORED SCALES OF THE ORANGE.

L. Sullivan del. A. Hoen & Co. lith. Baltimore

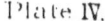

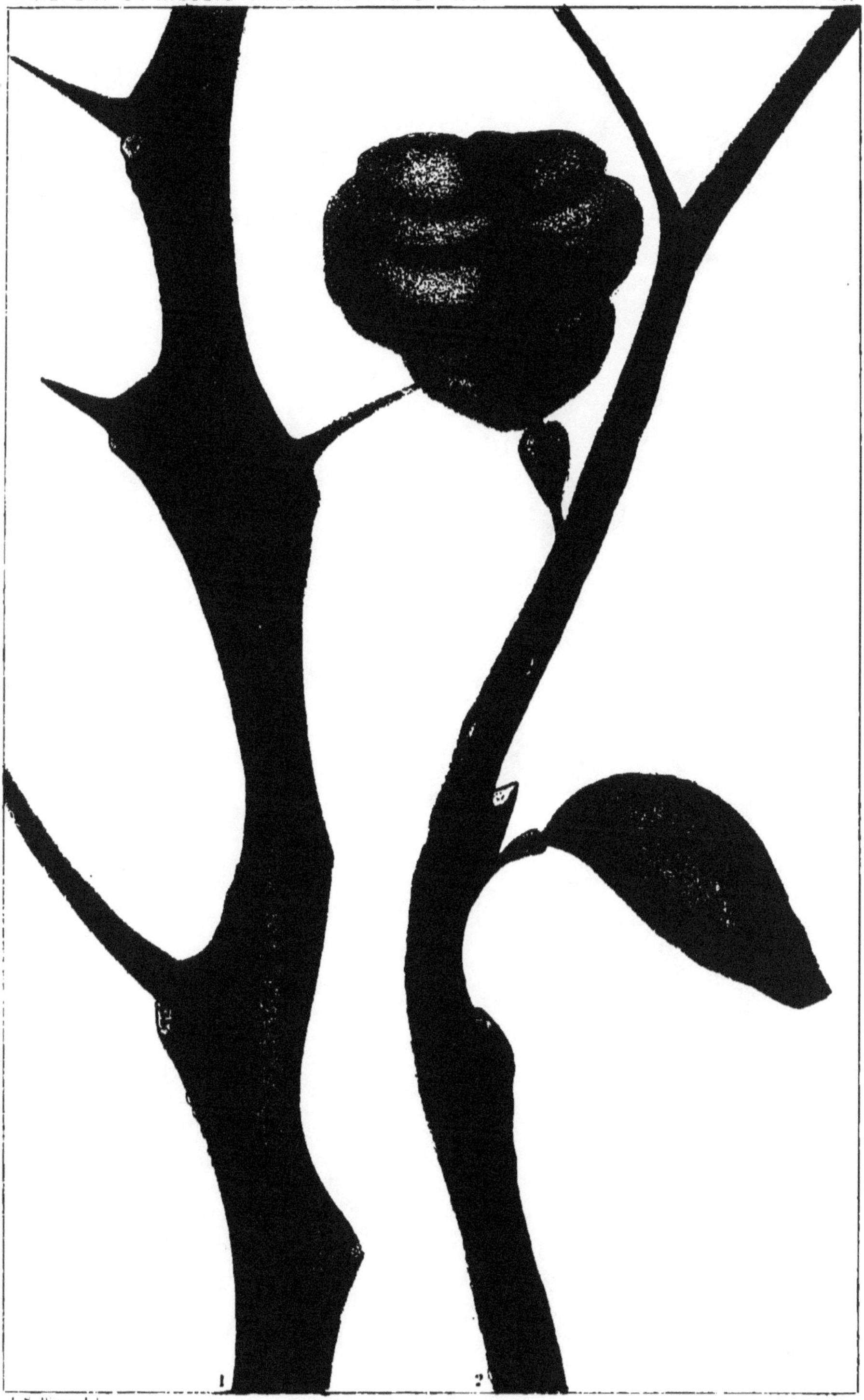

TWIGS OF ORANGE INFESTED WITH LONG SCALE.

"CHAFF SCALE" OF THE ORANGE.

ENEMIES OF BARK-LICE.

APPARATUS FOR SPRAYING ORANGE TREES.
(From a photograph taken in the field.)

1.

2.

KATYDIDS ON ORANGE.

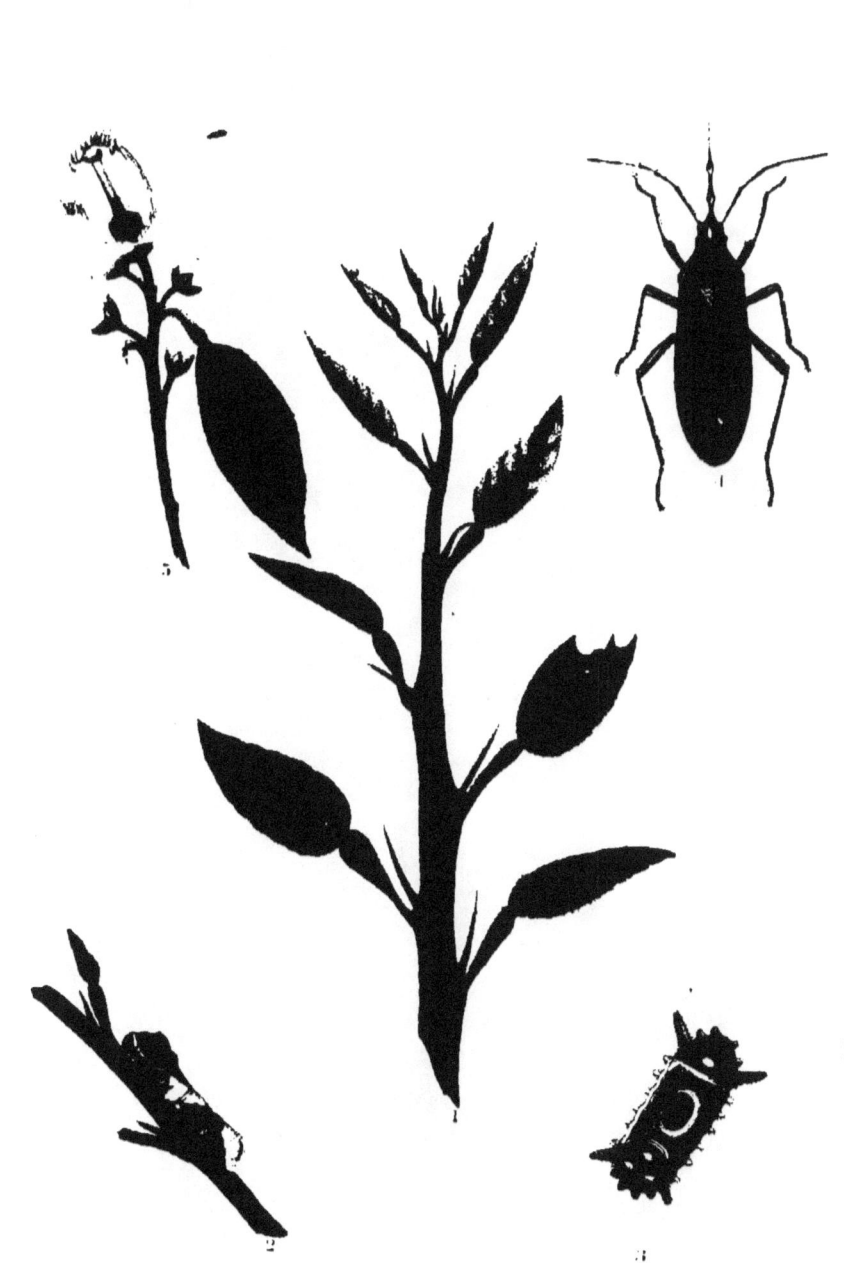

Report on Insects affecting the Orange.   PLATE XII.

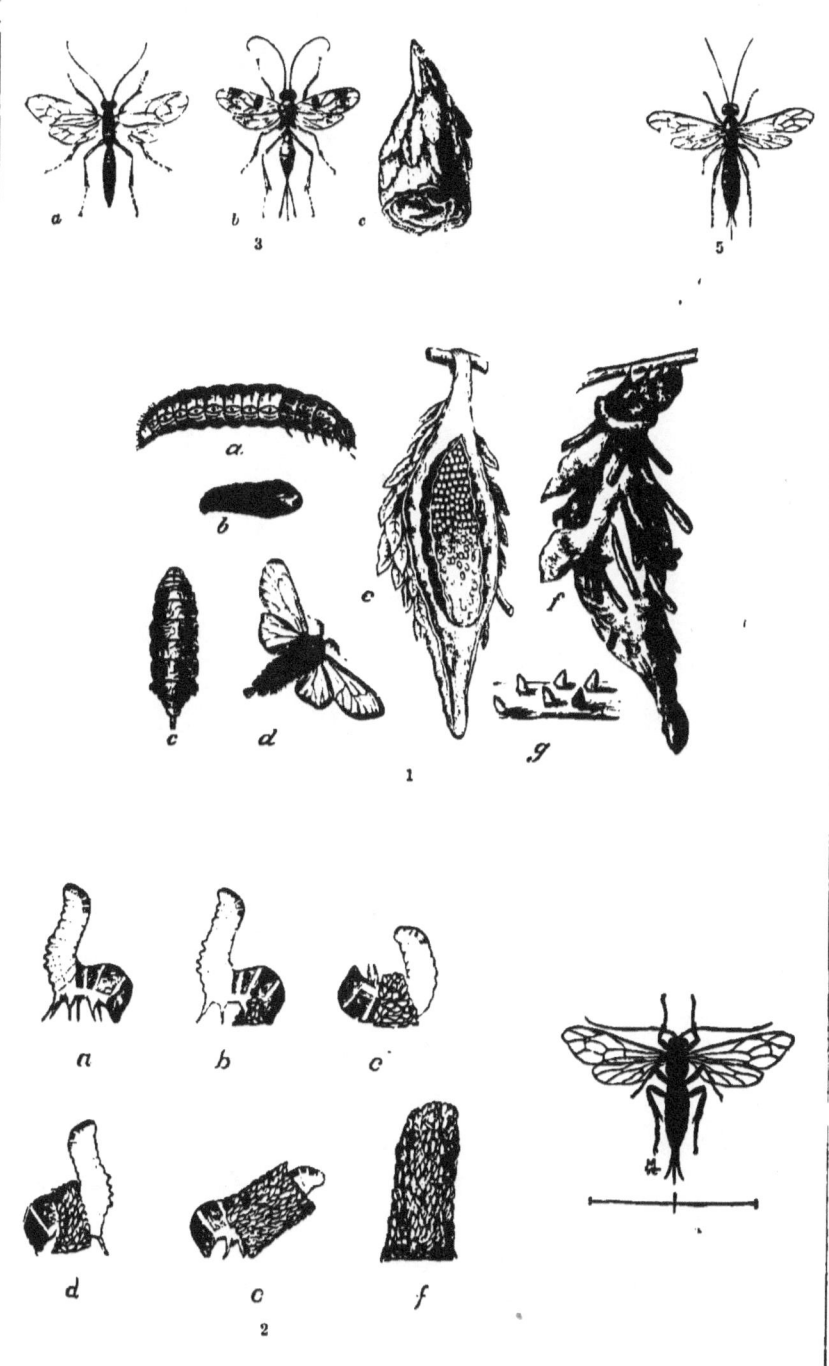

BAG WORM AND PARASITES.

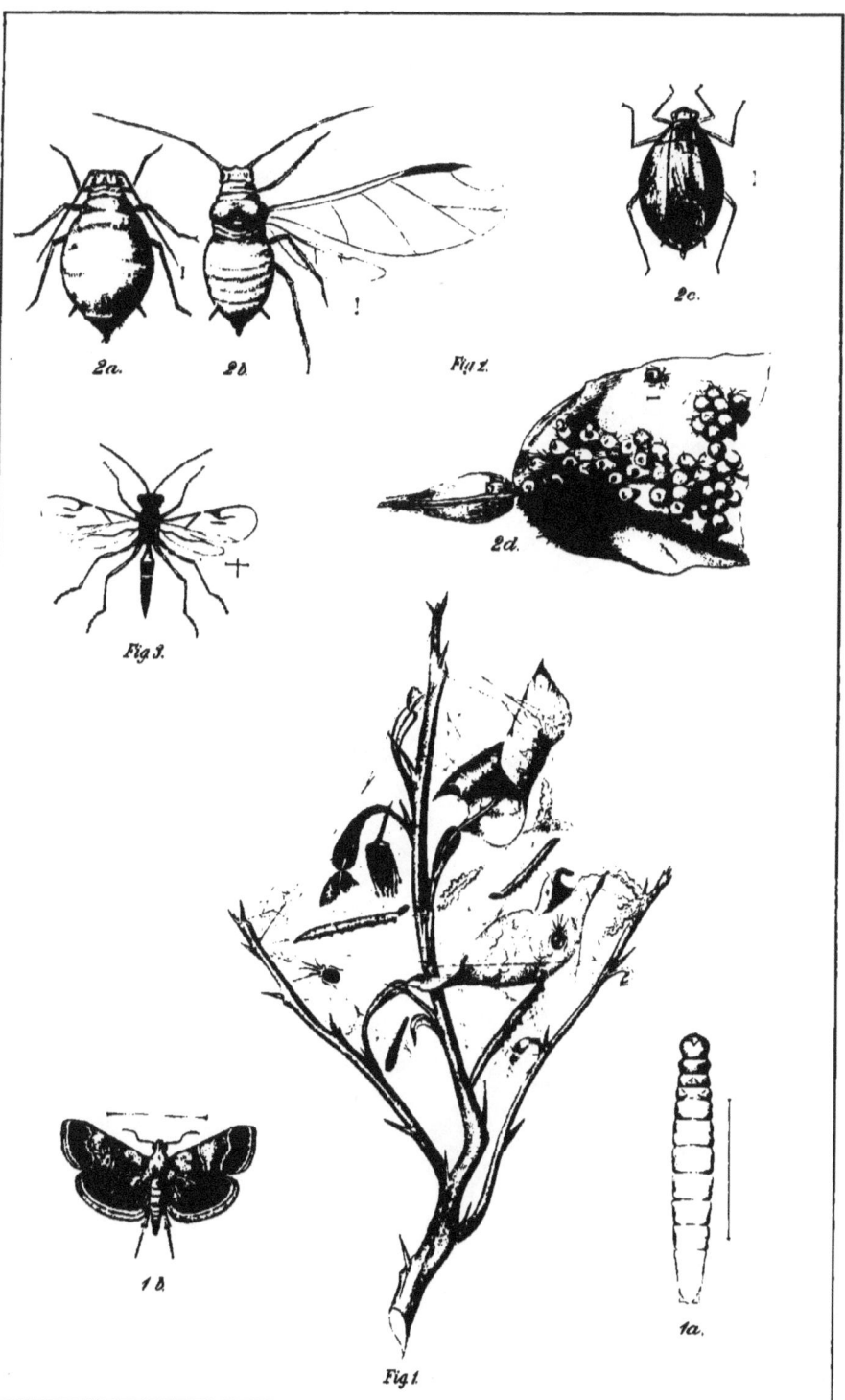

MISCELLANEOUS ORANGE INSECTS

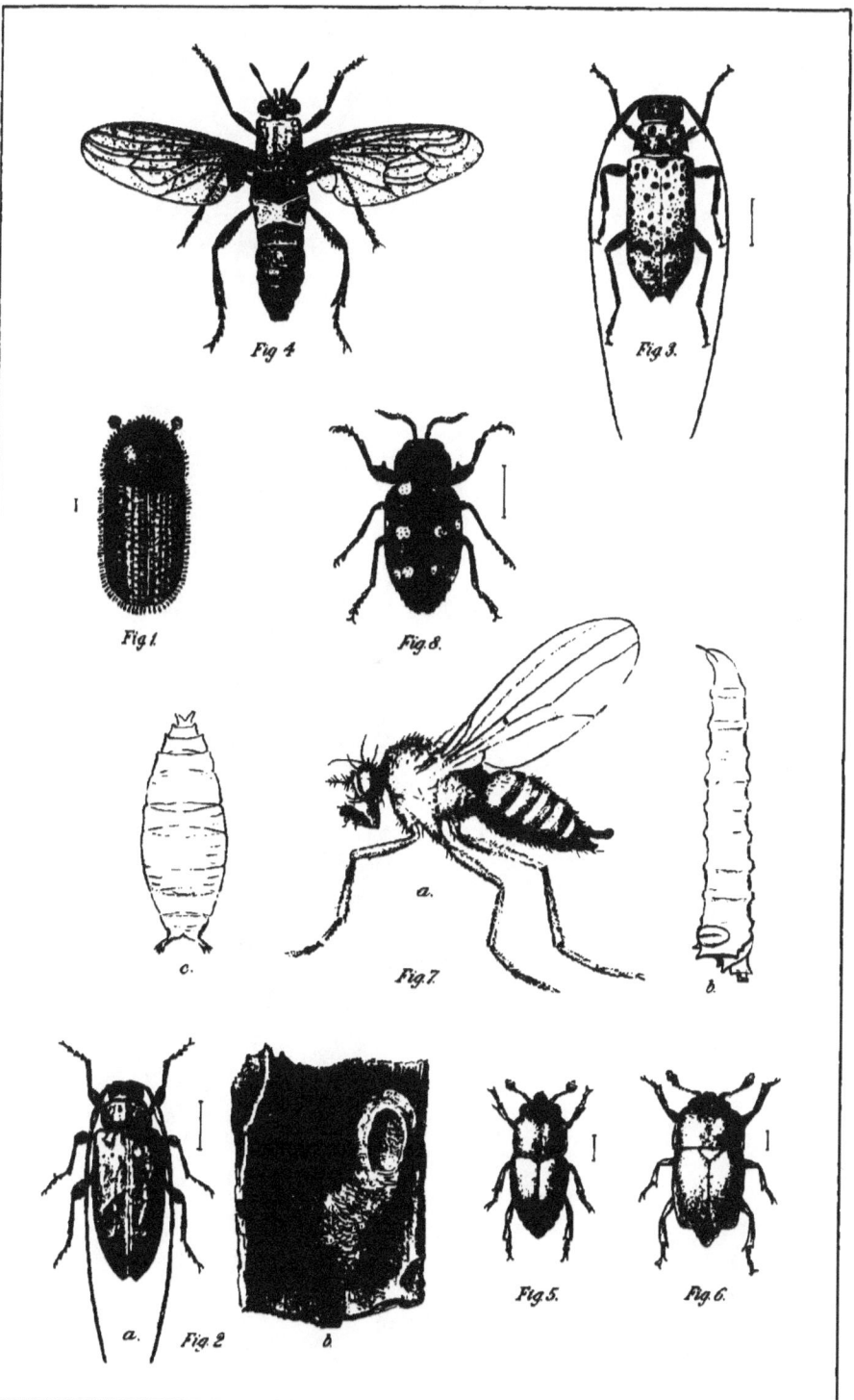

MISCELLANEOUS ORANGE INSECTS

INDEX.

Acarina feeding on Scale-insects, 81.
Acridiidæ injuring the Orange, 136.
Acridium alutaceum, 136.
    americanum, 136.
    obscurum, 136.
Aletia xylina, 9.
Ammonia as a remedy for Scale-insects, 99.
Amaurorhinus nitens, 175.
Anæglis, 77.
    demissalis, 80, 155.
Angular-winged Katydid, 134.
    Injury to the Orange, 134.
    Life-history, 134.
    Parasite, 134.
Anthomyid fly preying upon Aphis, 185.
Antigaster mirabilis, 134.
Ants attracted by honey secretion of plant-lice, 8, 130.
    Fruit-eating species, 177.
    indicating presence of injurious insects, 8.
    Injuries caused by, 129.
    preying upon Scale-insects, 70.
    Remedies and preventives, 130.
    sucked by Leptocorisa, 191.
    Tree-inhabiting species, 170.
Aphelinus aspidioticola, 24.
    fuscipennis, 24.
    mytilaspidis, 70.
Aphis, the Orange, 157.
Aphis-fly, Dusky-winged, 184.
    Four-spotted, 183.
    Pruinose, 185.
    Ruddy, 184.
Aphycus ceroplastis, 59.
    flavus, 24.
Apparatus for spraying trees, 101.
Apple Scale, 70.
Appendix I, 197.
    II, 199.
    III, 213.
Aquapult pump, 93.
Aræocerus fasciculatus, 178.
Armored Scales (see Diaspinæ).
Artace punctistriga, 150.
    Cocoon, 150.
    Moth, 150.
    Parasite, 150.
Artipus floridanus, 133.
Ashes as a remedy for Rust-mite, 120.
Ashmead, W. H., quoted, 44, 133.
Aspidiotus aurantii, 28, 32.
    citri, 34.
    ficus, 28, 34, 43, 86.
    nerii, 35.

Baccha babista, 183.
    cognata, 184.
    lugens, 184.
Bag-worms, 144.
    Coition of, 213.
    Common Bag-worm, 144.
    Cylindrical Bag-worm, 148.
    Northern Bag-worm, 147.
    Orange Basket-worm, 148.
    Unnamed species of, 149.
Bark-cleaners, 193.
Bark-fungus, 2.
Bark-lice (see Scale-insects).
Barnacle Scale, 59.
    Adult female, 59.
    Development, 60.
    Egg, 60.
    Food-plants, 61.
    Geographical distribution, 61.
    Young larva, 60.
Basket-worm (see Bag-worm).
Beneficial insects, general habits of, 6.
Birds transporting Scale-insects, 43.
Bisulphide of carbon as a remedy for ants, 130.
    for Scale-insects, 99.
    White-ants, 124.
    Table of experiments with, 209.
Black Scale of California, 53.
    Adult female, 53.
    Development, 54.
    Eggs, 54.
    Food-plants, 54.
    Geographical distribution, 54.
    Natural enemies, 55.
    Young larva, 54.
Blastobasis citricolella, 178.
    sp., 218.
Blood-red Lady-bird, 73.
    Habits, 73.
    Larva, 73.
    Pupa, 73.
Brachys ovata, 132.
Braconidæ bred from cells of Eumenes, 188.
Broad Scale, 48.
Cacœcia rosaceana, 217.
Calotermes castaneus, 125.
Camel-crickets, 188.
    Food, 188.
    Habits, 189.
Capnodium citri, 4, 50, 62, 63.
Carbolic acid as a remedy for Rust-mite, 118.
    Scale-insects, 97.
    Table of experiments with, 206.

INDEX.

Carpophilus mutilatus, 176.
    Habits, 176.
    Larva, 176.
Case-bearers on Orange, 193.
Caution in applying penetrating insecticides, 120.
Ceroplastes artemisiæ, 59.
    cirripediformis, 59, 62.
    fairmairii, 60.
    floridensis, 56, 60, 61, 62.
    rusci, 59, 60.
    vinsonii, 60.
Chaff-Scale, 2, 37, 42, 75, 86.
    Eggs, 38.
    Female insect, 37.
    Food-plants, 39.
    Introduction, 86.
    Habitat, 39.
    Life-history, 38.
    Number of generations, 38.
    Origin, 39.
    Parasites, 39.
    Scale of female, 37.
        male, 37.
    Winged male, 38.
    Young larva, 38.
Chalcis robusta, 139, 141.
Chalk, a band of, as a barrier for ants, 131.
Chapin, Dr. S. F., quoted, 67.
Chilocorus bivulnerus, 71, 72, 180.
Chiloneurus dactylopii, 66.
Chion cinctus, 121.
Chionaspis citri, 40.
    euonymi, 40, 41.
Chrysis parasitic on Eumenes fraterna, 158.
    fasciata, 218.
Chrysopa, 7, 69.
    Larva feeding on Scale-insects, 80.
    citri, 81.
    oculata, 80.
Chrysobothris chrysoela, 171.
Chrysomphalus ficus, 86.
Cicada septendecim, 216.
Coccid-eating Dakruma, 76.
    Earlier states, 76.
    Habits of larva, 76.
    Natural history, 76.
Coccidæ of the Orange tree, 13.
Coccinæ, A subfamily of Coccidæ, 14.
    General characteristics and habits, 63.
Coccinellidæ (*see* Lady-birds).
Coccophagus cognatus, 51.
    lecanii, 51.
    vividus, 215.
Coccus hesperidum, 4.
Cockroach associated with Orange Web-worm, 156.
Coition of Bag-worms, 213.
Cold, Effect of, on Scale-insects, 46.
Coleoptera injuring the twigs and leaves, 132.
    preying upon Scale-insects, 71.
Coleopterous borers, 121, 125.
Coleotechnites citriella, 193.
Common Bag-worm, 144.
    Larva, 144.
    Life-history, 145.
    Male moth, 145.
    Maternal instinct, 145.

Common Bag-worm.
    Parasites, 146.
    Process of forming the bag, 146.
Mealy-bug, 61, 86.
    introduced on living plants, 86.
Orange Sawyer, 125.
    Beetle, 126.
    Injuries, 127.
    Larva, 125.
    Precautions, 127.
    Remedies, 127.
Comstock, Prof. J. H., quoted, 18, 28, 33, 35, 40, 53, 55, 59, 64, 154, 178, 193.
Comys bicolor, 52.
Conops ? quadrimaculata, 183.
Cork-colored Orange Tortricid, 152.
    Larva, 152.
    Life history, 152.
    Moth, 152.
    Parasites, 153, 217.
    Remedy, 152.
Cossonidæ, Food-habits of, 175.
Cost of Kerosene wash, 202.
Cotton Stainer, 165.
    Attacks upon the Orange, 166.
    Effect of its puncture, 166.
    Egg and oviposition, 166.
    Food-habits, 166.
    General characteristics, 166.
    Geographical distribution, 167.
    Not a permanent enemy of the Orange, 168.
    Not subject to attacks of enemies, 167.
    Remedies, 167.
Cotton Worm, 9.
Cottony Cushion Scale, 66.
    Food-plants, 67.
    Life-history, 67.
    Male, 68.
    Number of broods, 68.
    Ravages, 67.
Crematogaster lineolata, 170.
Creosote, Oil of, as a remedy for Scale-insects, 97.
    Table of experiments with, 206.
Crude Carbolic Acid, Table of experiments with, 206.
Cyclone nozzle, 100.
Cycloneda sanguinea, 73, 180.
Cylindrical Bag-worm, 148.
Cylindrical Bark-borer, 173.
    Appearance of the beetle, 173.
    Gallery made by the larva, 173.
    Life-history, 173.
Dactylopius, 2, 4.
    adonidum, 66, 86.
    destructor, 14, 63, 64, 79.
    longifilis, 64.
Dakruma coccidivora, 76.
    pallida, 77.
Destructive Mealy-bug, 64.
    Adult female, 64.
    Eggs, 64.
    Food-plants, 64, 66.
    Life-history, 65.
    Male, 64.

Destructive Mealy-bug, Natural enemies, 66.
        Young larva, 64.
Diaspinæ, a subfamily of Coccidæ, 14.
        Agencies assisting their distribution, 43.
        Conditions favorable to their distribution, 45.
        Generally present on Orange trees, 42.
        Growth of the scale, 16.
        Influence of climate, 46.
        Larva, 15.
        Life-history, 15.
        Male and its development, 17.
        Natural checks, 47.
        Nature of the scale covering, 18.
        Ravages, 42.
        Usual course of the pest, 45.
Dichelia sulphureana, 154.
Die-back, 1.
Dropping of fruit, 5.
Dusky-winged Aphis-fly, 184.
        Chrysalis, 184.
        Imago, 184.
        Larva, 184.
Dysdercus suturellus, 165, 191.
Egg-parasite of Katydid, 134.
        Orange Leaf-roller, 153.
Elaphidion inerme, 125, 171.
        parallelum, 126, 171.
Empretia stimulea, 140.
        Cocoon, 142.
        Larva, 141.
        Moth, 142.
        Parasite, 142.
Encyrtus, 215.
        artaceæ, 150.
        flavus, 52, 59.
        inquisitor, 66.
Epitragus tomentosus, 75.
Epuræa æstiva, 176.
Eumenes fraterna, 187.
Eupelmus mirabilis, 134.
Euphoria sepulchralis, 175.
Europs pallipennis, 177.
Euthochtha galeator, 163, 192.
Exochomus contristatus, 72, 180.
        Habits, 72.
        Larva, 72.
Experiments with Insecticides, 199.
Farlow, Dr. W. G., on Orange smut, 4.
Flat-headed Borer of the Orange, 171.
        Beetle, 172.
        Gallery made by the larva, 171.
        Habits and life-history, 172.
        Larva, 172.
        Pupa cell, 171.
Foot-rot of the Orange, 3.
        Remedies, 3.
Forest trees affording protection against Scale-insects, 88.
Four-spotted Aphis-fly, 183.
        Chrysalis, 183.
        Egg, 183.
        Imago, 183.
        Larva, 183.
        Parasite, 183.
Franklin, James, on Green Soldier-bug, 160.

Fruit-eating ant, 177.
Fruit Worm, The Mexican, 169.
Fumago salicina, 4.
Fungus diseases of the Orange, 1.
        Bark-fungus, 2.
        Die-back, 1.
        Foot-rot, 3.
        Smut, 3.
Fur, A band of, as a barrier for ants, 131.
Glover's Orange Mite, 82.
        Changes in shape of body, 82.
        Eggs, 82.
Goniozus hubbardi, 153, 217.
Gossamer spiders transporting Scale-insects, 44.
Gossyparia mannipara, 13.
Grasshoppers injuring the Orange, 9, 135.
Grass-worm, 150.
Green Soldier-bug, 159, 190.
        Appearance in immense numbers, 159.
        Food-plants, 159.
        Nature of damage done, 161.
        Predaceous habits, 190.
Hadronotus leptocorisæ, 215.
Hag-moth caterpillar, 142.
Hairy Orange Mite, 83.
        Description, 216.
        Egg, 83.
        Young, 83.
Hedges as a protection against Scale-insects, 88.
Hemerobius feeding on Scale-insects, 81.
        Larva, 81.
Hemiptera injurious to the Orange, 157.
        Predatory species, 78, 190.
        Preying upon Scale-insects, 78, 79.
Hemipteron associated with Orange Web-worm, 79, 156.
Hemispherical Scale, 55.
        Adult female, 55.
        Egg, 56.
        Food-plants, 56.
        Geographical distribution, 56.
        Locomotive power, 56.
        Young larva, 56.
Hemiteles thyridopterygis, 146, 147.
        sp., 215.
Hermannia trinebulosa, 216.
Hesperobænus sp., 175.
Hippodamia convergens, 73, 180.
        Larva, 73.
        Parasite, 74.
        Pupa, 74.
Homalotylus obscurus, 74.
Howard, L. O., Description of Hymenopterous parasites, 215, 216, 217, 218.
Hymenoptera preying upon Scale-insects, 70.
        Predatory species, 186.
Hymenopterous parasites of Bark-lice, 70.
Hyperaspidius coccidivorus, 69, 75.
Hyperplatys maculatus, 174.
Hypothenemus eruditus, 173.
Icerya purchasi, 63, 66.
Ichneumon concitator, 148.
Injurious insects, General habits of, 6.
        Seasons of greatest activity, 9.
        Shade favorable to their increase, 8.
Innoxious insects, 7, 193.

INDEX.

Insecticides, Apparatus for applying, 100, 101.
    Application of liquid, 100.
    Caution in applying, 120.
    Experiments with, 199.
Insect-fauna of the Orange, Summary of, 5.
    Beneficial insects, 6.
    Distinguishing friends from foes, 7.
    Injurious insects, 6.
    Innoxious insects, 7.
Insects affecting the blossoms, 164.
    fruit, 165.
    root and crown, 121.
    trunk and branches, 125.
    twigs and leaves, 132.
    feeding upon dead wood and bark, 170.
    decaying fruit, 175.
    found in dry fruit, 178.
    wounds and foot-rot sores, 175.
    Predatory, 80.
    preying upon Aphis, 180.
    Bark-lice, 69.
Katydid, Protective resemblance of, 5.
    The Angular-winged, 134.
Kermes, 14.
Kerosene as a remedy for Rust-mite, 118.
    Scale-insects, 92.
    White ants, 124.
Kerosene emulsion, Best season for applying, 95.
    Effect of, upon the Orange, 94.
    Formula for improved, 94.
    Mode of applying, 100, 101.
    preparing, 93.
    Precautions in the use, 94.
    Table of experiments with, 199.

Lace-wings, 7, 69.
    Eggs, 81.
    Habits, 80.
    Imago, 80.
    Larva, 80.
    Life-history, 80.
    Pupa, 80.
    Parasite, 80.
Lady-birds, 7.
    preying upon Aphis, 180.
    Scale-insects, 69, 71.
    transporting Scale-insects, 43.
Læmophlœus, 175.
Lagoa opercularis, 140.
    Cocoon, 140.
    Larva, 140.
    Life-history, 141.
    Moth, 141.
    Parasites, 141.
Laphygma frugiperda, 150.
    Chrysalis, 151.
    Egg, 150.
    Larva, 151.
    Moth, 151.
Larger Leaf-roller, 154, 217.
Lathridius, 175.
Leaf-eating ant, 132.
Leaf-footed bug, 168.
    Attacking the Orange, 169.
    Characteristics, 168.
    Eggs, 168.

Leaf-footed bug.
    Habits, 169.
    Normal food-plants, 169.
    Prevention, 169.
Leaf-rollers injurious to the Orange, 151.
    General characteristics, 151.
    Life-history, 151.
Lecaninæ, a subfamily of Coccidæ, 14.
    Extent of injuries, 61.
    General characteristics, 48.
    Life-history, 48.
Lecanium hemisphæricum, 55.
    hesperidum, 14, 48, 78.
    oleæ, 53, 61.
    tiliæ, 218.
Lepidoptera injurious to the Orange, 137.
    preying upon Scale-insects, 76.
Leptocorisa tipuloides, 78, 191, 215.
Leptoglossus phyllopus, 164, 168.
Leptomastix dactylopii, 66.
Leptostylus biustus, 174.
    Beetle, 174.
    Larva, 174.
Limacodes scapha, 140, 143.
    Cocoon, 144.
    Larva, 143.
Lime as a remedy for Rust-mite, 120.
Liquid insecticides, 100.
    Fineness and force of spray, 100.
    Means of applying, 100.
    Proper seasons for applying, 102.
    Several applications necessary, 101.
Locusts injuring the Orange, 135.
Long Scale, 14, 42, 75, 77.
    Brood periods, 22.
    Eggs, 21.
    Female insect, 20.
    Geographical distribution, 24.
    Growth of the Scale, 19.
    Introduction into Florida, 25, 86.
    Life-history, 21.
    Parasites, 23.
    Scale of female, 20.
    male, 20.
    Winged male, 20.
    Young larva, 21.
Lubber Grasshopper, 135.
    Absence of enemies, 136.
    Life-history, 135.
    Remedies, 136.
    Wandering habits, 135.
Lye Solutions, Table of experiments with, 204.
Manna produced by a Scale-insect, 13.
Mantis carolina, 189.
    Characteristics, 189.
    Egg-mass, 190.
    missouriensis, 190.
    Characteristics, 190.
    Egg-mass, 191.
    Food, 191.
Mealy-bug, 2, 4, 14, 79.
    at Orange Lake, Florida, 197.
    The Common, 63, 86.
    Destructive, 64.
Mealy-bugs Food-plants, 63.
    General characteristics, 63.

INDEX. 225

Mealy-bugs, Habits, 63.
Metapodius femoratus, 162, 192.
        terminalis, 163, 192.
Mexican Fruit Worm, 169.
Microcentrum retinerve, 134.
Microgaster parasite of the Bag-worm, 147.
Midas clavatus, 175.
Miotropis platynotæ, 153, 217.
Mites preying upon Scale-insects, 69, 81.
    Glover's, 82.
    Habits, 82.
    Hairy Orange, 83, 216.
    Importance, 81.
    Orbicular, 85.
    Rhizoglyphus, 84.
    Spear-head, 83, 216.
    Spotted, 84, 216.
    Undetermined, 84, 216.
Monomorium carbonarium, 132.
Mytilaspis citricola, 26, 39, 42, 75.
    gloverii, 14, 19, 42, 75, 77, 86.
    pomorum, 15.
Naked Scales (*see* Lecaninæ).
Naphthaline for ants, 130.
Neuroptera preying upon Scale-insects, 80.
Northern Bag-worm, 147.
Nothris citrifoliella, 154.
Nothrus ovivorus, 85.
Notolomus basalis, 133.
Odontota rubra, 133.
Oiketicus abbotii, 144.
Oil of creosote as a remedy for Scale-insects, 97.
    Table of experiments with, 206.
Oncideres cingulatus, 128.
Ophideres fullonica, 170.
Orange Aphis, 157.
    Birth of the young, 158.
    Descriptive, 157.
    Enemies, 160.
    Influence of climate on development, 158.
    Injuries, 159.
    Natural history, 157.
    Parasite, 158.
    Remedy, 159.
Basket-worm, 148.
    preying upon Scale-insects, 69.
Case-bearing Tineid, 193.
Chionaspis, 40.
    Abundant in Louisiana, 40.
    Scale of female, 40.
        male, 40.
Dog, 5, 137.
    Descriptive, 137.
    Food-plants, 138.
    Life-history, 138.
    Parasites, 139.
    Protective resemblance, 5.
    Remedies, 139.
Orange-eating Tineid, 179.
    Flat-headed Borer, 171.
    Leaf-notcher, 133.
Orange leaf Nothris, 154.
    Mites, 81.
    Psocus, 194.
    Sawyer, 171.

Orange Thrips, 164.
    Beneficial rather than injurious 165.
    Injury done to the blossoms, 165.
    Remedies, 165.
tree, enfeebled condition of, fosters Scale-insects, 45.
    How affected by Scale-insects, 45.
    Organic diseases, 1.
    Systems of cultivation, 8.
Web worm, 155.
    Descriptive, 156.
    Earlier states, 156.
    Number of broods, 157.
    Other insects associated with it, 155, 156.
    Protective resemblance, 155.
    Remedies, 157.
    The web, 155.
Organic diseases of the Orange, 1.
    Bark-fungus, 1.
    Die-back, 1.
    Dropping of fruit, 5.
    Foot-rot, 3.
    Smut, 3.
    Splitting of fruit, 4.
Oyster-shell Bark-louse, 15, 85.
    Mode of growth, 15.
Pachnæus opalus, 133.
Pachyneuron altiscuta, 218.
        anthomyiæ, 218.
        aphidis, 218.
Pale Dakruma, 77.
Palmetto brushes for scrubbing the trees, 90.
Papilio cresphontes, 137.
Parasites, General importance of, 7.
Parlatoria pergandii, 2, 37, 42, 75, 86.
Penthalodes mytilaspidis, 216.
Pergande, Th., Notes on Orange Mites, 84.
Perilitus, 81, 215.
Phobetrum pithecium, 140, 142.
    Cocoon, 143.
    Larva, 142.
    Moth, 143.
Pimpla conquisitor, 147.
    inquisitor, 147.
Platœceticus gloverii, 69, 148.
Platynota rostrana, 152, 154, 217.
Polistes americanus, 186.
    Habits, 186.
    Nest, 186.
Polysphincta albipes, 153.
Pomace-fly of the Orange, 176.
    Life-history, 177.
Potash as a remedy for Rust-mite, 119.
    Scale-insects, 96.
Predatory insects, 180.
    Lepidoptera, 76.
    Wasps, 186.
Prionotus cristatus, 192.
Pruinose Aphis-fly, 185.
    Imago, 185.
    Larva, 185.
    Parasite, 186, 218.
    Puparium, 185.
Psocus citricola, 194.

Psocus venosus, 193.
Psyche confederata, 148.
    Unknown species, 148.
Purple Scale, 26, 42, 75.
    Egg, 26.
    Female, 26.
    Life-history, 27.
    Male, 26.
    Origin and spread, 27.
    Parasites, 27.
    Scale of female, 26.
        male, 26.
    Young larva, 27.
Pyrethrum as a remedy for ants, 130.
    Rust-mite, 119.
    White ants, 124.

Rapacious Soldier-bug, 191.
Raphigaster bilaris, 159, 163, 164, 190, 192.
Red Bug (*see* Cotton Stainer).
Red Scale of California, 32.
    Distribution, 34.
    Formation of Scale, 34.
    Scale of female, 33.
        male, 33.
Red Scale of Florida, 28, 86.
    Development, 28.
    Introduction, 86.
    Number of annual generations, 32.
    Origin and distribution, 32.
    Scales of male and female, 28.
    Winged male, 28.
    Young larva, 29.
Rhizacloa sp., 215.
Rhizoglyphus preying upon Scale-insects, 84, 216.
Riley, Prof. C. V., descriptions of mites, 216.
    on coition of bag worms, 214.
Romalea microptera, 135.
Ruddy Aphis-fly, 184.
Rust of the fig, 105.
    Orange, 105.
        Discoloration of the fruit, 105.
        not influenced by soil and cultivation, 113.
        preventive measures, 114.
        remedies, 113.
        the rust-mite its cause, 106.
        rings of rust on the fruit, 110.
        rusty oranges superior to bright fruit, 112.
Rust-mite of the Orange, 107.
    Confined to the Citrus family, 112.
    Description of the eggs, 108.
        mite, 107.
    Distribution, 113.
    Effect of attacks upon the foliage, 112.
        fruit, 107, 110.
    Food, 109.
    Influence of weather, 111.
    Life-history, 108.
    Modes of spreading, 111.
    Numerical abundance, 109.
    Periods of increase, 113.
    Preference for half shade, 110.
    Rapidity in development, 115.
    Transported by birds and spiders, 111.
    Uncertainty as to its origin, 113.

Rust-mite of the Orange.
    Wandering habits, 107, 109.
Sacium, 175.
Saddle-back Caterpillar, 141.
Sap-beetles, 175.
Sap-feeding insects, 175.
Sawyers, 121, 125.
Scale-devouring Hyperaspidius, 75.
    Habits, 75.
    Larva, 75.
    Pupa, 75.
Scale-eating Tineid, 77.
    Earlier states, 78.
    Habits of larva, 77.
    Moth, 78.
    Number of broods, 78.
Scale-insects affecting the Orange, 13.
    Agencies assisting their distribution, 43.
    Characteristics, 13.
    Conditions favorable to their increase, 45.
    Division into subfamilies, 14.
    Enemies, 69.
    Generally present on Orange trees, 42.
    Infection from nursery stock, 87.
    Influence of climate, 46.
        cold, 46.
    Insect enemies, 69.
    Introduced on imported plants, 86.
    Oscillations in numerical increase, 46.
    Parasites, 47.
    Precautionary measures, 87.
    Protected by Spider-webs, 43.
    Ravages, 42.
    Remedies, 91.
        Effective remedies, 92.
        Popular fallacies, 91.
    Secretions, 13.
    Spreading, 87.
Scavenger insects, 170.
Scolytidæ, General habits of, 173.
Scymnus bioculatus, 66.
    caudalis, 180.
    Larva and habits, 180.
    Various species preying on Aphis, 180.
Sejus sp., 216.
Silicate of soda as a remedy for Scale-insects, 99.
    Table of experiments with, 211.
Sinea multispinosa, 191.
Siphonophora multispinosa, 191.
Skiff-caterpillar, 143.
Slug-caterpillar, 140.
Smicrips hypocoproides, 177.
Smut of the Orange, 3, 62, 63.
Soda lye as a remedy for Scale-insects, 96.
Soldier-bug, The Green, 159, 190.
Soldier-bugs as predatory insects, 190.
Solenopsis xyloni, 129.
    Destroying their colonies, 130.
    Habits, 130.
    Preventive measures, 131.
Soothsayers, 188.
Spear-head Mite, 83.
Spider associated with Orange Web-worm, 155.
Spider-webs protecting Scale-insects, 43.
Spider-legged Soldier-bug, 78, 191.
    Eggs, 79.

INDEX.

Spider-legged Soldier-bug.
    Food-habits, 78, 191.
    Life-history, 79.
    Parasite, 79.
Spiders transporting Rust-mites, 111.
    Scale-insects, 43.
Splitting of fruit, 4.
Spotted Mite, 83, 216.
    Description, 216.
Stenomesius (?) aphidicola, 159.
Stinging caterpillars, 149.
Sulphate of iron as a remedy for Scale-insects, 99.
Sulphur as a remedy for Rust-mite, 116.
    Scale-insects, 91.
Sulphur-colored Tortricid, 154.
Sulphurated lime as a remedy for Scale-insects, 98.
Sulphuric acid as a remedy for Scale-insects, 99.
Syrphus, 7, 181.
Syrphus-fly larvæ, 181.
    Characteristics, 181.
    Change of color, 181.
    Mode of feeding, 181.
    Number of broods, 181.
    Rapid development, 181.
    Transformations, 181.
Tachina-fly parasitic on Orange Dog, 139.
Tap-root borers, 121.
Telenomus, 215.
Termes flavipes, 122.
Termites (see White ants).
Tetrastichus, 59, 215.
Thick-legged Metapodius, 162.
    Egg, 163.
    Insectivorous habits, 163.
    Young bug, 163.
Thrips tritici, 164.
Thyridopteryx ephemeræformis, 147.
    Coition of, 214.
Tineid, Case-bearing, on Orange, 193.
    larvæ preying on Scale-insects, 69, 77, 78.
    The Orange-eating, 178.
    Scale-eating, 77.
Tomocera californica, 55.
Tortricidæ injurious to the Orange, 151.
Treecockroach associated with Orange Web-worm, 156.
Tree-inhabiting ants, 170.
Trichogramma minuta, 153.
    pretiosa, 153.
Trioxys testaceipes, 159.
Turtle-back Scale, 14, 48, 61.
    Attended by ants, 50.
    Brood periods, 50.
    Excretion of honey, 50.
    Food-plants, 52.
    Full-grown insect, 48.
    Geographical distribution, 52.
    Gregarious habits, 49.
    Injury, 61.
    Metamorphosis, 49.
    Parasites, 50.

Turtle-back Scale.
    Young larva, 49.
Twice-stabbed Ladybird, 71.
    Habits, 72.
    Larva, 71.
    Pupa, 72.
Twig-girdler, 128.
    Food-plants, 128.
    Natural history, 128.
    Remedies, 129.
Typhlodromus oleivorus, 107.
Tyroglyphus (?) gloverii, 82.
    mali, 84, 85.
    sp., 216.
Vase-maker wasp, 187.
    Cell, 187.
    Habits, 187.
    Parasites, 186.
Voyle, Jos., on effect of cold on Scale-insects, 47.
    on Mealy-bug, 197.
Wax Scale, 56.
    Adult female, 56.
    Eggs, 57.
    Food-plants, 58.
    Geographical distribution, 58.
    Life-history, 57.
    Natural checks, 59.
    Nature of waxy covering, 58.
    Number of annual broods, 58.
    Parasites, 59.
    Young Larva, 57.
Waxy Scales (see Lecaninæ).
Web-makers injurious to the Orange, 156.
Whale-oil soap as a remedy for Rust-mites, 115.
    Scale-insects, 95.
    Table of experiments with, 202.
Wheel-bug, 192.
    Characteristics, 192.
    Eggs, 192.
White ants, 3, 6, 9, 121, 178.
    Found in the fruit, 178.
    Habits, 121.
    Injuries, 122.
    Nature of their galleries, 123.
    Precautionary measures, 123.
    Remedies, 124.
White Scale, 35, 56.
    Distribution, 35.
    Food-plants, 36.
    Number of annual generations, 37.
    Scales of male and female, 35.
    Winged male, 35.
Wiley, Prof. H. W., on reactions of sulphur on lime, 217.
Williston, Dr. S. W., on an Anthomyid fly, 185.
Wine Fly of the Orange, 176.
    Life-history, 177.
Winter-killed branches, 5.
Wood-lice (see White ants).
Yellow-banded Ichneumon, 147.

www.ingramcontent.com/pod-product-compliance
Lightning Source LLC
Chambersburg PA
CBHW032140230426
43672CB00011B/2402